THE
INSIDE
STORY

IN MODERN ENGLISH
AS TOLD IN
LUKE, JOHN, ACTS AND ROMANS

A Translation by

J. B. Phillips

AMERICAN BIBLE SOCIETY
New York

The Gospels of Luke and John,
The Acts of the Apostles,
The Letter to the Christians at Rome

From *The New Testament in Modern English*
a translation by J. B. Phillips
© The Macmillan Company
1952, 1957, New York

Eng. Lk-Rom.MEV470P
ABS-1966-100M-L-1

CONTENTS

THE GOSPEL OF LUKE

Prefatory note

Dear Theophilus,
 Many people have already written an account of the events which have happened among us, basing their work on the evidence of those who we know were eyewitnesses as well as teachers of the message. I have therefore decided, since I have traced the course of these happenings carefully from the beginning, to set them down for you myself in their proper order, so that you may have reliable information about the matters in which you have already had instruction.

A vision comes to an old priest of God

The story begins in the days when Herod was king of Judaea with a priest called Zacharias (who belonged to the Abijah section of the priesthood), whose wife Elisabeth was, like him, a descendant of Aaron. They were both truly religious people, blamelessly observing all God's commandments and require-ments. They were childless through Elisabeth's infertility, and both of them were getting on in years. One day, while Zacharias was performing his priestly functions (it was the turn of his division to be on duty), it fell to him to go into the sanctuary and burn the incense. The crowded congregation outside was praying at the actual time of the incense burning, when an angel of the Lord appeared on the right side of the incense altar. When Zacharias saw him, he was terribly agitated and a sense of awe swept over him. But the angel spoke to him:

"Do not be afraid, Zacharias; your prayers have been heard. Elisabeth your wife will bear you a son, and you are to call him John. This will be joy and delight to you and many more will be glad because he is born. He will be one of Gods. great men; he will touch neither wine nor strong drink and he will be filled with the Holy Spirit from the moment of his birth' He will turn many of Israel's children to the Lord their God. He will go out before God in the spirit and power of Elijah—to reconcile fathers and children, and bring back the disobedient to the wisdom of good men—and he will make a people fully ready for their Lord."

But Zacharias replied to the angel:

"How can I know that this is true? I am an old man myself and my wife is getting on in years . . ."

"I am Gabriel," the angel answered. "I stand in the presence of God, and I have been sent to speak to you and tell you this good news. Because you do not believe what I have said, you shall live in silence, and you shall be unable to speak a word until the day that it happens. But be sure that everything that I have told you will come true at the proper time."

Meanwhile, the people were waiting for Zacharias, wondering why he stayed so long in the sanctuary. But when he came out and was unable to speak a word to them—for although he kept making signs, not a sound came from his lips—they realized that he had seen a vision in the Temple. Later, when his days of duty were over, he went back home, and soon afterward his wife Elisabeth became pregnant and kept herself secluded for five months.

"How good the Lord is to me," she would say, "now that he has taken away the shame that I have suffered!"

A vision comes to a young woman in Nazareth   1.26

Then, six months after Zacharias' vision, the angel Gabriel was sent from God to a Galilean town, Nazareth by name, to a young woman who was engaged to a man called Joseph (a descendant of David). The girl's name was Mary. The angel entered her room and said,

"Greetings to you, Mary. O favored one!—the Lord be with you!"

Mary was deeply perturbed at these words and wondered what such a greeting could possibly mean. But the angel said to her:

"Do not be afraid, Mary; God loves you dearly. You are going to be the mother of a son, and you will call him Jesus. He will be great and will be known as the Son of the most high. The Lord God will give him the throne of his forefather, David, and he will be king over the people of Jacob for ever. His reign shall never end."

Then Mary spoke to the angel,

"How can this be?" she said. "I am not married!"

But the angel made this reply to her:

"The Holy Spirit will come upon you, the power of the most high will overshadow you. Your child will therefore be called holy—the Son of God. Your cousin Elisabeth has also conceived a son, old as she is. Indeed, this is the sixth month for her, a woman who was called barren. For no promise of God can fail to be fulfilled."

"I belong to the Lord, body and soul," replied Mary, "let it happen as you say." And at this the angel left her.

With little delay Mary got ready and hurried off to the hillside town in Judaea where Zacharias and Elisabeth lived. She went into their house and greeted her cousin. When Elisabeth heard her greeting, the unborn child stirred inside her and she herself was filled with the Holy Spirit, and cried out:

"Blessed are you among women, and blessed is your child! What an honor it is to have the mother of my Lord come to see me! Why, as soon as your greeting reached my ears, the child within me jumped for joy! Oh, how happy is the woman who believes in God, for he does make his promises to her come true!"

Then Mary said: "My heart is overflowing with praise of my Lord; my soul is full of joy in God my Savior. For he has deigned to notice me, his humble servant and, after this, all the people who ever shall be will call me the happiest of women! The one who can do all things has done great things for me—oh, holy is his Name! Truly, his mercy rests on those who fear him in every generation. He has shown the strength of his arm, he has swept away the high and mighty. He has set kings down from their thrones and lifted up the humble. He has satisfied the hungry with good things and sent the rich away with empty hands. Yes, he has helped Israel, his child: he has remembered the mercy that he promised to our fore-fathers, to Abraham and his sons for evermore!"

The old woman's son, John, is born   **1.56**

So Mary stayed with Elisabeth about three months, and then went back to her own home. Then came the time for Elisabeth's child to be born, and she gave birth to a son. Her neighbors and relations heard of the great mercy the Lord had shown her and shared her joy.

When the eighth day came, they were going to circumcise the child and call him Zacharias, after his father, but his mother said,

"Oh, no! He must be called John."

"But none of your relations is called John," they replied. And they made signs to his father to see what name he wanted the child to have. He beckoned for a writing tablet and wrote the words, "His name is John," which greatly surprised every-body. Then his power of speech suddenly came back, and his first words were to thank God. The neighbors were awestruck at this, and all these incidents were reported in the hill country of Judaea. People turned the whole matter over in their hearts, and said,

"What is this child's future going to be?" For the Lord's blessing was plainly upon him.

Then Zacharias, his father, filled with the Holy Spirit and speaking like a prophet, said:

"Blessings on the Lord, the God of Israel, because he has turned his face toward his people and has set them free! And he has raised up for us a standard of salvation in his servant David's house! Long, long ago, through the words of his holy prophets, he promised to do this for us, so that we should be safe from our enemies and secure from all who hate us. So does he continue the mercy he showed to our forefathers. So does he remember the holy agreement he made with them and the oath which he swore to our father Abraham, to make us this gift: that we should be saved from the hands of our enemies, and in his presence should serve him unafraid in holiness and righteousness all our lives.

"And you, little child, will be called the prophet of the most high, for you will go before the Lord to prepare the way for his coming. It will be for you to give his people knowledge of their salvation through the forgiveness of their sins. Because the heart of our God is full of mercy toward us, the first light of Heaven shall come to visit us—to shine on those who lie in darkness and under the shadow of death, and to guide our feet into the path of peace."

The little child grew up and became strong in spirit. He lived in lonely places until the day came for him to show himself to Israel.

The census brings Mary and Joseph to Bethlehem   2.1

At that time a proclamation was made by Caesar Augustus that all the inhabited world should be registered. This was the first census, undertaken while Cyrenius was governor of Syria; and everybody went to the town of his birth to be registered. Joseph went up from the town of Nazareth in Galilee to David's town, Bethlehem, in Judaea, because he was a direct descendant of David, to be registered with his future wife, Mary, now in the later stages of her pregnancy. So it happened that it was while they were there in Bethlehem that she came to the end of her time. She gave birth to her first child, a son. And as there was no place for them inside the inn, she wrapped him up and laid him in a manger.

A vision comes to shepherds on the hillside   2.8

There were some shepherds living in the same part of the country, keeping guard throughout the night over their flock in the open fields. Suddenly an angel of the Lord stood by their side, the splendor of the Lord blazed around them, and they were terror-stricken. But the angel said to them:

"Do not be afraid! Listen, I bring you glorious news of great joy which is for all the people. This very day, in David's town, a Savior has been born for you. He is Christ, the Lord. Let this prove it to you: you will find a baby, wrapped up and lying in a manger."

And in a flash there appeared with the angel a vast host of the armies of Heaven, praising God, saying,

"Glory to God in the highest Heaven! Peace upon earth among men of goodwill!"

When the angels left them and went back into Heaven, the shepherds said to each other,

"Now let us go straight to Bethlehem and see this thing which the Lord has made known to us."

So they came as fast as they could and they found Mary and Joseph—and the baby lying in the manger. And when they had seen this sight, they told everybody what had been said to them about the little child. And those who heard them were amazed at what the shepherds said. But Mary treasured all these things and turned them over in her mind. The shepherds went back to work, glorifying and praising God for everything that they had heard and seen, which had happened just as they had been told.

Mary and Joseph bring their newly born son   **2.21**
to the Temple

At the end of the eight days, the time came for circumcising the child and he was called Jesus, the name given to him by the angel before his conception.

When the "purification" time, stipulated by the Law of Moses, was completed, they brought Jesus to Jerusalem to present him to the Lord. This was to fulfill a requirement of the Law—

Every male that openeth the womb shall be called holy to the Lord.

They also offered the sacrifice prescribed by the Law—

A pair of turtle doves, or two young pigeons.

In Jerusalem was a man by the name of Simeon. He was an upright man, devoted to the service of God, living in expectation of the "salvation of Israel." His heart was open to the

Holy Spirit, and it had been revealed to him that he would not die before he saw the Lord's Christ. He had been led by the Spirit to go into the Temple, and when Jesus' parents brought the child in to have done to him what the Law required, he took him up in his arms, blessed God and said—

"At last, Lord, you can dismiss your servant in peace, as you promised! For with my own eyes I have seen your salvation which you have made ready for every people—a light to show truth to the gentiles and bring glory to your people Israel."

The child's father and mother were still amazed at what was said about him, when Simeon gave them his blessing. He said to Mary, the child's mother,

"This child is destined to make many fall and many rise in Israel and to set up a standard which many will attack—for he will expose the secret thoughts of many hearts. And for you . . . your very soul will be pierced by a sword."

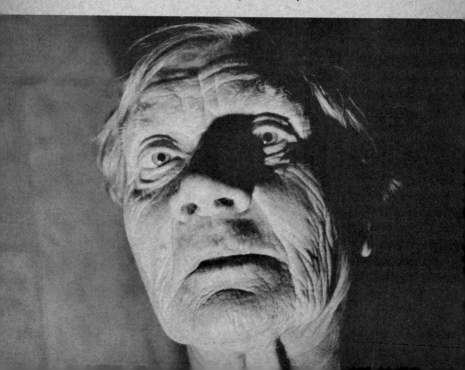

There was also present, Anna, the daughter of Phanuel of the tribe of Asher, who was a prophetess. She was a very old woman, having had seven years' married life, and was now a widow of eighty-four. She spent her whole life in the Temple and worshiped God night and day with fastings and prayers. She came up at this very moment, praised God and spoke about Jesus to all those in Jerusalem who were expecting redemption.

When they had completed all the requirements of the Law of the Lord, they returned to Galilee, to their own town of Nazareth. The child grew up and became strong and full of wisdom. And God's blessing was upon him.

Twelve years later: the boy Jesus goes with his parents to Jerusalem 2.41

Every year at the Passover festival, Jesus' parents used to go to Jerusalem. When he was twelve years old they went up to the city as usual for the festival. When it was over they started back home, but the boy Jesus stayed behind in Jerusalem, without his parents' knowledge. They went a day's journey assuming that he was somewhere in their company, and then they began to look for him among their relations and acquaintances. They failed to find him, however, and turned back to the city, looking for him as they went. Three days later they found him—in the Temple, sitting among the teachers, listening to them and asking them questions. All those who heard him were astonished at his powers of comprehension and at the answers that he gave. When Joseph and Mary saw him, they could hardly believe their eyes, and his mother said to him:

"Why have you treated us like this, my son? Here have your father and I been very worried, looking for you everywhere!"

And Jesus replied,

"But why were you looking for me? Did you not know that I must be in my Father's house?"

But they did not understand his reply. Then he went home with them to Nazareth and was obedient to them. And his mother treasured all these things in her heart. And as Jesus continued to grow in body and mind, he grew also in the love of God and of those who knew him.

Several years later: John prepares the way of Christ 3.1

In the fifteenth year of the reign of the Emperor Tiberius (a year when Pontius Pilate was governor of Judaea, Herod tetrarch of Galilee, Philip, his brother, tetrarch of the territory of Ituraea and Trachonitis, and Lysanias tetrarch of Abilene, while Annas and Caiaphas were the High Priests), the word of God came to John, the son of Zacharias, while he was in the desert. He went into the whole country round about the Jordan proclaiming baptism as a mark of a complete change of heart and of the forgiveness of sins, as the book of the prophet Isaiah says—

The voice of one crying in the wilderness,
Make ye ready the way of the Lord,
Make his paths straight.
Every valley shall be filled,
And every mountain and hill shall be brought low:
And the crooked shall become straight,
And the rough ways smooth:
And all flesh shall see the salvation of God.

So John used to say to the crowds who came out to be baptized by him:

"Who warned you, you serpent's brood, to escape from the wrath to come? See that you do something to show that your hearts are really changed! Don't start thinking that you can say to yourselves, 'We are Abraham's children,' for I tell you that God could produce children of Abraham out of these stones! The ax already lies at the root of the tree, and the tree that fails to produce good fruit is cut down and thrown into the fire."

Then the crowds would ask him, "Then what shall we do?"

And his answer was, "The man who has two shirts must share with the man who has none, and the man who has food must do the same."

Some of the tax collectors also came to him to be baptized, and they asked him,

"Master, what are we to do?"

"You must not demand more than you are entitled to," he replied.

And the soldiers asked him, "And what are we to do?"

"Don't bully people, don't bring false charges, and be content with your pay," he replied.

The people were in a great state of expectation and were inwardly discussing whether John could possibly be Christ. But John answered them all in these words:

"It is true that I baptize you with water, but the one who follows me is stronger than I am—indeed I am not fit to undo his shoelaces—he will baptize you with the fire of the Holy Spirit. He will come all ready to separate the wheat from the chaff, and to clear the rubbish from his threshing floor. The wheat he will gather into his barn and the chaff he will burn with a fire that cannot be put out."

These and many other things John said to the people as he exhorted them and announced the good news. But the tetrarch Herod, who had been condemned by John in the affair of Herodias, his brother's wife, as well as for the other evil things that he had done, crowned his misdeeds by putting John in prison.

Jesus is himself baptized   3.21

When all the people had been baptized, and Jesus was praying after his own baptism, Heaven opened and the Holy Spirit came down upon him in the bodily form of a dove. Then there came a voice from Heaven, saying,

"You are my dearly loved Son, in whom I am well pleased."
Jesus himself was about thirty years old at this time when he
began his work.

The ancestry of Jesus traced to Adam   3.23b

People assumed that Jesus was the son of Joseph, who was
the son of Heli, who was the son of Matthat, who was the son
of Levi, who was the son of Melchi, who was the son of Jannai,
who was the son of Joseph, who was the son of Mattathias,
who was the son of Amos, who was the son of Nahum, who was
the son of Esli, who was the son of Naggai, who was the son
of Maath, who was the son of Mattathias, who was the son of
Semein, who was the son of Josech, who was the son of Joda,
who was the son of Joanan, who was the son of Rhesa, who
was the son of Zerubbabel, who was the son of Shealtiel,
who was the son of Neri, who was the son of Melchi, who was
the son of Addi, who was the son of Cosam, who was the son
of Elmadam, who was the son of Er, who was the son of Jesus,
who was the son of Eliezer, who was the son of Jorim, who was
the son of Matthat, who was the son of Levi, who was the son
of Symeon, who was the son of Judas, who was the son of
Joseph, who was the son of Jonam, who was the son of Eliakim,
who was the son of Melea, who was the son of Menna, who was
the son of Mattatha, who was the son of Nathan, who was the
son of David, who was the son of Jesse, who was the son of
Obed, who was the son of Boaz, who was the son of Salmon,
who was the son of Nahshon, who was the son of Amminadab,
who was the son of Arni, who was the son of Hezron, who was
the son of Perez, who was the son of Judah, who was the son
of Jacob, who was the son of Isaac, who was the son of
Abraham, who was the son of Terah, who was the son of
Nahor, who was the son of Serug, who was the son of Reu,
who was the son of Peleg, who was the son of Eber, who was
the son of Shelah, who was the son of Cainan, who was the
son of Arphaxad, who was the son of Shem, who was the son
of Noah, who was the son of Lamech, who was the son of

Methuselah, who was the son of Enoch, who was the son of
Jared, who was the son of Mahalaleel, who was the son of
Cainan, who was the son of Enos, who was the son of Seth,
who was the son of Adam, who was the son of God.

Jesus faces temptation 4.1

Jesus returned from the Jordan full of the Holy Spirit and
he was led by the Spirit to spend forty days in the desert,
where he was tempted by the devil. He ate nothing during
that time and afterward he felt very hungry.

"If you really are the Son of God," the devil said to him,
"tell this stone to turn into a loaf."

Jesus answered,

"The scripture says, 'Man shall not live by bread alone.' "

Then the devil took him up and showed him all the kingdoms
of mankind in a sudden vision, and said to him:

"I will give you all this power and magnificence, for it
belongs to me and I can give it to anyone I please. It shall all
be yours if you will fall down and worship me."

To this Jesus replied,

"It is written, 'Thou shalt worship the Lord thy God and him
only shalt thou serve.' "

Then the devil took him to Jerusalem and set him on the
highest ledge of the Temple.

"If you really are the Son of God," he said, "throw yourself
down from here, for the scripture says, 'He shall give his angels
charge concerning thee, to guard thee,' and 'On their hands
they shall bear thee up, lest haply thou dash thy foot against
a stone.' "

To which Jesus replied,

"It is also said, 'Thou shalt not tempt the Lord thy God.' "

And when the devil had exhausted every kind of temptation, he withdrew until his next opportunity.

Jesus begins his ministry in Galilee   4.14

And now Jesus returned to Galilee in the power of the Spirit, and news of him spread through all the surrounding district. He taught in their synagogues, to everyone's great admiration.

Then he came to Nazareth where he had been brought up and, according to his custom, went to the synagogue on the Sabbath day. He stood up to read the scriptures, and the book of the prophet Isaiah was handed to him. He opened the book and found the place where these words are written—

The Spirit of the Lord is upon me,
Because he anointed me to preach good tidings to the poor:
He hath sent me to proclaim release to the captives,
And recovering of sight to the blind,
To set at liberty them that are bruised,
To proclaim the acceptable year of the Lord.

Then he shut the book, handed it back to the attendant and resumed his seat. Every eye in the synagogue was fixed upon him and he began to tell them, "This very day this scripture has been fulfilled, while you have been listening to it!"

Everybody noticed what he said and was amazed at the beautiful words that came from his lips, and they kept saying,

"Isn't this Joseph's son?"

So he said to them,

"I expect you will quote this proverb to me, 'Cure yourself, doctor! Let us see you do in your own country all that we have heard that you did in Capernaum!' " Then he added: "I assure you that no prophet is ever welcomed in his own country. I tell you the plain fact that in Elijah's time, when the heavens were shut up for three and a half years and there was a great famine through the whole country, there were plenty of widows in Israel, but Elijah was not sent to any of them. But he was sent to Sarepta, to a widow in the country of Sidon. In the time of Elisha the prophet, there were a great many lepers in Israel, but not one of them was healed—only Naaman, the Syrian."

But when they heard this, everyone in the synagogue was furiously angry. They sprang to their feet and drove him right out of the town, taking him to the brow of the hill on which it was built, intending to hurl him down bodily. But he walked straight through the whole crowd and went on his way.

Jesus heals in Capernaum   4.31

So he came down to Capernaum, a town in Galilee, and taught them on the Sabbath day. They were astonished at his teaching, for his words had the ring of authority.

There was a man in the synagogue under the influence of some evil spirit and he yelled at the top of his voice, "Hi! What have you got to do with us, Jesus, you Nazarene—have you come to kill us? I know who you are all right, you're God's holy one!"

Jesus cut him short and spoke sharply:

"Be quiet! Get out of him!"

And after throwing the man down in front of them, the devil did come out of him without hurting him in the slightest. At this everybody present was amazed and they kept saying to each other:

"What sort of words are these? He speaks to these evil spirits with authority and power and out they come."

And his reputation spread over the whole surrounding district.

When Jesus got up and left the synagogue he went into Simon's house. Simon's mother-in-law was suffering from a high fever, and they asked Jesus about her. He stood over her as she lay in bed, brought the fever under control and it left her. At once she got up and began to see to their needs.

Then, as the sun was setting, all those who had friends suffering from every kind of disease brought them to Jesus and he laid his hands on each one of them separately and healed them. Evil spirits came out of many of these people, shouting, "You are the Son of God!"

But he spoke sharply to them and would not allow them to say any more, for they knew perfectly well that he was Christ.

Jesus attempts to be alone—in vain   4.42

At daybreak he went off to a deserted place, but the crowds tried to find him and, when they did discover him, tried to prevent him from leaving them. But he told them, "I must tell the good news of the kingdom of God to other towns as well—that is my mission."

And he continued proclaiming his message in the synagogues of Judaea.

Simon, James and John become Jesus' followers   5.1

One day the people were crowding closely round Jesus to hear God's message, as he stood on the shore of Lake Gennesaret. Jesus noticed two boats drawn up on the beach, for the fishermen had left them there while they were cleaning their nets. He went aboard one of the boats, which belonged to Simon, and asked him to push out a little from the shore. Then he sat down and continued his teaching of the crowds from the boat.

When he had finished speaking, he said to Simon, "Push out now into deep water and let down your nets for a catch."

Simon replied, "Master! We've worked all night and never caught a thing, but if you say so I'll let the nets down."

And when they had done this, they caught an enormous shoal of fish—so big that the nets began to tear. So they signaled to their friends in the other boat to come and help them. They came and filled both the boats to sinking point. When Simon Peter saw this, he fell on his knees before Jesus and said,

"Keep away from me, Lord, for I'm only a sinful man!"

For he and his companions (including Zebedee's sons, James and John, Simon's partners) were staggered at the haul of fish that they had made.

Jesus said to Simon: "Don't be afraid, Simon. From now on your catch will be *men*."

So they brought the boats ashore, left everything and followed him.

Jesus cures leprosy   5.12

While he was in one of the towns, Jesus came upon a man who was a mass of leprosy. When the man saw Jesus he prostrated himself before him and begged,

"If you want to, Lord, you can make me clean."

Jesus stretched out his hand, placed it on the leper, saying: "Certainly I want to. Be clean!"

Immediately the leprosy left him and Jesus warned him not to tell anybody, but to go and show himself to the priest and to make the offerings for his recovery that Moses prescribed, as evidence to the authorities.

Yet the news about him spread all the more, and enormous crowds collected to hear Jesus and to be healed of their diseases. But he slipped quietly away to deserted places for prayer.

Jesus cures a paralytic in soul and body   5.17

One day while Jesus was teaching, some Pharisees and experts in the Law were sitting near him. They had come out of every village in Galilee and Judaea as well as from Jerusalem. God's power to heal people was with him. Soon some men arrived carrying a paralytic on a small bed and they kept trying to carry him in to put him down in front of Jesus. When they failed to find a way of getting him in because of the dense crowd, they went up onto the top of the house and let him down, bed and all, through the tiles, into the middle of the crowd in front of Jesus. When Jesus saw their faith, he said to the man,

"My friend, your sins are forgiven."

The scribes and the Pharisees began to argue about this,

saying: "Who is this man who talks blasphemy? Who can forgive sins? Only God can do that."

Jesus realized what was going on in their minds and spoke straight to them.

"Why must you argue like this in your minds? Which do you suppose is easier—to say, 'Your sins are forgiven' or to say, 'Get up and walk'? But to make you realize that the Son of Man has full authority on earth to forgive sins—I tell *you*," he said to the man who was paralyzed, "get up, pick up your bed and go home!"

Instantly the man sprang to his feet before their eyes, picked up the bedding on which he used to lie, and went off home, praising God. Sheer amazement gripped every man present, and they praised God and said in awed voices, "We have seen incredible things today."

Jesus calls Levi to be his disciple   5.27

Later on, Jesus went out and looked straight at a tax collector called Levi, as he sat at his office desk.

"Follow me," he said to him.

And he got to his feet at once, left everything behind and followed him.

Then Levi gave a big reception for Jesus in his own house, and there was a great crowd of tax collectors and others at table with them. The Pharisees and their companions the scribes kept muttering indignantly about this to Jesus' disciples, saying,

"Why do you have your meals with tax collectors and sinners?"

Jesus answered them,

"It is not the healthy who need the doctor, but those who are ill. I have not come to invite the 'righteous' but the 'sinners'—to change their ways."

Jesus hints at who he is   5.33

Then people said to him,

"Why is it that John's disciples are always fasting and praying, just like the Pharisees' disciples, but yours both eat and drink?"

Jesus answered,

"Can you expect wedding guests to fast while they have the bridegroom with them? The day will come when they will lose the bridegroom; that will be the time for them to fast!"

Then he gave them this illustration.

"Nobody tears a piece from a new coat to patch up an old one. If he does, he ruins the new one and the new piece does not match the old.

"Nobody puts new wine into old wineskins. If he does, the new wine will burst the skins—the wine will be spilled and the skins ruined. No, new wine must be put into new wineskins. Of course, nobody who has been drinking old wine will want the new at once. He is sure to say, 'The old is a good sound wine.' "

Jesus speaks of the Sabbath—   **6.1**

One Sabbath day, as Jesus happened to be passing through the cornfields, his disciples began picking the ears of corn, rubbing them in their hands, and eating them. Some of the Pharisees remarked,

"Why are you doing what the Law forbids men to do on the Sabbath day?"

Jesus answered them and said:

"Have you never read what David and his companions did when they were hungry? How he went into the house of God, took the presentation loaves, ate some bread himself and gave some to his companions, even though the Law does not permit anyone except the priests to eat it?"

Then he added, "The Son of Man is master even of the Sabbath."

—and provokes violent antagonism   **6.6**

On another Sabbath day when he went into a synagogue

to teach, there was a man there whose right hand was wasted away. The scribes and the Pharisees were watching Jesus closely to see whether he would heal on the Sabbath day, which would, of course, give them grounds for an accusation. But he knew exactly what was going on in their minds and said to the man with the wasted hand,

"Stand up and come out in front."

And he got up and stood there. Then Jesus said to them:

"I am going to ask you a question. Does the Law command us to do good on Sabbath days or do harm—to save life or destroy it?"

He looked round, meeting all their eyes, and said to the man,

"Now stretch out your hand."

He did so, and his hand was restored as sound as the other one. But they were filled with insane fury and kept discussing with one another what they could do to Jesus.

After a night of prayer Jesus selects the twelve   6.12

It was in those days that he went up the hillside to pray, and spent the whole night in prayer to God. When daylight came, he summoned his disciples to him and out of them he chose twelve whom he called apostles. They were—

Simon (whom he called Peter),
Andrew, his brother,
James,
John,
Philip,
Bartholomew,
Matthew,
Thomas,
James, the son of Alphaeus,
Simon, called the patriot,
Judas, the son of James, and
Judas Iscariot, who later betrayed him.

Then he came down with them and stood on a level piece of ground, surrounded by a large crowd of his disciples and a great number of people from all parts of Judaea and Jerusalem and the coastal district of Tyre and Sidon, who had come to hear him and to be healed of their diseases. (And even those who were troubled with evil spirits were cured.) The whole crowd were trying to touch him with their hands, for power was going out from him and he was healing them all.

**Jesus declares who is happy and who is to be   6.20
pitied, and defines a new attitude toward life**

Then Jesus looked steadily at his disciples and said,

"How happy are you who own nothing, for the kingdom of
God is yours!

"How happy are you who are hungry now, for you will be
satisfied!

"How happy are you who weep now, for you are going to
laugh!

"How happy you are when men hate you and turn you out
of their company; when they slander you and detest all that
you stand for because you are loyal to the Son of Man. Be
glad when that happens and jump for joy—your reward in
Heaven is magnificent. For that is exactly how their fathers
treated the prophets.

"But how miserable for you who are rich, for you have had
all your comforts!

"How miserable for you who have all you want, for you
are going to be hungry!

"How miserable for you who are laughing now, for you will
know sorrow and tears!

"How miserable for you when everybody says nice things about you, for that is exactly how their fathers treated the false prophets.

"But I say to all of you who will listen to me: love your enemies, do good to those who hate you, bless those who curse you, and pray for those who treat you badly.

"As for the man who hits you on one cheek, offer him the other one as well! And if a man is taking away your coat, do not stop him from taking your shirt as well. Give to everyone who asks you, and when a man has taken what belongs to you, don't demand it back.

"Treat men exactly as you would like them to treat you. If you love only those who love you, what credit is that to you? Even sinners love those who love them! And if you do good only to those who do good to you, what credit is that to you? Even sinners do that. And if you lend only to those from whom you hope to get your money back, what credit is that to you? Even sinners lend to sinners and expect to get their money back. No, you are to love your *enemies* and do good and lend without hope of return. Your reward will be wonderful and you will be sons of the most high. For he is kind to the ungrateful and the wicked!

"You must be merciful, as your Father in Heaven is merciful. Don't judge other people and you will not be judged your-selves. Don't condemn and you will not be condemned. Make allowances for others and people will make allowances for you. Give and men will give to you—yes, good measure, pressed down, shaken together and running over will they pour into your lap. For whatever measure you use with other people, they will use in their dealings with you."

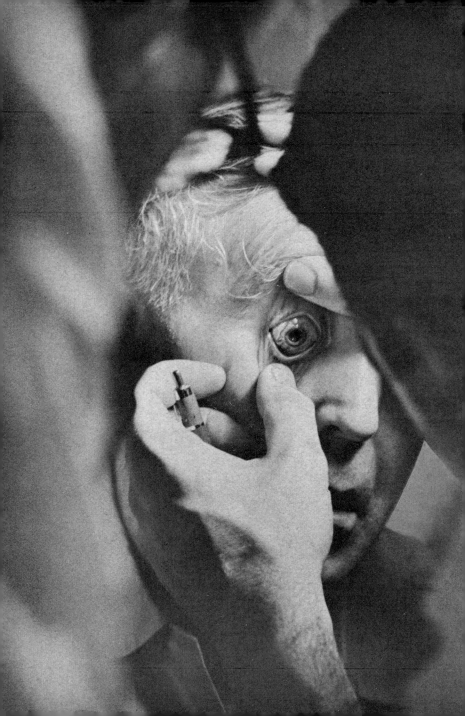

The need for thoroughgoing sincerity   6.39

Then he gave them an illustration—

"Can one blind man be guide to another blind man? Surely they will both fall into the ditch together. A disciple is not above his teacher, but when he is fully trained he will be like his teacher.

"Why do you look at the speck of sawdust in your brother's eye and fail to notice the plank in your own? How can you say to your brother, 'Let me take the speck out of your eye' when you cannot see the plank in your own? You fraud, take the plank out of your own eye first and then you can see clearly enough to remove your brother's speck.

"It is impossible for a good tree to produce bad fruit—as impossible as it is for a bad tree to produce good fruit. Do not men know what a tree is by its fruit? You cannot pick figs from briars, or gather a bunch of grapes from a blackberry bush! A good man produces good things from the good stored up in his heart, and a bad man produces evil things from his own stores of evil. For a man's words will always express what has been treasured in his heart.

"And what is the point of calling me, 'Lord, Lord,' without doing what I tell you to do? Let me show you what the man who comes to me, hears what I have to say, and puts it into practice, is really like. He is like a man building a house, who dug down to rock bottom and laid the foundation of his house upon it. Then when the flood came and the flood water swept down upon that house, it could not shift it because it was properly built. But the man who hears me and does nothing about it is like a man who built his house with its foundation upon soft earth. When the flood water swept down upon it, it collapsed and the whole house crashed down in ruins."

A Roman centurion's extraordinary faith in Jesus   7.1

When Jesus had finished these talks to the people, he came to Capernaum, where it happened that there was a man very seriously ill and in fact at the point of death. He was the slave of a centurion who thought very highly of him. When the centurion heard about Jesus, he sent some Jewish elders to him with the request that he would come and save his servant's life. When they came to Jesus, they urged him strongly to grant this request, saying that the centurion deserved to have this done for him. "He loves our nation and has built us a synagogue out of his own pocket," they said.

So Jesus went with them, but as he approached the house the centurion sent some of his personal friends with the message:

"Don't trouble yourself, sir! I'm not important enough for you to come into my house—I didn't think I was fit to come to you in person. Just give the order, please, and my servant will recover. I am used to working under orders, and I have soldiers under me. I can say to one, 'Go,' and he goes, or I can say to another, 'Come here,' and he comes; or I can say to my slave, 'Do this job,' and he does it."

These words amazed Jesus and he turned to the crowd who were following behind him, and said,

"I have never found faith like this anywhere, even in Israel!"

Then those who had been sent by the centurion returned to the house and found the slave perfectly well.

Jesus brings a dead youth back to life   7.11

Not long afterward, Jesus went into a town called Nain, accompanied by his disciples and a large crowd. As they approached the city gate, it happened that some people were carrying out a dead man, the only son of his widowed mother. The usual crowd of fellow townsmen was with her. When the Lord saw her, his heart went out to her, and he said,

"Don't cry."

Then he walked up and put his hand on the bier while the bearers stood still. Then he said,

"Young man, *wake up!*"

And the dead man sat up and began to talk, and Jesus handed him to his mother. Everybody present was awestruck and they praised God, saying,

"A great prophet has arisen among us and God has turned his face toward his people."

And this report of him spread through the whole of Judaea and the surrounding countryside.

Jesus sends John a personal message   7.18

John's disciples reported all these happenings to him. Then he summoned two of them and sent them to the Lord with this message,

"Are you the one who was to come, or are we to look for someone else?"

When the men came to Jesus, they said,

"John the Baptist has sent us to you with this message, 'Are you the one who was to come, or are we to look for someone else?' "

At that very time Jesus was healing many people of their diseases and ailments and evil spirits, and he restored sight to many who were blind. Then he answered them:

"Go and tell John what you have seen and heard. The blind are recovering their sight, cripples are walking again, lepers being healed, the deaf hearing, dead men are being brought to life again, and the good news is being given to those in need. *And happy is the man who never loses his faith in me.*"

Jesus emphasizes the greatness of John—and   7.24
the greater importance of the kingdom of God

When these messengers had gone back, Jesus began to talk to the crowd about John.

"What did you go out into the desert to look at? Was it a

reed waving in the breeze? Well, *what* was it you went out to see? A man dressed in fine clothes? But the men who wear fine clothes live luxuriously in palaces. But what *did* you really go to see? A prophet? Yes, I tell you, a prophet and far more than a prophet! This is the man of whom the scripture says,

> Behold, I send my messenger before thy face,
> Who shall prepare thy way before thee.

Believe me, no one greater than John has even been born, and yet a humble member of the kingdom of God is greater than he.

"All the people, yes, even the tax collectors, when they heard John, acknowledged God and were baptized by his baptism. But the Pharisees and the experts in the Law frustrated God's purpose for them, for they refused John's baptism.

"What can I say that the men of this generation are like—what sort of men are they? They are like children sitting in the market place and calling out to one another, 'We played at weddings for you, but you wouldn't dance, and we played at funerals for you, and you wouldn't cry!' For John the Baptist came in the strictest austerity and you say he is crazy. Then the Son of Man came, enjoying life, and you say, 'Look, a drunkard and a glutton, a bosom friend of the tax collector and the outsider!' Ah, well, wisdom's reputation is entirely in the hands of her children!"

Jesus contrasts unloving righteousness with loving penitence   7.36

Then one of the Pharisees asked Jesus to a meal with him. When Jesus came into the house, he took his place at the table and a woman, known in the town as a bad woman, found out that Jesus was there and brought an alabaster flask of perfume and stood behind him crying, letting her tears fall on his feet and then drying them with her hair. Then she kissed them and anointed them with the perfume. When the Pharisee who had invited him saw this, he said to himself, "If this man were really a prophet, he would know who this woman is and what sort of person is touching him. He would have realized that she is a bad woman." Then Jesus spoke to him,

"Simon, there is something I want to say to you."

"Very well, master," he returned, "say it."

"Once upon a time, there were two men in debt to the same moneylender. One owed him fifty dollars and the other five. And since they were unable to pay, he generously canceled both of their debts. Now, which one of them do you suppose will love him more?"

"Well," returned Simon, "I suppose it will be the one who has been more generously treated."

"Exactly," replied Jesus, and then turning to the woman, he said to Simon:

"You can see this woman? I came into your house but you provided no water to wash my feet. But she has washed my feet with her tears and dried them with her hair. There was no warmth in your greeting, but she, from the moment I came in, has not stopped covering my feet with kisses. You gave me no oil for my head, but she has put perfume on my feet. That is why I tell you, Simon, that her sins, many as they are, are forgiven; for she has shown me so much love. But the man who has little to be forgiven has only a little love to give."

Then he said to her,

"Your sins are forgiven."

And the men at table with him began to say to themselves,

"And who is this man, who even forgives sins?"

But Jesus said to the woman:

"It is your faith that has saved you. Go in peace."

Not long after this incident, Jesus went through every town and village preaching and telling the people the good news of the kingdom of God. He was accompanied by the twelve and some women who had been cured of evil spirits and illnesses—Mary, known as "the woman from Magdala" (who had once been possessed by seven evil spirits), Joanna the wife of Chuza, Herod's agent; Susanna, and many others who used to look after his comfort from their own resources.

Jesus' parable of the mixed reception given to the truth   8.4

When a large crowd had collected and people were coming to him from one town after another, he spoke to them and gave them this parable:

"A sower went out to sow his seed, and while he was sowing, some of the seed fell by the roadside and was trodden down and the birds gobbled it up. Some fell on the rock, and when it sprouted it withered for lack of moisture. Some fell among thornbushes which grew up with the seeds and choked the life out of them. But some seed fell on good soil and grew and produced a crop—a hundred times what had been sown."

And when he had said this, he called out,

"Let the man who has ears to hear use them!"

Then his disciples asked him the meaning of the parable. To which Jesus replied,

"You have been given the chance to understand the secrets of the kingdom of God, but the others are given parables so that they may go through life with their eyes open and see nothing, and with their ears open, and understand nothing of what they hear.

"This is what the parable means. The seed is the message of God. The seed sown by the roadside represents those who hear the message, and then the devil comes and takes it away from their hearts so that they cannot believe it and be saved. That sown on the rock represents those who accept the message with great delight when they hear it, but have no real root. They believe for a little while but when the time of temptation comes, they lose faith. And the seed sown among the thorns represents the people who hear the message and go on their way, and with the worries and riches and pleasures of living, the life is choked out of them, and in the end they produce nothing. But the seed sown on good soil means the men who hear the message and accept it with a good and honest heart, and go on steadily producing a good crop.

Truth is not a secret to be hidden but a gift to be used   8.16

"Nobody lights a lamp and covers it with a basin or puts it under the bed. No, a man puts his lamp on a lampstand so that those who come in can see the light. For there is nothing hidden now which will not become perfectly plain and there are no secrets now which will not become as clear as daylight.

So take care how you listen—more will be given to the man
who has something already, but the man who has nothing will
lose even what he thinks he has."

Then his mother and his brothers arrived to see him, but
could not get near him because of the crowd. So a message
was passed to him,

"Your mother and your brothers are standing outside wanting to see you."

To which he replied,

"My mother and my brothers? That means those who listen
to God's message and obey it."

Jesus' mastery of wind and water   8.22

It happened on one of these days that he embarked on a
boat with his disciples and said to them,

"Let us cross over to the other side of the lake."

So they set sail, and when they were under way he dropped
off to sleep. Then a squall of wind swept down upon the lake
and they were in grave danger of being swamped. Coming
forward, they woke him up, saying,

"Master, master, we're drowning!"

Then he got up and reprimanded the wind and the stormy
waters, and they died down, and everything was still. Then he
said to them,

"What has happened to your faith?"

But they were frightened and bewildered and kept saying
to one another:

"Who ever can this be? He gives orders even to the winds
and waters and *they obey him*."

Jesus encounters and heals a dangerous lunatic   8.26

They sailed on to the country of the Gerasenes which is on
the opposite side of the lake to Galilee. And as Jesus disembarked, a man from the town who was possessed by evil spirits
met him. He had worn no clothes for a long time and did not

live inside a house, but among the tombs. When he saw Jesus, he let out a howl and fell down in front of him, yelling:

"What have you got to do with me, you Jesus, Son of the most high God? Please, please, don't torment me."

For Jesus was commanding the evil spirit to come out of the man. Again and again the evil spirit had taken control of him, and though he was bound with chains and fetters and closely watched, he would snap his bonds and go off into the desert with the devil at his heels. Then Jesus asked him,

"What is your name?"

"Legion!" he replied. For many evil spirits had gone into him, and were now begging Jesus not to order them off to the bottomless pit. It happened that there was a large herd of pigs feeding on the hillside, so they implored him to allow them to go into the pigs, and he let them go. And when the evil spirits came out of the man and went into the pigs, the whole herd rushed down the cliff into the lake and were drowned. When the swineherds saw what had happened, they took to their heels, pouring out the story to the people in the town and countryside. These people came out to see what had happened, and approached Jesus. They found the man, whom the evil spirits had left, sitting down at Jesus' feet, properly clothed and quite sane. That frightened them. Those who had seen it told the others how the man with the evil spirits had been cured. And the whole crowd of people from the district surrounding the Gerasenes' country begged Jesus to go away from them, for they were thoroughly frightened. Then he re-embarked on the boat and turned back. The man who had had the evil spirits kept begging to go with Jesus, but he sent him away with the words,

"Go back home and tell them all what wonderful things God has done for you."

So the man went away and told the marvelous story of what Jesus had done for him, all over the town.

On Jesus' return, the crowd welcomed him back, for they had all been looking for him.

Jesus heals in response to faith   8.41

Then up came Jairus (who was president of the synagogue), and fell at Jesus' feet, begging him to come into his house, for his daughter, an only child about twelve years old, was dying.

But as he went, the crowds nearly suffocated him. Among them was a woman who had had a hemorrhage for twelve years and who had derived no benefit from anybody's treatment. She came up behind Jesus and touched the edge of his cloak, with the result that her hemorrhage stopped at once.

"Who was that who touched me?" said Jesus.

And when everybody denied it, Peter remonstrated,

"Master, the crowds are all round you and are pressing you on all sides. . . ."

But Jesus said,

"Somebody touched me, for I felt that power went out from me."

When the woman realized that she had not escaped notice, she came forward trembling, and fell at his feet and admitted before everybody why she had had to touch him, and how she had been instantaneously cured.

"Daughter," said Jesus, "it is your faith that has healed you —go in peace."

While he was still speaking, somebody came from the synagogue president's house to say,

"Your daughter is dead—there is no need to trouble the master any further."

But when Jesus heard this, he said to him,

"Now don't be afraid, go on believing and she will be all right."

Then when he came to the house, he would not allow anyone to go in with him except Peter, John and James, and the child's parents. All those already there were weeping and wailing over her, but he said,

"Stop crying! She is not dead, she is fast asleep."

This drew a scornful laugh from them, for they were quite certain that she had died. But he turned them all out, took the little girl's hand and called out to her,

"Wake up, my child!"

And her spirit came back and she got to her feet at once, and Jesus ordered food to be given to her. Her parents were nearly out of their minds with joy, but Jesus told them not to tell anyone what had happened.

Jesus commissions the twelve to preach and heal   9.1

Then he called the twelve together and gave them power and authority over all evil spirits and the ability to heal disease. He sent them out to preach the kingdom of God and to heal the sick, with these words:

"Take nothing for your journey—neither a stick nor a purse nor food nor money, nor even extra clothes! When you come to stay at a house, remain there until you go on your way again. And where they will not welcome you, leave that town, and shake the dust off your feet as a protest against them!"

So they set out, and went from village to village preaching the gospel and healing people everywhere.

Herod's uneasy conscience after his execution of   9.7
John

All these things came to the ears of Herod the tetrarch and caused him acute anxiety, because some people were saying that John had risen from the dead, some maintaining that the prophet Elijah had appeared, and others that one of the old-time prophets had come back.

"I beheaded John," said Herod. "Who can this be that I hear all these things about?"

And he tried to find a way of seeing Jesus.

The twelve return and tell their story   9.10

Then the apostles returned, and when they had made their report to Jesus of what they had done, he took them with him privately and retired into a town called Bethsaida.

Jesus welcomes the crowds, teaches, heals and   9.11
feeds them

But the crowds observed this and followed him. And he welcomed them and talked to them about the kingdom of God, and cured those who were in need of healing. As the day drew to its close the twelve came to him and said,

"Please dismiss the crowd now so that they can go to the villages and country round about and find some food and shelter, for we're quite in the wilds here."

"You give them something to eat!" returned Jesus.

"But we've nothing here," they replied, "except five loaves and two fish, unless you want us to go and buy food for all this crowd." (There were approximately five thousand men there.)

Then Jesus said to the disciples,

"Get them to sit down in groups of about fifty."

This they did, making them all sit down. Then he took the five loaves and the two fish and looked up to Heaven, blessed them, broke them into pieces and passed them to his disciples to serve to the crowd. Everybody ate and was satisfied. Afterward they collected twelve baskets full of broken pieces which were left over.

Jesus asks a question and receives Peter's   9.18
momentous answer

Then came this incident. While Jesus was praying by himself, having only the disciples near him, he asked them this question:

"Who are the crowd saying that I am?"

"Some say that you are John the Baptist," they replied. "Others that you are Elijah, and others think that one of the old-time prophets has come to life again."

Then he said,
"And who do you say that I am?"
"*God's Christ!*" said Peter.

Jesus foretells his own suffering: the paradox   9.21
of losing life to find it

But Jesus expressly told them not to say a word to anybody,
at the same time warning them of the inevitability of the Son
of Man's great suffering, of his repudiation by the elders, chief
priests and scribes, and of his death and of being raised to
life again on the third day. Then he spoke to them all:

"If anyone wants to follow in my footsteps, he must give up
all right to himself, carry his cross every day and keep close
behind me. For the man who wants to save his life will lose it,
but the man who loses his life for my sake will save it. For what
is the use of a man gaining the whole world if he loses or
forfeits his own soul? If anyone is ashamed of me and my
words, the Son of Man will be ashamed of him, when he comes
in his glory and the glory of the Father and the holy angels.
I tell you the simple truth—there are men standing here today
who will not taste death until they have seen the kingdom of
God!"

Peter, John and James are allowed to see the   9.28
glory of Jesus

About eight days after these sayings, Jesus took Peter,
James and John and went off with them to the hillside to pray.
And then, while he was praying, the whole appearance of his
face changed and his clothes became white and dazzling.
And two men were talking with Jesus. They were Moses and
Elijah—revealed in heavenly splendor, and their talk was
about the way he must take and the end he must fulfill in
Jerusalem. But Peter and his companions had been overcome
by sleep and it was as they struggled into wakefulness that
they saw the glory of Jesus and the two men standing with
him. Just as they were parting from him, Peter said to Jesus:

"Master, it is wonderful for us to be here! Let us put up three shelters—one for you, one for Moses and one for Elijah." But he did not know what he was saying. While he was still talking, a cloud overshadowed them and awe swept over them as it enveloped them. A voice came out of the cloud, saying,

"This is my Son, my chosen! Listen to him!"

And while the voice was speaking, they found there was no one there at all but Jesus. The disciples were reduced to silence, and in those days never breathed a word to anyone of what they had seen.

Jesus heals an epileptic boy   9.37

Then on the following day, as they came down the hillside, a great crowd met him. Suddenly a man from the crowd shouted out:

"Master, please come and look at my son! He's my only child, and without any warning some spirit gets hold of him and he calls out suddenly. Then it convulses him until he foams at the mouth, and only after a fearful struggle does it go away and leave him bruised all over. I begged your disciples to get rid of it, but they couldn't."

"You really are an unbelieving and difficult people," replied Jesus. "How long must I be with you, how long must I put up with you? Bring him here to me."

But even while the boy was on his way, the spirit hurled him to the ground in a dreadful convulsion. Then Jesus reprimanded the evil spirit, healed the lad and handed him back to his father. And everybody present was amazed at this demonstration of the power of God.

The realism of Jesus in the midst of enthusiasm   9.43b

And while everybody was full of wonder at all the things they saw him do, Jesus was saying to the disciples,

"Store up in your minds what I tell you nowadays, for the Son of Man is going to be handed over to the power of men."

But they made no sense of this saying—something made it impossible for them to understand it, and they were afraid to ask him what he meant.

Jesus and "greatness"   9.46

Then an argument arose among them as to who should be the greatest. But Jesus, knowing what they were arguing about, took a little child and made him stand by his side. And then he said to them:

"Anyone who accepts a little child in my name is really accepting me, and the man who accepts me is really accepting the one who sent me. It is the humblest among you all who is really the greatest."

Then John broke in,

"Master, we saw a man driving out evil spirits in your name, but we stopped him, for he is not one of us who follow you."

But Jesus told him,

"You must not stop him. The man who is not against you is on your side."

He sets off for Jerusalem to meet inevitable death 9.51

Now as the days before he should be taken back into Heaven were running out, he resolved to go to Jerusalem, and sent messengers in front of him. They set out and entered a Samaritan village to make preparations for him. But the people there refused to welcome him because he was obviously intending to go to Jerusalem. When the disciples James and John saw this, they said,

"Master, do you want us to call down fire from heaven and burn them all up?"

But Jesus turned and reproved them, and they all went on to another village.

As the little company made its way along the road, a man said to him,

"I'm going to follow you wherever you go."

And Jesus replied,

"Foxes have earths, birds have nests, but the Son of Man has nowhere that he can call his own."

But he said to another man,

"Follow me."

And he replied,

"Let me go and bury my father first."

But Jesus told him:

"Leave the dead to bury their own dead. You must come away and preach the kingdom of God."

Another man said to him,

"I am going to follow you, Lord, but first let me bid farewell to my people at home."

But Jesus told him,

"Anyone who puts his hand to the plow and then looks behind him is useless for the kingdom of God."

Jesus now dispatches thirty-five couples   10.1
to preach and heal the sick

Later on, the Lord commissioned seventy other disciples, and sent them off in twos as advance parties into every town and district where he intended to go.

"There is a great harvest," he told them, "but only a few are working in it—which means you must pray to the Lord of the harvest that he will send out more reapers.

"Now go on your way. I am sending you out like lambs among wolves. Don't carry a purse or a bag or a pair of shoes, and don't stop to pass the time of day with anyone you meet on the road. When you go into a house, say first of all, 'Peace be to this household!' If there is a lover of peace there, he will accept your words of blessing, and if not, they will come back to you. Stay in the same house and eat and drink whatever they put before you—a workman deserves his wages. But don't move from one house to another.

"Whatever town you go into and the people welcome you, eat the meals they give you and heal the people who are ill there. Tell them, 'The kingdom of God is very near to you now.' But whenever you come into a town and they will not welcome you, you must go into the streets and say, 'We brush off even the dust of your town from our feet as a protest against you. But it is still true that the kingdom of God has arrived!' I assure you that it will be better for Sodom in 'that day' than for that town.

"Alas for you, Chorazin, and alas for you, Bethsaida! For if Tyre and Sidon had seen the demonstrations of God's power that you have seen, they would have repented long ago and sat in sackcloth and ashes. It will be better for Tyre and Sidon in the judgment than for you! As for you, Capernaum, are you on your way up to heaven? I tell you you will go hurtling down among the dead!"

Then he added to the seventy:

"Whoever listens to you is listening to me, and the man who has no use for you has no use for me either. And the man who has no use for me has no use for the one who sent me!"

Jesus tells the returned missioners not to be   10.17
enthusiastic over mere power

Later the seventy came back full of joy.

"Lord," they said, "even evil spirits obey us when we use your name!"

"Yes," returned Jesus, "I was watching and saw Satan fall from heaven like a flash of lightning! It is true that I have given you the power to tread on snakes and scorpions and to over-come all the enemy's power—there is nothing at all that can do you any harm. Yet it is not your power over evil spirits which should give such joy, but the fact that your names are written in Heaven."

Jesus prays aloud to his Father   10.21

At that moment Jesus himself was inspired with joy, and exclaimed:

"O Father, Lord of Heaven and earth, I thank you for hiding these things from the clever and intelligent and for showing them to mere children! Yes, I thank you, Father, that this was your will." Then he went on:

"Everything has been put in my hands by my Father; and nobody knows who the Son really is except the Father. Nobody knows who the Father really is except the Son—and the man to whom the Son chooses to reveal him!"

Then he turned to his disciples and said to them quietly:

"How fortunate you are to see what you are seeing! I tell you that many prophets and kings have wanted to see what you are seeing but they never saw it, and to hear what you are hearing but they never heard it."

Jesus shows the relevance of the Law   10.25
to actual living

Then one of the experts in the Law stood up to test him and said,

"Master, what must I do to be sure of eternal life?"

"What does the Law say and what has your reading taught you?" said Jesus.

"The Law says, 'Thou shalt love the Lord thy God with all thy heart and with all thy soul and with all thy strength and with all thy mind—and thy neighbor as thyself,' " he replied.

"Quite right," said Jesus. "Do that and you will live."

But the man, wanting to justify himself, continued,

"But who is my 'neighbor'?"

And Jesus gave him the following reply:

"A man was once on his way down from Jerusalem to Jericho. He fell into the hands of bandits who stripped off his clothes, beat him up, and left him half dead. It so happened that a priest was going down that road, and when he saw him he passed by on the other side. A Levite also came on the scene, and when he saw him he too passed by on the other side. But then a Samaritan traveler came along to the place where the man was lying, and at the sight of him he was touched with pity. He went across to him and bandaged his wounds, pouring on oil and wine. Then he put him on his own mule, brought him to an inn and did what he could for him. Next day he took out two silver coins and gave them to the innkeeper with the words: 'Look after him, will you? I will pay you back whatever more you spend, when I come through here on my return.' Which of these three seems to you to have been a neighbor to the bandits' victim?"

"The man who gave him practical sympathy," he replied.

"Then you go and give the same," returned Jesus.

Yet emphasizes the need for quiet listening to his words   10.38

As they continued their journey, Jesus came to a village and a woman called Martha welcomed him to her house. She had a sister by the name of Mary who settled down at the Lord's feet and was listening to what he said. But Martha was very worried about her elaborate preparations and she burst in, saying:

"Lord, don't you *mind* that my sister has left me to do everything by myself? Tell her to get up and help me!"

But the Lord answered her:

"Martha, my dear, you are worried and bothered about providing so many things. Only a few things are really needed, perhaps only one. Mary has chosen the best part and you must not tear it away from her!"

Jesus gives a model prayer   11.1

One day it happened that Jesus was praying in a certain place, and after he had finished, one of his disciples said,

"Lord, teach us how to pray, as John used to teach his disciples."

"When you pray," returned Jesus, "you should say, 'Father, may your name be honored—may your kingdom come! Give us each day the bread we need, and forgive us our sins, for we forgive anyone who owes anything to us; and keep us clear of temptation.' "

The willingness of the Father to answer prayer   11.5

Then he added:

"If any of you has a friend, and goes to him in the middle of the night and says, 'Lend me three loaves, my dear fellow, for a friend of mine has just arrived after a journey and I have no food to put in front of him'; and then he answers from inside the house: 'Don't bother me with your troubles. The front door is locked and my children and I have gone to bed. I simply cannot get up now and give you anything!' Yet, I tell you, that even if he won't get up and give him what he wants simply because he is his friend, yet if he persists, he will rouse himself and give him everything he needs. And so I tell you, ask and it will be given you, search and you will find, knock and the door will be opened to you. The one who asks will always receive; the one who is searching will always find, and the door is opened to the man who knocks. Some of you are fathers, and if your son asks you for some fish would you give him a snake instead, or if he asks you for an egg would you make him a present of a scorpion? So, if you, for all your evil, know how to give good things to your children, how much more likely is it that your Heavenly Father will give the Holy Spirit to those who ask him!"

Jesus shows the absurdity of "his being   **11.14**
in league with the devil"

Another time, Jesus was expelling an evil spirit which was preventing a man from speaking, and as soon as the evil spirit left him the dumb man found his speech, to the amazement of the crowds.

But some of them said,

"He expels these spirits because he is in league with Beelzebub, the chief of the evil spirits."

Others among them, to test him, tried to get a sign from Heaven out of him. But he knew what they were thinking, and told them:

"Any kingdom divided against itself is doomed, and a disunited household will collapse. And if Satan disagrees with Satan, how does his kingdom continue?—for I know you are saying that I expel evil spirits because I am in league with Beelzebub. But if I do expel devils because I am an ally of Beelzebub, who is your own sons' ally when they do the same thing? They can settle that question for you. But if it is by the finger of God that I am expelling evil spirits, *then the kingdom of God has swept over you unawares!*

"When a strong man armed to the teeth guards his own house, his property is in peace. But when a stronger man comes and conquers him, he removes all the arms on which he pinned his faith and divides the spoil among his friends.

"Anyone who is not with me is against me, and the man who does not gather with me is really scattering.

The danger of a spiritual vacuum in a man's soul   11.24

"When the evil spirit comes out of a man, it wanders through waterless places looking for rest, and when it fails to find any, it says, 'I will go back to my house from which I came.' When it arrives, it finds it cleaned and all in order. Then it goes and collects seven other spirits more evil than itself to keep it company, and they all go in and make themselves at home. The last state of that man is worse than the first."

Jesus brings sentimentality down to earth   11.27

And while he was still saying this, a woman in the crowd called out and said,

"Oh, what a blessing for a woman to have brought you into the world and nursed you!"

But Jesus replied,

"Yes, but a far greater blessing to hear the word of God and obey it."

His scathing judgment on his contemporary   11.29
generation

Then as the people crowded closely around him, he continued:

"This is an evil generation! It looks for a sign and it will be given no sign except that of Jonah. Just as Jonah was a sign to the people of Nineveh, so will the Son of Man be a sign to this generation. When the judgment comes, the Queen of the South will rise up with the men of this generation and she will condemn them. For she came from the ends of the earth to listen to the wisdom of Solomon, and there is more than the wisdom of Solomon with you now! The men of Nineveh will stand up at the judgment with this generation and will condemn it. For they did repent when Jonah preached to them, and there is something more than Jonah's preaching with you now!

The need for complete sincerity   **11.33**

"No one takes a lamp and puts it in a cupboard or under a bucket, but on a lampstand, so that those who come in can see the light. The lamp of your body is your eye. When your eye is sound, your whole body is full of light, but when your eye is evil your whole body is full of darkness. So be very careful that your light never becomes darkness. For if your whole body is full of light, with no part of it in shadow, it will all be radiant —it will be like having a bright lamp to give you light."

While he was talking, a Pharisee invited him to dinner. So he went into his house and sat down at table. The Pharisee noticed with some surprise that he did not wash before the meal. But the Lord said to him:

"You Pharisees are fond of cleaning the outside of your cups and dishes, but inside yourselves you are full of greed and wickedness! Have you no sense? Don't you realize that the one who made the outside is the maker of the inside as well? If you would only make the inside clean by doing good to others, the outside things become clean as a matter of course! But alas for you Pharisees, for you pay out your tithe of mint and rue and every little herb, and lose sight of the justice and the love of God. Yet these are the things you ought to have been concerned with—it need not mean leaving the lesser duties undone. Yes, alas for you Pharisees, who love the front seats in the synagogues and having men bow down to you in public! Alas for you, for you are like unmarked graves—men walk over your corruption without ever knowing it is there."

Jesus denounces the learned for obscuring the truth   11.45

Then one of the experts in the Law said to him,

"Master, when you say things like this, you are insulting us as well."

And he returned:

"Yes, and I do blame you experts in the Law! For you pile up back-breaking burdens for men to bear, but you yourselves will not raise a finger to lift them. Alas for you, for you build memorial tombs for the prophets—the very men whom your fathers murdered. You show clearly enough how you approve your fathers' actions. They did the actual killing and you put up a memorial to it. That is why the wisdom of God has said, 'I will send them prophets and apostles; some they will kill and some they will persecute!' So that the blood of all the prophets shed from the foundation of the earth, from Abel to Zachariah who died between the altar and the sanctuary, shall be charged to this generation!

"Alas for you experts in the Law, for you have taken away the key of knowledge. You have never gone in yourselves and you have hindered everyone else who was at the door!"

And when he left the house, the scribes and the Pharisees began to regard him with bitter animosity and tried to draw him out on a great many subjects, waiting to pounce on some incriminating remark.

Meanwhile, the crowds had gathered in thousands, so that they were actually treading on one another's toes, and Jesus, speaking primarily to his disciples, said:

"Be on your guard against yeast—I mean the yeast of the Pharisees, which is sheer pretense. For there is nothing covered up which is not going to be exposed, nor anything private which is not going to be made public. Whatever you may say in the dark will be heard in daylight, and whatever you whisper within four walls will be shouted from the housetops.

Man need only fear God   12.4

I tell you, as friends of mine, that you need not be afraid of those who can kill the body, but afterward cannot do anything more. I will show you the only one you need to fear—the one who, after he has killed, has the power to throw you into destruction! Yes, I tell you, it is right to stand in awe of him. The market price of five sparrows is two cents, isn't it? Yet not one of them is forgotten in God's sight. Why, the very hairs of your heads are all numbered! Don't be afraid, then; you are worth more than a great many sparrows! I tell you that every man who publicly acknowledges me, I, the Son of Man, will acknowledge in the presence of the angels of God. But the man who publicly disowns me will find himself disowned before the angels of God!

"Anyone who speaks against the Son of Man will be forgiven, but there is no forgiveness for the man who speaks evil against the Holy Spirit. And when they bring you before the synagogues and magistrates and authorities, don't worry as to what defense you are going to put up or what words you are going to use. For the Holy Spirit will tell you at the time what is the right thing for you to say."

Jesus gives a warning about the love of material security   12.13

Then someone out of the crowd said to him,

"Master, tell my brother to share his legacy with me."

But Jesus replied,

"My dear man, who appointed me a judge or arbitrator in your affairs?"

And then, turning to the disciples, he said to them:

"Notice that, and be on your guard against covetousness in any shape or form. For a man's real life in no way depends upon the number of his possessions."

Then he gave them a parable in these words:

"Once upon a time a rich man's farmland produced heavy crops. So he said to himself, 'What shall I do, for I have no room to store this harvest of mine?' Then he said: 'I know what I'll do. I'll pull down my barns and build bigger ones where I can store all my grain and my goods and I can say to my soul, Soul, you have plenty of good things stored up there for years to come. Relax! Eat, drink and have a good time!' But God said to him, 'You fool, this very night you will be asked for *your soul!* Then who is going to possess all that you have prepared?' That is what happens to the man who hoards things for himself and is not rich where God is concerned."

And then he added to the disciples:

"That is why I tell you; don't worry about life, wondering what you are going to eat. And stop bothering about what clothes you will need. Life is much more important than food, and the body more important than clothes. Think of the ravens. They neither sow nor reap, and they have neither store nor barn, but God feeds them. And how much more valuable do you think you are than birds? Can any of you make himself an inch taller however much he worries about it? And if you can't manage a little thing like this, why do you worry about anything else? Think of the wild flowers, and how they neither work nor weave. Yet I tell you that Solomon in all his glory was

never arrayed like one of these. If God so clothes the grass, which flowers in the field today and is burned in the stove tomorrow, is he not much more likely to clothe you, you little-faiths? You must not set your heart on what you eat or drink, nor must you live in a state of anxiety. The whole heathen world is busy about getting food and drink, and your Father knows well enough that you need such things. No, set your heart on his kingdom, and your food and drink will come as a matter of course. Don't be afraid, you tiny flock! Your Father plans to give you the kingdom. Sell your possessions and give the money away. Get yourselves purses that never grow old, inexhaustible treasure in Heaven, where no thief can ever reach it, or moth ruin it. For wherever your treasure is, you may be certain that your heart will be there too!

Jesus' disciples must be on the alert   12.35

"You must be ready dressed and have your lamps alight, like men who wait to welcome their lord and master on his return from the wedding feast, so that when he comes and knocks at the door they may open it for him at once. Happy are the servants whom their lord finds on the alert when he arrives. I assure you that he will then take off his outer clothes, make them sit down to dinner, and come and wait on them. And if he should come just after midnight or in the very early morning and find them still on the alert, their happiness is assured. But be certain of this, that if the householder had known the time when the burglar would come, he would not have let his house be broken into. So you must be on the alert, for the Son of Man is coming at a time when you may not expect him."

Then Peter said to him,

"Lord, do you mean this parable for us or for everybody?"

But the Lord continued:

"Well, who will be the faithful, sensible steward whom his master will put in charge of his household to give them their

supplies at the proper time? Happy is the servant if his master finds him so doing when he returns. I tell you he will promote him to look after all his property. But suppose the servant says to himself, 'My master takes his time about returning,' and then begins to beat the men and women servants and to eat and drink and get drunk, that servant's lord and master will return suddenly and unexpectedly, and he will punish him severely and send him to share the penalty of the unfaithful. The slave who knows his master's plan but does not get ready or act upon it will be severely punished, but the servant who did not know the plan, though he has done wrong, will be let off lightly. Much will be expected from the one who has been given much, and the more a man is trusted, the more people will expect of him.

"It is fire that I have come to bring upon the earth—how I could wish it were already ablaze! There is a baptism that I must undergo and how strained I am until it is over!

Jesus declares that his coming is bound   **12.51**
to bring division

"Do you think I have come to bring peace on the earth? No, I tell you, not peace, but division! For from now on, there will be five people divided against each other in one house, three against two, and two against three. It is going to be father against son, and son against father, and mother against daughter, and daughter against mother; mother-in-law against her daughter-in-law, and daughter-in-law against mother-in-law!"

Intelligence should be used not only about   **12.54**
the weather but about the times in which men live

Then he said to the crowds:

"When you see a cloud rising in the west, you say at once that it is going to rain, and so it does. And when you feel the south wind blowing, you say that it is going to be hot, and so it is. You frauds! You know how to interpret the look of the earth and the sky. Why can't you interpret the meaning of the times in which you live?

"And why can't you decide for yourselves what is right? For instance, when you are going before the magistrate with your opponent, do your best to come to terms with him while you have the chance, or he may rush you off to the judge, and the judge hand you over to the police officer, and the police officer throw you into prison. I tell you you will never get out again until you have paid your last penny."

Jesus is asked about the supposed significance   13.1
of disasters

It was just at this moment that some people came up to tell him the story of the Galileans whose blood Pilate had mixed with that of their own sacrifices. Jesus made this reply to them:

"Are you thinking that these Galileans were worse sinners than any other men of Galilee because this happened to them? I assure you that is not so. You will all die just as miserable a death unless your hearts are changed! You remember those eighteen people who were killed at Siloam when the tower collapsed upon them? Are you imagining that they were worse offenders than any of the other people who lived in Jerusalem? I assure you they were not. You will all die as tragically unless your whole outlook is changed!"

And hints at God's patience with the Jewish nation 13.6

Then he gave them this parable:

"Once upon a time a man had a fig tree growing in his garden, and when he came to look for the figs he found none at all. So he said to his gardener, 'Look, I have come expecting fruit on this fig tree for three years running and never found any. Better cut it down. Why should it use up valuable space!' And the gardener replied: 'Master, don't touch it this year till I have had a chance to dig round it and give it a bit of manure. Then, if it bears after that, it will be all right. But if it doesn't, then you can cut it down.' "

Jesus reduces the sabbatarians to silence 13.10

It happened that he was teaching in one of the synagogues on the Sabbath day. In the congregation was a woman who for eighteen years had been ill from some psychological cause; she was bent double and was quite unable to straighten herself up. When Jesus noticed her, he called her and said,

"You are set free from your illness!"

And he put his hands upon her, and at once she stood upright and praised God. But the president of the synagogue, in his annoyance at Jesus' healing on the Sabbath, announced to the congregation:

"There are six days in which men may work. Come on one of them and be healed, and not on the Sabbath day!"

But the Lord answered him, saying:

"You hypocrites, every single one of you unties his ox or his ass from the stall on the Sabbath day and leads him away to water! This woman, a daughter of Abraham, whom you all know Satan has kept bound for eighteen years—surely she should be released from such bonds on the Sabbath day!"

These words reduced his opponents to shame, but the crowd was thrilled at all the glorious things he did.

Then he went on:

"What is the kingdom of God like? What illustration can I use to make it plain to you? It is like a grain of mustard seed which a man took and dropped in his own garden. It grew and became a tree and the birds came and nested in its branches."

Then again he said:

"What can I say the kingdom of God is like? It is like the yeast which a woman took and covered up in three measures of flour until the whole lot had risen."

The kingdom is not entered by drifting but   13.22
by decision

So he went on his way through towns and villages, teaching as he went and making his way toward Jerusalem. Someone remarked,

"Lord, are only a few men to be saved?"

And Jesus told them:

"You must do your utmost to get in through the narrow door, for many, I assure you, will try to do so and will not succeed, once the master of the house has got up and shut the door. Then you may find yourselves standing outside and knocking at the door crying, 'Lord, please open the door for us.' He will reply to you, 'I don't know who you are or where you come from.' 'But...' you will protest, 'we have had meals with you, and you taught in our streets!' Yet he will say to you, 'I tell you I do not know where you have come from. Be off, you scoundrels!' At that time there will be tears and bitter regret—to see Abraham and Isaac and Jacob and all the prophets inside the kingdom of God, and you yourselves excluded, outside! Yes, and people will come from the east and the west, and from the north and the south, and take their seats in the kingdom of God. There are some at the back now who will be in front then, and there are some in front now who will then be far behind."

The Pharisees warn Jesus of Herod; he replies   13.31

Just then some Pharisees arrived to tell him,

"You must get right away from here, for Herod intends to kill you."

"Go and tell that fox," returned Jesus, "today and tomorrow I am expelling evil spirits and continuing my work of healing, and on the third day my work will be finished. But I must journey on today, tomorrow and the next day, for it would never do for a prophet to meet his death outside Jerusalem!

"O Jerusalem, Jerusalem, you murder the prophets and stone the messengers that are sent to you! How often have I longed to gather your children round me like a bird gathering her brood together under her wings, but you would never have it. Now, all that is left is yourselves, and your house. For I tell you that you will never see me again till the day when you cry, 'Blessed is he who comes in the name of the Lord!' "

Strict sabbatarianism is again rebuked   14.1

One Sabbath day he went into the house of one of the leading Pharisees for a meal, and they were all watching him closely. Right in front of him was a man afflicted with dropsy. So Jesus spoke to the scribes and Pharisees and said,

"Well, is it right to heal on the Sabbath day or not?"

But there was no reply. So Jesus took the man and healed him and let him go. Then he said to them,

"If an ass or a cow belonging to one of you fell into a well, wouldn't you rescue him without the slightest hesitation even though it were the Sabbath?"

And this again left them quite unable to reply.

A lesson in humility   14.7

Then he gave a little word of advice to the guests when he noticed how they were choosing the best seats.

"When you are invited to a wedding reception, don't sit down in the best seat. It might happen that a more distinguished man than you has also been invited. Then your host might say, 'I am afraid you must give up your seat for this man.' And then, with considerable embarrassment, you will have to sit in the humblest place. No, when you are invited, go and take your seat in an inconspicuous place, so that when your host comes in he may say to you, 'Come on, my dear fellow, we have a much better seat than this for you.' That is the way to be important in the eyes of all your fellow guests! For everyone who makes himself important will become insignificant, while the man who makes himself insignificant will find himself important."

Then, addressing his host, Jesus said:

"When you give a luncheon or a dinner party, don't invite your friends or your brothers or relations or wealthy neighbors, for the chances are they will invite you back, and you will be fully repaid. No, when you give a party, invite the poor, the lame, the crippled and the blind. That way lies real happiness for you. They have no means of repaying you, but you will be repaid when good men are rewarded—at the resurrection."

Then, one of the guests, hearing these remarks of Jesus, said, "What happiness for a man to eat a meal in the kingdom of God!"

Men who are "too busy" for the kingdom of God 14.16

But Jesus said to him:

"Once upon a time, a man planned a big dinner party and invited a great many people. At dinnertime, he sent his servant out to tell those who were invited, 'Please come, everything is ready now.' But they all, as one man, began to make their excuses. The first one said to him: 'I have bought some land. I must go and look at it. Please excuse me.' Another one said: 'I have bought five yoke of oxen and am on my way to try them out. Please convey my apologies.' And another one said, 'I have just got married and I am sure you will understand I cannot come.' So the servant returned and reported all this to his master. The master of the house was extremely annoyed and said to his servant, 'Hurry out now into the streets and alleys of the town, and bring here the poor and crippled and blind and lame.' Then the servant said, 'I have done what you told me, sir, and there are still empty places.' Then the master replied: 'Now go out to the roads and hedgerows and make them come inside, so that my house may be full. For I tell you that not one of the men I invited shall have a taste of my dinner.' "

Now as Jesus proceeded on his journey, great crowds accompanied him, and he turned and spoke to them:

"If anyone comes to me without 'hating' his father and mother and wife and children and brothers and sisters, and even his own life, he cannot be a disciple of mine. The man who will not take up his cross and follow in my footsteps cannot be my disciple.

"If any of you wanted to build a tower, wouldn't he first sit down and work out the cost of it, to see if he can afford to finish it? Otherwise, when he has laid the foundation and found himself unable to complete the building, everyone who sees it will begin to jeer at him, saying, 'This is the man who started to build a tower but couldn't finish it!' Or, suppose there is a king who is going to war with another king, doesn't he sit down first and consider whether he can engage the twenty thousand of the other king with his own ten thousand? And if he decides he can't, then, while the other king is still a long way off, he sends messengers to him to ask for conditions of peace. So it is with you; only the man who says goodbye to all his possessions can be my disciple.

"Salt is a very good thing, but if salt loses its flavor, what can you use to restore it? It is no good for the ground and no good as manure. People just throw it away. Every man who has ears should use them!"

Jesus speaks of the love of God for "the lost"   15.1

Now all the tax collectors and "outsiders" were crowding around to hear what he had to say. The Pharisees and the scribes complained of this, remarking,

"This man accepts sinners and even eats his meals with them."

So Jesus spoke to them, using this parable:

"Wouldn't any man among you who owned a hundred sheep, and lost one of them, leave the ninety-nine to themselves in the open, and go after the one which is lost until he finds it? And when he has found it, he will put it on his shoulders with great joy, and as soon as he gets home, he will call his friends and neighbors together. 'Come and celebrate with me,' he will say, 'for I have found that sheep of mine which was lost.' I tell you that it is the same in Heaven—there is more joy over one sinner whose heart is changed than over ninety-nine righteous people who have no need of repentance.

"Or if there is a woman who has ten silver coins, if she should lose one, won't she take a lamp and sweep and search the house from top to bottom until she finds it? And when she has found it, she calls her friends and neighbors together. 'Come and celebrate with me,' she says, 'for I have found that coin I lost.' I tell you, it is the same in Heaven—there is rejoicing among the angels of God over one sinner whose heart is changed."

Then he continued:

"Once there was a man who had two sons. The younger one said to his father, 'Father, give me my share of the property that will come to me.' So he divided up his property between the two of them. Before very long, the younger son collected all his belongings and went off to a foreign land, where he squandered his wealth in the wildest extravagance. And when he had run through all his money, a terrible famine arose in that country, and he began to feel the pinch. Then he went and hired himself out to one of the citizens of that country who sent him out into the fields to feed the pigs. He got to the point of longing to stuff himself with the food the pigs were eating, and not a soul gave him anything. Then he came to his senses and cried aloud, 'Why, dozens of my father's hired men have got more food than they can eat, and here am I dying of hunger! I will get up and go back to my father, and I will say to him: "Father, I have done wrong in the sight of Heaven and in your eyes. I don't deserve to be called your son any more. Please take me on as one of your hired men." ' So he got up and went to his father. But while he was still some distance off, his father saw him and his heart went out to him, and he ran and fell on his neck and kissed him. But his son said: 'Father, I have done wrong in the sight of Heaven and in your eyes. I don't deserve to be called your son any more. . . .' 'Hurry!' called out his father to the servants, 'fetch the best clothes and put them on him! Put a ring on his finger and shoes on his feet, and get that calf we've fattened and kill it, and we will have a feast and a celebration! For this is my son—I thought he was dead, and he's alive again. I thought I had lost him, and he's found!' And they began to get the festivities going.

"But his elder son was out in the fields, and as he came near the house, he heard music and dancing. So he called one of the servants across to him and inquired what was the meaning of it all. 'Your brother has arrived, and your father has killed the calf we fattened because he has got him home again safe and sound,' was the reply. But he was furious and refused to go inside the house. So his father came outside and called him. Then he burst out: 'Look, how many years have I slaved for you and never disobeyed a single order of yours, and yet you have never given me so much as a young goat, so that I could give my friends a dinner! But when that son of yours arrives, who has spent all your money on prostitutes, for *him* you kill the calf we've fattened!' But the father replied: 'My dear son, you have been with me all the time and everything I have is yours. But we *had* to celebrate and show our joy. For this is your brother; I thought he was dead—and he's alive. I thought he was lost—and he is found!' "

A clever rogue, and the right use of money 16.1

Then there is this story he told his disciples:
"Once there was a rich man whose agent was reported to him to be mismanaging his property. So he summoned him and said: 'What's this that I hear about you? Give me an account of your stewardship—you're not fit to manage my

household any longer.' At this the agent said to himself: 'What am I going to do now that my employer is taking away the stewardship from me? I am not strong enough to dig and I can't sink to begging. Ah, I know what I'll do so that when I lose my position people will welcome me into their homes!' So he sent for each one of his master's debtors. 'How much do you owe my master?' he said to the first. 'A hundred barrels of oil,' he replied. 'Here,' replied the agent, 'take your bill, sit down, hurry up and write in fifty.' Then he said to another, 'And what's the size of your debt?' 'A thousand bushels of wheat,' he replied. 'Take your bill,' said the agent, 'and write in eight hundred.' Now the master praised this rascally steward because he had been so careful for his own future. For the children of this world are considerably more shrewd in dealing with their contemporaries than the children of light. Now my advice to you is to use 'money,' tainted as it is, to make yourselves friends, so that when it comes to an end they may welcome you into eternal habitations.

"The man who is faithful in the little things will be faithful in the big things, and the man who cheats in the little things will cheat in the big things too. So that if you are not fit to be trusted to deal with the wicked wealth of this world, who will trust you with the true riches? And if you are not trustworthy with someone else's property, who will give you property of your own? No servant can serve two masters. He is bound to hate one and love the other, or give his loyalty to one and despise the other. You cannot serve God and the power of money at the same time."

Now the Pharisees, who were very fond of money, heard all this with a sneer. But he said to them:

"You are the people who advertise your goodness before men, but God knows your hearts. Remember, there are things men consider perfectly splendid which are detestable in the sight of God!

MONEY
LOANED

DIAMONDS

JEWELRY

Jesus states that the kingdom of God has superseded "the Law and the Prophets"   16.16

"The Law and the Prophets were in force until John's day. From then on the good news of the kingdom of God has been proclaimed and men are forcing their way into it.

"Yet it would be easier for Heaven and earth to disappear than for a single point of the Law to become a dead letter.

"Any man who divorces his wife and marries another woman commits adultery. And so does any man who marries the woman who was divorced from her husband.

Jesus shows the fearful consequence of social injustice   16.19

"There was once a rich man who used to dress in purple and fine linen and lead a life of daily luxury. And there was a poor man called Lazarus who was put down at his gate. He was covered with sores. He used to long to be fed with the scraps from the rich man's table. Yes, and the dogs used to come and lick his sores. Well, it happened that the poor man died, and was carried by the angels into Abraham's bosom. The rich man also died and was buried. And from among the dead he looked up and saw Abraham a long way away, and Lazarus in his arms. 'Father Abraham!' he cried out, 'please pity me. Send Lazarus to dip the tip of his finger in water and cool my tongue, for I am in agony in these flames.' But Abraham replied: 'Remember, my son, that you used to have the good things in your lifetime, while Lazarus suffered the bad. Now he is being comforted here, while you are in agony. And besides this, a great chasm has been set between you and us, so that those who want to go to you from this side cannot do so, and people cannot come to us from your side.' At this he said: 'Then I beg you, father, to send him to my father's house, for I have five brothers. He could warn them about all this and prevent their coming to this place of torture.' But Abraham said, 'They have Moses and the Prophets: they can listen to them.' 'Ah no, father Abraham,' he said, 'if only someone were to go to them from the dead, they would change completely.' But Abraham told him, 'If they will not listen to Moses and the Prophets, they would not be convinced even if somebody were to rise from the dead.' "

Jesus warns his disciples about spoiling   17.1
the spirit of the new kingdom

Then Jesus said to his disciples:
"It is inevitable that there should be pitfalls, but alas for the man who is responsible for them! It would be better for that man to have a millstone hung round his neck and be thrown into the sea, than that he should trip up one of these little ones. So be careful how you live. If your brother offends you, take him to task about it, and if he is sorry forgive him. Yes, if he wrongs you seven times in one day and turns to you and says, 'I am sorry' seven times, you must forgive him."

And the apostles said to the Lord,
"Give us more faith."
And he replied,
"If your faith were as big as a grain of mustard seed, you could say to this fig tree, 'Pull yourself up by the roots and plant yourself in the sea,' and it would do what you said!

Work in the kingdom must be taken   17.7
as a matter of course

"If any of you have a servant plowing or looking after the sheep, are you likely to say to him when he comes in from the fields, 'Come straight in and sit down to your meal'? Aren't you more likely to say, 'Get my supper ready: change your coat, and wait while I eat and drink: and then, when I've finished, you can have your meal'? Do you feel particularly grateful to your servant for doing what you tell him? I don't think so. It is the same with yourselves—when you have done everything that you are told to do, you can say, 'We are not much good as servants, for we have only done what we ought to do.' "

**Jesus heals ten men of leprosy: only one   17.11
shows his gratitude**

In the course of his journey to Jerusalem, Jesus crossed the
boundary between Samaria and Galilee, and as he was
approaching a village ten lepers met him. They kept their
distance but shouted out,

"Jesus, Master, have pity on us!"

When Jesus saw them, he said,

"Go and show yourselves to the priests."

And it happened that as they went on their way they were
cured. One of their number, when he saw that he was cured,
turned round and praised God at the top of his voice, and
then fell on his face before Jesus and thanked him. This man
was a Samaritan. And at this Jesus remarked:

"Weren't there ten men healed? Where are the other nine?
Is nobody going to turn and praise God for what has been
done, except this stranger?"

And he said to the man:

"Stand up now, and go on your way. It is your faith that has
made you well."

**Jesus tells the Pharisees that the kingdom   17.20
is here and now**

Later, he was asked by the Pharisees when the kingdom of
God was coming, and he gave them this reply:

"The kingdom of God never comes by watching for it. Men
cannot say, 'Look, here it is,' or 'There it is,' for the kingdom of
God is inside you."

Jesus tells his disciples about the future   17.22

Then he said to the disciples:

"The time will come when you will long to see again a single
day of the Son of Man, but you will not see it. People will say
to you, 'Look, there he is,' or 'Look, here he is.' Stay where

you are and don't go off looking for him! For the day of the Son of Man will be like lightning flashing from one end of the sky to the other. But before that happens, he must go through much suffering and be utterly rejected by this generation. In the time of the coming of the Son of Man, life will be as it was in the days of Noah. People ate and drank, married and were given in marriage, right up to the day when Noah entered the ark—and then came the flood and destroyed them all. It will be just the same as it was in the days of Lot. People ate and drank, bought and sold, planted and built, but on the day that Lot left Sodom fire and brimstone rained from heaven, and destroyed them all. That is how it will be on the day when the Son of Man is revealed. When that day comes, the man who is on the roof of his house, with his goods inside it, must not come down to get them. And the man out in the fields must not turn back for anything. Remember what happened to Lot's wife. Whoever tries to preserve his life will lose it, and the man who is prepared to lose his life will preserve it. I tell you, that night there will be two men in one bed; one man will be taken and the other will be left. Two women will be turning the grinding mill together; one will be taken and the other left."

"But where, Lord?" they asked him.

" 'Wherever there is a dead body, there the vultures will flock,' " he replied.

Jesus urges his disciples to persist in prayer   18.1

Then he gave them an illustration to show that they must always pray and never lose heart.

"Once upon a time," he said, "there was a magistrate in a town who had neither fear of God nor respect for his fellow men. There was a widow in the town who kept coming to him, saying, 'Please protect me from the man who is trying to ruin me.' And for a long time he refused. But later he said to himself, 'Although I don't fear God and have no respect for men, yet this woman is such a nuisance that I shall give judgment in her favor, or else her continual visits will be the death of me!' "

Then the Lord said:

"Notice how this dishonest magistrate behaved. Do you suppose God, patient as he is, will not see justice done for his chosen, who appeal to him day and night? I assure you he will not delay in seeing justice done. Yet, when the Son of Man comes, will he find men on earth who believe in him?"

Jesus tells a story against the self-righteous   18.9

Then he gave this illustration to certain people who were confident of their own goodness and looked down on others:

"Two men went up to the Temple to pray, one was a Pharisee, the other was a tax collector. The Pharisee stood and prayed like this with himself, 'O God, I do thank thee that I am not like the rest of mankind, greedy, dishonest, impure, or even like that tax collector over there. I fast twice every week; I give away a tenth part of all my income.' But the tax collector stood in a distant corner, scarcely daring to look up to Heaven, and with a gesture of despair, said, 'God, have mercy on a sinner like me.' I assure you that he was the man who went home justified in God's sight rather than the other one. For everyone who sets himself up as somebody will become a nobody, and the man who makes himself nobody will become somebody."

Jesus welcomes babies   18.15

Then people began to bring babies to him so that he could put his hands on them. But when the disciples noticed it, they frowned on them. But Jesus called them to him, and said:

"You must let little children come to me, and you must never prevent their coming. The kingdom of Heaven belongs to little children like these. I tell you, the man who will not accept the kingdom of God like a little child will never get into it at all."

Jesus and riches   18.18

Then one of the Jewish rulers put this question to him,

"Master, I know that you are good; tell me, please, what must I do to be sure of eternal life?"

"I wonder why you call me good?" returned Jesus. "No one is good—only the one God. You know the commandments—

"Thou shalt not commit adultery.

"Thou shalt not commit murder.

"Thou shalt not steal.

"Thou shalt not bear false witness.

"Honor thy father and thy mother."

"All these," he replied, "I have carefully kept since I was quite young."

And when Jesus heard that, he said to him:

"There is still one thing you have missed. Sell everything you possess and give the money away to the poor, and you will have riches in Heaven. Then come and follow me."

But when the man heard this, he was greatly distressed, for he was very rich.

And when Jesus saw how his face fell, he remarked:
"How difficult it is for those who have great possessions to enter the kingdom of God! A camel could squeeze through the eye of a needle more easily than a rich man could get into the kingdom of God."
Those who heard Jesus say this, exclaimed,
"Then who can possibly be saved?"
Jesus replied,
"What men find impossible is perfectly possible with God."
"Well," rejoined Peter, "we have left all that we ever had and followed you."
And Jesus told them,
"Believe me, nobody has left his home or wife, or brothers or parents or children for the sake of the kingdom of God, without receiving very much more in this present life—and eternal life in the world to come."

Jesus foretells his death and resurrection   18.31

Then Jesus took the twelve to one side and spoke to them:
"Listen to me. We are now going up to Jerusalem, and everything that has been written by the prophets about the Son of Man will come true. For he will be handed over to the heathen, and he is going to be jeered at and insulted and spat upon, and then they will flog him and kill him. But he will rise again on the third day."
But they did not understand any of this. His words were quite obscure to them and they had no idea of what he meant.

On the way to Jericho he heals a blind beggar   18.35

Then, as he was approaching Jericho, it happened that there was a blind man sitting by the roadside, begging. He heard the crowd passing and inquired what it was all about. And they told him, "Jesus the man from Nazareth is going past you." So he shouted out,

"Jesus, Son of David, have pity on me!"

Those who were in front tried to hush his cries. But that made him call out all the more,

"Son of David, have pity on me!"

So Jesus stood quite still and ordered the man to be brought to him. And when he was quite close, he said to him,

"What do you want me to do for you?"

"Lord, make me see again," he cried.

"You can see again! Your faith has cured you," returned Jesus.

And his sight was restored at once, and he followed Jesus, praising God. All the people who saw it thanked God too.

The chief tax collector is converted to faith in Jesus   19.1

Then he went into Jericho and was making his way through it. And here we find a wealthy man called Zacchaeus, a chief collector of taxes, wanting to see what sort of person Jesus was. But the crowd prevented him from doing so, for he was very short. So he ran ahead and climbed up into a sycamore tree to get a view of Jesus as he was heading that way. When Jesus reached the spot, he looked up and saw the man and said:

"Zacchaeus, hurry up and come down. I must be your guest today."

So Zacchaeus hurriedly climbed down and gladly welcomed him. But the bystanders muttered their disapproval, saying,

"Now he has gone to stay with a real sinner."

But Zacchaeus himself stopped and said to the Lord:

"Look, sir, I will give half my property to the poor. And if I have swindled anybody out of anything I will pay him back four times as much."

Jesus said to him:

"Salvation has come to this house today! Zacchaeus is a descendant of Abraham, and it was the lost that the Son of Man came to seek—and to save."

Life requires courage, and is hard on those   19.11
who dare not use their gifts

Then as the crowd still listened attentively, Jesus went on to give them this parable. For the fact that he was nearing Jerusalem made them imagine that the kingdom of God was on the point of appearing.

"Once upon a time a man of good family went abroad to accept a kingdom and then return. He summoned ten of his servants and gave them each ten dollars, with the words, 'Use this money to trade with until I come back.' But the citizens detested him and they sent a delegation after him, to say, 'We will not have this man to be our king.' Then later, when he had received his kingdom, he returned and gave orders for the servants to whom he had given the money to be called to him, so that he could find out what profit they had made. The first came into his presence, and said, 'Sire, your ten dollars have made a hundred dollars more.' 'Splendid, my good fellow,' he said, 'since you have proved trustworthy over this small amount, I am going to put you in charge of ten towns.' The second came in and said, 'Sire, your ten dollars have made fifty dollars.' And he said to him, 'Good, you're appointed governor of five towns.' When the last came, he said, 'Sire, here are your ten dollars, which I have been keeping wrapped up in a handkerchief. I have been scared—I know you're a hard man, getting something for nothing and reaping where you never sowed.' To which he replied: 'You scoundrel, your own words condemn you! You knew perfectly well, did you, that I am a hard man who gets something for nothing and reaps where he never sowed? Then why didn't you put my money into the bank, and then when I returned I could have had it back with interest?' Then he said to those who were standing by, 'Take away his ten dollars and give it to the fellow who has a hundred.'

" 'But, sire, he has a hundred dollars already,' they said to him. 'Yes,' he replied, 'and I tell you that the man who has something will get more given to him. But as for the man who has nothing, even his "nothing" will be taken away. And as for these enemies of mine who objected to my being their king, bring them here and execute them in my presence.' "

After these words, Jesus walked on ahead of them on his way to Jerusalem.

Jesus arranges his own entrance into Jerusalem   19.29

Then as he was approaching Bethphage and Bethany, near the hill called the Mount of Olives, he sent off two of his disciples, telling them:

"Go into the village just ahead of you, and there you will find a colt tied on which no one has ever yet ridden. Untie it and bring it here. And if anybody asks you, 'Why are you untying it?' just say, 'The Lord needs it.' "

So the messengers went off and found things just as he had told them. In fact, as they were untying the colt, the owners did say, "Why are you untying it?" and they replied, "The Lord needs it." So they brought it to Jesus and, throwing their cloaks upon it, mounted Jesus on its back. Then as he rode along, people spread out their coats in the roadway. And as he approached the city, where the road slopes down from the Mount of Olives, the whole crowd of his disciples joyfully shouted praises to God for all the marvelous things that they had seen him do.

"God bless the king who comes in the name of the Lord!" they cried. "There is peace in Heaven and glory on high!"

There were some Pharisees in the crowd who said to Jesus, "Master, restrain your disciples!"

To which he replied,

"I tell you that if they kept quiet, the very stones in the road would burst out cheering!"

The sight of the city moves him to tears   19.41

And as he came still nearer to the city, he caught sight of it and wept over it, saying:

"Ah, if you only knew, even at this eleventh hour, on what your peace depends—but you cannot see it. The time is coming when your enemies will encircle you with ramparts, surrounding you and hemming you in on every side. And they will hurl you and all your children to the ground—yes, they will not leave you one stone standing upon another—all because you did not know when God Himself was visiting you!"

Then he went into the Temple, and proceeded to throw out the traders there.

"It is written," he told them, " *'My house shall be a house of prayer,'* but you have turned it into a thieves' kitchen."

Jesus teaches daily in the Temple   19.47

Then day after day he was teaching inside the Temple. The chief priests, the scribes and the national leaders were all the time trying to get rid of him, but they could not find any way to do it since all the people hung upon his words.

Then one day as he was teaching the people in the Temple, and preaching the gospel to them, the chief priests, the scribes and elders confronted him in a body and asked him this direct question,

"Tell us by whose authority you act as you do—who gave you such authority?"

"I have a question for you, too," replied Jesus. "John's baptism, now—tell me, did it come from Heaven or was it purely human?"

At this they began arguing with one another, saying:

"If we say, 'from Heaven,' he will say to us, 'Then why didn't you believe in him?' but if we say it was purely human, this mob will stone us to death, for they are convinced that John was a prophet." So they replied that they did not know where it came from.

"Then," returned Jesus, "neither will I tell you by what authority I do what I am doing."

He tells the people a pointed story   20.9

Then he turned to the people and told them this parable:
"There was once a man who planted a vineyard, let it
out to farm workers, and went abroad for some time. Then,
when the season arrived, he sent a servant to the farm workers
so that they could give him the proceeds of the vineyard. But
the farm workers beat him up and sent him back empty-
handed. So he sent another servant, and they beat him up as
well, manhandling him disgracefully, and sent him back empty-
handed. Then he sent a third servant, but after wounding him
severely they threw him out. Then the owner of the vineyard
said, 'What shall I do now? I will send them my son who is so
dear to me. Perhaps they will respect *him*.' But when the farm
workers saw him they talked the matter over with one another
and said, 'This man is the heir—come on let's kill him, and we
shall get everything that he would have had!' And they threw
him outside the vineyard and killed him. What then do you
suppose the owner will do to them? He will come and destroy
the men who were working his property, and hand it over
to others."

When they heard this, they said,
"God forbid!"
But he looked them straight in the eyes and said,
"Then what is the meaning of this scripture—

The stone which the builders rejected,
The same was made the head of the corner?

The man who falls on that stone will be broken, and the man
on whom it falls will be crushed to powder."

The authorities resort to trickery   20.19

The scribes and chief priests longed to get their hands on
him at that moment, but they were afraid of the people. They
knew well enough that his parable referred to them. They
watched him, however, and sent some spies into the crowd,

pretending that they were honest men, to fasten on something that he might say which could be used to hand him over to the authority and power of the governor.

These men asked him:

"Master, we know that what you say and teach is right, and that you teach the way of God truly without fear or favor. Now, *is it right for us to pay taxes to Caesar or not?*"

But Jesus saw through their cunning and said to them:

"Show me one of the coins. Whose face is this, and whose name is in the inscription?"

"Caesar's," they said.

"Then give to Caesar," he replied, "what belongs to Caesar, and to God what belongs to God."

So his reply gave them no sort of handle that they could use against him publicly. And in fact they were so taken aback by his answer that they had nothing more to say.

Jesus exposes the ignorance of the Sadducees   20.27

Then up came some of the Sadducees (who deny that there is any resurrection) and they asked him:

"Master, Moses told us in the scripture, 'If a man's brother should die without any children, he should marry the widow and raise up a family for his brother.' Now, there were once seven brothers. The first got married and died childless, and the second and the third married the woman, and in fact all the seven married her and died without leaving any children. Lastly, the woman herself died. Now, in this 'resurrection' whose wife is she of these seven men, for she belonged to all of them?"

"People in this world," Jesus replied, "marry and are given in marriage. But those who are considered worthy of reaching that world, which means rising from the dead, neither marry nor are they given in marriage. They cannot die any more but live like the angels; for being children of the resurrection, they are the sons of God. But that the dead are raised, even Moses showed to be true in the story of the bush, when he calls the

Lord the God of Abraham, the God of Isaac and the God of Jacob. For God is not God of the dead, but of the living. For all men are alive to him."

To this some of the scribes replied,

"Master, that was a good answer."

And indeed nobody had the courage to ask him any more questions. But Jesus went on to say,

"How can they say that Christ is David's *son*? For David himself says in the book of psalms—

The Lord said unto my *Lord*,
Sit thou on my right hand,
Till I make thine enemies the footstool of thy feet.

David is plainly calling him 'Lord.' How then can he be his *son*?"

Jesus warns his disciples against religious pretentiousness   20.45

Then while everybody was listening, Jesus remarked to his disciples:

"Be on your guard against the scribes, who enjoy walking round in long robes and love having men bow to them in public, getting front seats in the synagogue, and the best places at dinner parties—while all the time they are battening on widows' property and covering it up with long prayers. These men are only heading for deeper damnation."

Then he looked up and saw the rich people dropping their gifts into the treasury, and he noticed a poor widow drop in two coppers, and he commented,

"I assure you that this poor widow has put in more than all of them, for they have all put in what they can easily spare, but she in her poverty has given away her whole living."

Jesus foretells the destruction of the Temple   21.5

Then when some of them were talking about the Temple and pointing out the beauty of its lovely stonework and the various ornaments that people had given, he said,

"Yes, you can gaze on all this today, but the time is coming when not a single stone will be left upon another, without being thrown down."

So they asked him,

"Master, when will this happen, and what sign will there be that these things are going to take place?"

"Be careful that you are not deceived," he replied. "There will be many coming in my name, saying 'I am he' and 'The time is very near now.' Never follow men like that. And when you hear about wars and disturbances, don't be alarmed. These things must indeed happen first, but the end will not come immediately."

And prophesies world-wide suffering   21.10

Then he continued:

"Nation will rise up against nation, and kingdom against kingdom; there will be great earthquakes and famines and plagues in this place or that. There will be dreadful sights, and great signs from heaven. But before all this happens, men will arrest you and persecute you, handing you over to synagogue or prison, or bringing you before kings and governors, for my name's sake. This will be your chance to witness for me. So make up your minds not to think out your defense beforehand. I will give you such eloquence and wisdom that none of your opponents will be able to resist or contradict it. But you will be betrayed, even by parents and brothers and kinsfolk and friends, and there will be some of you who will be killed and you will be hated everywhere for my name's sake. Yet, not a hair of your head will perish. Hold on, and you will win your souls!

"But when you see Jerusalem surrounded by armed forces, then you will know that the time of her devastation has arrived. Then is the time for those who are in Judaea to fly to the hills. And those who are in the city itself must get out of it, and those who are already in the country must not try to get into the city.

For these are the days of vengeance, when all that the scriptures have said will come true. Alas for those who are pregnant
and those who have tiny babies in those days! For there will
be bitter misery in the land and great anger against this
people. They will die by the sword. They will be taken off as
prisoners into all nations. Jerusalem will be trampled under-
foot by the heathen until the heathen's day is over. There will
be signs in the sun and moon and stars, and on the earth there
will be dismay among the nations and bewilderment at the
roar of the surging sea. Men's courage will fail completely as
they realize what is threatening the world, for the very powers
of heaven will be shaken. Then men will see the Son of Man
coming in a cloud with great power and splendor! But when
these things begin to happen, look up, hold your heads high,
for you will soon be free."

Vigilance is essential   21.29

Then he gave them a parable.

"Look at a fig tree, or indeed any tree, when it begins to
burst its buds, and you realize without anybody telling you
that summer is nearly here. So, when you see these things
happening, you can be equally sure that the kingdom of God
has nearly come. Believe me, this generation will not disappear
until all this has taken place. Earth and heaven will pass away,
but my words will never pass away.

"Be on your guard—see to it that your minds are never
clouded by dissipation or drunkenness or the worries of this
life, or else that day may catch you like the springing of a
trap—for it will come upon every inhabitant of the whole earth.

"You must be vigilant at all times, praying that you may be
strong enough to come safely through all that is going to
happen, and stand in the presence of the Son of Man."

And every day he went on teaching in the Temple, and every
evening he went off and spent the night on the hill which is
called the Mount of Olives. And the people used to come early
in the morning to listen to him in the Temple.

Judas Iscariot becomes the tool of the authorities   22.1

Now as the feast of unleavened bread, called the Passover, was approaching, fear of the people made the
chief priests and scribes try desperately to find a way of
getting rid of Jesus. Then a diabolical plan came into the mind
of Judas Iscariot, who was one of the twelve. He went and
discussed with the chief priests and officers a method of getting
Jesus into their hands. They were delighted and arranged to
pay him for it. He agreed, and began to look for a suitable
opportunity for betrayal when there was no crowd present.

Jesus makes arrangements for his last   22.7
Passover with his disciples

Then the day of unleavened bread arrived, on which the
Passover lamb had to be sacrificed, and Jesus sent off Peter
and John with the words, "Go and make all the preparations
for us to eat the Passover."

"Where would you like us to do this?" they asked.

And he replied:

"Listen, just as you're going into the city a man carrying a
jug of water will meet you. Follow him to the house he is making
for. Then say to the owner of the house, 'The master has this
message for you—which is the room where my disciples and
I may eat the Passover?' And he will take you upstairs and
show you a large room furnished for our needs. Make all the
preparations there."

So they went off and found everything exactly as he had
told them it would be, and they made the Passover preparations.

Then, when the time came, he took his seat at table with the apostles, and spoke to them:

"With all my heart I have longed to eat this Passover with you before the time comes for me to suffer. Believe me, I shall not eat the Passover again until all that it means is fulfilled in the kingdom of God."

Then taking a cup from them, he thanked God and said,

"Take this and share it amongst yourselves, for I tell you that I shall drink no more wine until the kingdom of God comes."

The mysterious words which were remembered later   22.19

Then he took a loaf and, after thanking God, he broke it and gave it to them, with these words,

"This is my body which is given for you: do this in remembrance of me."

So too, he gave them a cup after supper with the words:

"This cup is the new agreement made in my own blood which is shed for you. Yet the hand of the man who is betraying me lies with mine at this moment on the table. The Son of Man goes on his appointed way: yet alas for the man by whom he is betrayed!"

Jesus again teaches humility   22.23

And at this they began to debate among themselves as to which of them would do this thing.

And then a dispute arose among them as to who should be considered the most important.

But Jesus said to them:

"Among the heathen it is their kings who lord it over them, and their rulers are given the title of 'benefactors.' But it must not be so with you! *Your* greatest man must become like a junior and your leader must be a servant. Who is the greater, the man who sits down to dinner or the man who serves him? Obviously, the man who sits down to dinner—yet *I* am the one who is the servant among you. But you are the men who have stood by me in all that I have gone through, and as surely as my Father has given me my kingdom, so I give you the right to eat and drink at my table in that kingdom. Yes, you will sit on thrones and rule the twelve tribes of Israel!

The personal warning to Simon   22.31

"Oh, Simon, Simon, do you know that Satan has asked to have you all to sift like wheat?—But I have prayed for *you* that you may not lose your faith. Yes, when you have turned back to me, you must strengthen these brothers of yours."

Peter said to him,

"Lord, I am ready to go to prison, or even to die with you!"

"I tell you, Peter," returned Jesus, "before the cock crows today you will deny three times that you know me!"

Jesus tells his disciples that the crisis has arrived   22.35

Then he continued to them all,

"That time when I sent you out without any purse or wallet or shoes—did you find you needed anything?"

"No, not a thing," they replied.

"But now," Jesus continued, "if you have a purse or wallet, take it with you, and if you have no sword, sell your coat and buy one! for I tell you that this scripture must be fulfilled in me—

And he was reckoned with transgressors.

So comes the end of what they wrote about me."
Then the disciples said,
"Lord, look, here are two swords."
And Jesus returned,
"That is enough."
Then he went out of the city and up onto the Mount of Olives,
as he had often done before, with the disciples following him.
And when he reached his usual place, he said to them,
"Pray that you may not have to face temptation!"
Then he went off by himself, about a stone's throw away,
and falling on his knees, prayed in these words—
"Father, if you are willing, take this cup away from me—
but it is not my will, but yours, that must be done."
And an angel from Heaven appeared, strengthening him.
He was in agony and prayed even more intensely so that his
sweat was like great drops of blood falling to the ground.
Then he got to his feet from his prayer and walking back to
the disciples, he found them sleeping through sheer grief.
"Why are you sleeping?" he said to them. "You must get up
and go on praying that you may not have to face temptation."

The mob arrives and Judas betrays   22.47

While he was still speaking a crowd of people arrived, led
by the man called Judas, one of the twelve. He stepped up to
Jesus to kiss him.
"Judas, would you betray the Son of Man with a kiss?" said
Jesus to him.
And the disciples, seeing what was going to happen, cried.

"Lord, shall we use our swords?"

And one of them did slash at the High Priest's servant, cutting off his right ear. But Jesus retorted,

"That will do!"

And he touched his ear and healed him. Then he spoke to the chief priests, Temple officers and elders who were there to arrest him:

"So you have come out with your swords and staves as if I were a bandit. Day after day I was with you in the Temple and you never laid a finger on me—but this is your hour and the power of darkness is yours!"

Jesus is arrested: Peter follows but denies his   22.54 master three times

Then they arrested him and marched him off to the High Priest's house. Peter followed at a distance, and sat down among some people who had lighted a fire in the middle of the courtyard and were sitting round it. A maidservant saw him sitting there in the firelight, peered into his face and said,

"This man was with him too."

But he denied it and said,

"I don't know him, girl!"

A few minutes later someone else noticed Peter, and said,

"You're one of these men too."

But Peter said,

"Man, I am not!"

Then about an hour later someone else insisted,

"I am convinced this fellow was with him. Why, he is a Galilean!"

"Man," returned Peter, "I don't know what you're talking about."

And immediately, while he was still speaking, the cock crew.

The Lord turned his head and looked straight at Peter, into whose mind flashed the words that the Lord had said to him . . . "You will disown me three times before the cock crows today." And he went outside and wept bitterly.

Then the men who held Jesus made a great game of knocking him about. And they blindfolded him and asked him,

"Now, prophet, guess who hit you that time!"

And that was only the beginning of the way they insulted him.

In the early morning Jesus is formally   22.66
interrogated

Then when daylight came, the assembly of the elders of the people, which included both chief priests and scribes, met and marched him off to their own council. There they asked him,

"If you really are Christ, tell us!"

"If I tell you, you will never believe me, and if I ask you a question, you will not answer me. But from now on the Son of Man will take his seat at the right hand of almighty God."

Then they all said,

"So you are the Son of God then?"

"You are right; I am," Jesus told them.

Then they said,

"Why do we need to call any more witnesses, for we ourselves have heard this thing from his own lips?"

Jesus is taken before Pilate and Herod   23.1

Then they rose up in a body and took him off to Pilate, and began their accusation in these words,

"Here is this man whom we have found corrupting our people, and telling them that it is wrong to pay taxes to Caesar, claiming that he himself is Christ, a king."

But Pilate addressed his question to Jesus,
"Are you the king of the Jews?"
"Yes, I am," he replied.
Then Pilate spoke to the chief priests and the crowd,
"I find nothing criminal about this man."
But they pressed their charge, saying:
"He's a troublemaker among the people. He teaches through the whole of Judaea, all the way from Galilee to this place."

When Pilate heard this, he inquired whether the man were a Galilean, and when he discovered that he came under Herod's jurisdiction, he passed him on to Herod who happened to be in Jerusalem at that time. When Herod saw Jesus, he was delighted, for he had been wanting to see him for a long time. He had heard a lot about Jesus and was hoping to see him perform a miracle. He questioned him very thoroughly, but Jesus gave him absolutely no reply, though the chief priests and scribes stood there making the most violent accusations. So Herod joined his own soldiers in scoffing and jeering at Jesus. Finally, they dressed him up in a gorgeous cloak, and sent him back to Pilate. On that day Herod and Pilate became firm friends, though previously they had been at daggers drawn.

Pilate declares Jesus' innocence   23.13

Then Pilate summoned the chief priests, the officials and the people, and addressed them in these words:

"You have brought this man to me as a mischief-maker among the people, and I want you all to realize that, after examining him in your presence, I have found nothing criminal about him, in spite of all your accusations. And neither has Herod, for he has sent him back to us. Obviously, then, he has

done nothing to deserve the death penalty. I propose, therefore, to teach him a sharp lesson and let him go."

But they all yelled as one man:

"Take this man away! We want Barabbas set free!"

(Barabbas was a man who had been put in prison for
causing a riot in the city and for murder.) But Pilate wanted
to set Jesus free and he called out to them again, but they
shouted back at him,

"Crucify, crucify him!"

Then he spoke to them, for the third time:

"What is his crime, then? I have found nothing in him that
deserves execution; I am going to teach him his lesson and let
him go."

But they shouted him down, yelling their demand that he
should be crucified.

Their shouting won the day, and Pilate pronounced the
official decision that their request should be granted. He
released the man for whom they asked, the man who had
been imprisoned for rioting and murder, and surrendered
Jesus to their demands.

And as they were marching him away, they caught hold of
Simon, a native of Cyrene in Africa, who was on his way home
from the fields, and put the cross on his back for him to carry
behind Jesus.

On the way to the cross   23.27

A huge crowd of people followed him, including women
who wrung their hands and wept for him. But Jesus turned to
them and said:

"Women of Jerusalem, do not shed your tears for me, but
for yourselves and for your children! For the days are coming
when men will say, 'Lucky are the women who are childless—

the bodies which have never borne, and the breasts which have never given nourishment.' Then men will begin to say to the mountains, 'Fall upon us!' and will say to the hills, 'Cover us up!' For if this is what men do when the wood is green, what will they do when it is seasoned?"

Jesus is crucified with two criminals   23.32

Two criminals were also led out with him for execution, and when they came to the place called The Skull, they crucified him with the criminals, one on either side of him. But Jesus himself was saying,

"Father, forgive them; they do not know what they are doing."

Then they shared out his clothes by casting lots.

The people stood and stared while their rulers continued to scoff, saying, "He saved other people, let's see him save himself, if he is really God's Christ—his chosen!"

The soldiers also mocked him by coming up and presenting sour wine to him, saying,

"If you are the king of the Jews, why not save yourself?" For there was a placard over his head which read, "THIS IS THE KING OF THE JEWS."

One of the criminals hanging there covered him with abuse, and said,

"Aren't you Christ? Why don't you save yourself—and us?"

But the other one checked him with the words:

"Aren't you afraid of God even when you're getting the same punishment as he is? And it's fair enough for us, for we've only got what we deserve, but this man never did anything wrong in his life."

Then he said,

"Jesus, remember me when you come into your kingdom."

And Jesus answered,

"I tell you truly, this very day you will be with me in paradise."

The darkness, and the death of Jesus   23.44

It was now about midday, but darkness came over the whole countryside until three in the afternoon, for there was an eclipse of the sun. The veil in the Temple sanctuary was split in two. Then Jesus gave a great cry and said,

"Father, I commend my spirit into your hands."

And with these words, he died.

When the centurion saw what had happened, he exclaimed reverently,

"That was indeed a good man!"

And the whole crowd who had collected for the spectacle, when they saw what had happened, went home in deep distress. And those who had known him, as well as the women who had followed him from Galilee, remained standing at a distance and saw all this happen.

Joseph from Arimathaea lays the body   23.50
of Jesus in a tomb

Now there was a man called Joseph, a member of the Jewish council. He was a good and just man, and had neither agreed with their plan nor voted for their decision. He came from the Jewish City of Arimathaea and was awaiting the kingdom of God. He went to Pilate and asked for Jesus' body. He took it down and wrapped it in linen and placed it in a rock-hewn tomb which had not been used before.

It was now the day of the preparation and the Sabbath was beginning to dawn, so the women who had accompanied Jesus from Galilee followed Joseph, noted the tomb and the position of the body, and then went home to prepare spices and perfumes. On the Sabbath they rested, in obedience to the commandment.

The first day of the week: the empty tomb   24.1

But at the first signs of dawn on the first day of the week, they went to the tomb, taking with them the aromatic spices they had prepared. They discovered that the stone had been rolled away from the tomb, but on going inside, the body of the Lord Jesus was not to be found. While they were still puzzling over this, two men suddenly stood at their elbow, dressed in dazzling light. The women were terribly frightened, and turned their eyes away and looked at the ground. But the two men spoke to them,

"Why do you look for the living among the dead? He is not here: he has risen! Remember that he said to you, while he was still in Galilee—that the Son of Man must be betrayed into the hands of sinful men, and must be crucified, and must rise again on the third day."

Then they did remember what he had said, and they turned their backs on the tomb and went and told all this to the eleven and the others who were with them.

It was Mary of Magdala, Joanna, Mary, the mother of

James, and their companions who made this report to the apostles. But it struck them as sheer imagination, and they did not believe the women. Only Peter got up and ran to the tomb. He stooped down and saw the linen clothes lying there all by themselves, and he went home wondering what had happened.

The walk to Emmaus   24.13

Then on the same day we find two of them going off to Emmaus, a village about seven miles from Jerusalem. As they went they were deep in conversation about everything that had happened. While they were absorbed in their serious talk and discussion, Jesus himself approached and walked along with them, but something prevented them from recognizing him. Then he spoke to them,

"What is all this discussion that you are having on your walk?"

They stopped, their faces drawn with misery, and the one called Cleopas replied,

"You must be the only stranger in Jerusalem who hasn't heard all the things that have happened there recently!"

"What things?" asked Jesus.

"Oh, all about Jesus, from Nazareth. There was a man—a prophet strong in what he did and what he said, in God's eyes as well as the people's. Haven't you heard how our chief priests and rulers handed him over for execution, and had him crucified? But we were hoping he was the one who was to come and set Israel free. . . .

"Yes, and as if that were not enough, it's getting on for three days since all this happened; and some of our women-folk have disturbed us profoundly. For they went to the tomb at dawn, and then when they couldn't find his body they said that they had had a vision of angels who said that he was alive. Some of our people went straight off to the tomb and found things just as the women had described them—but they didn't see *him!*"

Then he himself spoke to them:

"Aren't you failing to understand, and slow to believe in all that the prophets have said? Was it not inevitable that Christ should suffer like that and so find his glory?"

Then, beginning with Moses and all the prophets, he explained to them everything in the scriptures that referred to himself.

They were by now approaching the village to which they were going. He gave the impression that he meant to go on further, but they stopped him with the words,

"Do stay with us. It is nearly evening and soon the day will be over."

So he went indoors to stay with them. Then it happened! While he was sitting at table with them he took the loaf, gave thanks, broke it and passed it to them. Their eyes opened wide and they knew him! But he vanished from their sight. Then they said to each other,

"Weren't our hearts glowing while he was with us on the road, and when he made the scriptures so plain to us?"

And they got to their feet without delay and turned back to Jerusalem. There they found the eleven and their friends all together, full of the news—

"The Lord is really risen—he has appeared to Simon now!"

Then they told the story of their walk, and how they recognized him when he broke the loaf.

Jesus suddenly appears to the disciples   24.36

And while they were still talking about these things, Jesus himself stood among them and said,

"Peace be to you all!"

But they shrank back in terror, for they thought they were

seeing a ghost.

"Why are you so worried?" said Jesus, "and why do doubts arise in your minds? Look at my hands and my feet—it is really I myself! Feel me and see; ghosts have no flesh or bones as you can see that I have."

But while they still could not believe it through sheer joy, and were quite bewildered, Jesus said to them,

"Have you anything here to eat?"

They gave him a piece of broiled fish and part of a honeycomb, which he took and ate before their eyes. Then he said,

"Here and now are fulfilled the words that I told you when I was with you: that everything written about me in the Law of Moses and in the prophets and psalms must come true."

Then he opened their minds so that they could understand the scriptures, and added:

"That is how it was written, and that is why it was inevitable that Christ should suffer, and rise from the dead on the third day. So must the change of heart which leads to the forgiveness of sins be proclaimed in his name to all nations, beginning at Jerusalem.

Jesus commissions them with the new message   24.48

"You are eyewitnesses of these things. Now I hand over to you the command of my Father. Stay in the city, then, until you are clothed with power from on high."

Then he led them outside as far as Bethany, where he blessed them with uplifted hands. While he was in the act of blessing them he was parted from them and was carried up to Heaven. They worshiped him, and turned back to Jerusalem with great joy, and spent their days in the Temple, praising and blessing God.

THE GOSPEL OF JOHN

Prologue   **1.1**

At the beginning God expressed himself. That personal expression, that word, was with God and was God, and he existed with God from the beginning. All creation took place through him, and none took place without him. In him appeared life and this life was the light of mankind. The light still shines in the darkness, and the darkness has never put it out.

The gospel's beginning on earth   **1.6**

A man called John was sent by God as a witness to the light, so that any man who heard his testimony might believe in the light. This man was not himself the light: he was sent simply as a personal witness to that light.

That was the true light which shines upon every man as he comes into the world. He came into the world—the world he had created—and the world failed to recognize him. He came into his own creation, and his own people would not accept him. Yet wherever men did accept him he gave them the power to become sons of God. These were the men who truly believed in him, and their birth depended not on the course of nature nor on any impulse or plan of man, but on God.

So the word of God became a human being and lived among us. We saw his splendor (the splendor as of a father's only son), full of grace and truth. And it was about him that John stood up and testified, exclaiming: "Here is the one I was speaking about when I said that although he would come after me he would always be in front of me; for he existed before I was born!" Indeed, every one of us has shared in his riches—there is a grace in our lives because of his grace. For while the Law was given by Moses, love and truth came through Jesus Christ. It is true that no one has ever seen God at any time. Yet the divine and only Son, who lives in the closest intimacy with the Father, has made him known.

John's witness   1.19

This then is the testimony of John, when the Jews sent priests and Levites to ask him who he was. He admitted with complete candor, "I am not Christ."

So they asked him, "Who are you then? Are you Elijah?"

"No, I am not," he replied.

"Are you the Prophet?"

"No," he replied.

"Well, then," they asked again, "who are you? We want to give an answer to the people who sent us. What would you call yourself?"

"I am a voice shouting in the desert, 'Make straight the way of the Lord!' as Isaiah the prophet said."

Now some of the Pharisees had been sent to John, and they questioned him, "What is the reason, then, for your baptizing people if you are not Christ and not Elijah and not the Prophet?"

To which John returned, "I do baptize—with water. But somewhere among you stands a man you do not know. He comes after me, it is true, but I am not fit to undo his shoes!" (All this happened in the Bethany on the far side of the Jordan where the baptisms of John took place.)

On the following day, John saw Jesus coming toward him and said, "Look, there is the lamb of God who will take away the sin of the world! This is the man I meant when I said 'A man comes after me who is always in front of me, for he existed before I was born!' It is true I have not known him, yet it was to make him known to the people of Israel that I came and baptized people with water."

Then John gave this testimony: "I have seen the Spirit come down like a dove from Heaven and rest upon him. Indeed, it is true that I did not recognize him by myself, but he who sent me to baptize with water told me this: 'The one on whom you will see the Spirit coming down and resting is the man who baptizes with the Holy Spirit!' Now I have seen this happen and I declare publicly before you all that he is the Son of God!"

Men begin to follow Jesus 1.35

On the following day John was again standing with two of his disciples. He looked straight at Jesus as he walked along and said, "There is the lamb of God!" The two disciples heard what he said and followed Jesus. Then Jesus turned round and when he saw them following him, spoke to them. "What do you want?" he said.

"Master, where are you staying?" they replied.

"Come and see," returned Jesus.

So they went and saw where he was staying and remained with him the rest of that day. (It was then about four o'clock in the afternoon.) One of the two men who had heard what John said and had followed Jesus was Andrew, Simon Peter's brother. He went straight off and found his own brother, Simon, and told him, "We have found the Messiah!" (meaning, of course, Christ). And he brought him to Jesus.

Jesus looked steadily at him and said: "You are Simon, the son of John. From now on your name is Cephas" (that is, Peter, meaning "a rock").

The following day Jesus decided to go into Galilee. He found Philip and said to him, "Follow me!" Philip was a man from Bethsaida, the town that Andrew and Peter came from. Now Philip found Nathanael and told him. "We have discovered the man whom Moses wrote about in the Law and about whom the Prophets wrote too. He is Jesus, the son of Joseph, and comes from Nazareth."

"Can anything good come out of Nazareth?" retorted Nathanael.

"You come and see," replied Philip.

Jesus saw Nathanael coming toward him and remarked, "Now here is a true man of Israel; there is no deceit in him!"

"How can you know me?" returned Nathanael.

"When you were underneath that fig tree," replied Jesus, "before Philip called you, I saw you."

At which Nathanael exclaimed, "Master, you are the Son of God, you are the king of Israel!"

"Do you believe in me," replied Jesus, "because I said I had seen you underneath that fig tree? You are going to see something greater than that! Believe me," he added, "I tell you all that you will see Heaven wide open and God's angels ascending and descending around the Son of Man!"

The Son of God and a village wedding   2.1

Two days later there was a wedding in the Galilean village of Cana. Jesus' mother was there and he and his disciples were invited to the festivities. Then it happened that the supply of wine gave out, and Jesus' mother told him, "They have no more wine."

"Is that your concern, or mine?" replied Jesus. "My time has not come yet."

So his mother said to the servants, "Mind you do whatever he tells you."

In the room six very large stone water jars stood on the floor (actually for the Jewish ceremonial cleansing), each holding about twenty gallons. Jesus gave instructions for these jars to be filled with water, and the servants filled them to the brim. Then he said to them, "Now draw some out and take it to the master of ceremonies," which they did. When this man tasted the water, which had now become wine, without knowing where it came from (though naturally the servants who had drawn the water knew), he called out to the bridegroom and said to him, "Everybody I know puts his good wine on first and then when men have had plenty to drink, he brings out the poor stuff. But you have kept back your good wine till now!" Jesus gave this, the first of his signs, at Cana in Galilee. He demonstrated his power and his disciples believed in him.

Jesus in the Temple   2.12

After this incident, Jesus, accompanied by his mother, his brothers and his disciples, went down to Capernaum and stayed there a few days. The Jewish Passover was approaching and Jesus made the journey up to Jerusalem. In the Temple he discovered cattle and sheep dealers and pigeon sellers, as well as money-changers sitting at their tables. So he made a rough whip out of rope and drove the whole lot of them, sheep and cattle as well, out of the Temple. He sent the coins of the money-changers flying and turned their tables upside down. Then he said to the pigeon dealers, "Take those things out of here. Don't you dare turn my Father's house into a market!" His disciples remembered the scripture—

The zeal of thine house shall eat me up.

As a result of this, the Jews said to him, "What sign can you give us to justify what you are doing?"

"Destroy this temple," Jesus retorted, "and I will rebuild it in three days!"

To which the Jews replied, "This Temple took forty-six years to build, and are you going to rebuild it in three days?"

He was, in fact, speaking about the temple of his own body,

and when he was raised from the dead the disciples remembered what he had said to them and that made them believe both the scripture and what Jesus had said.

While he was in Jerusalem at Passover time, during the festivities, many believed in him as they saw the signs that he gave. But Jesus, on his side, did not trust himself to them—for he knew them all. He did not need anyone to tell him what people were like: he understood human nature.

Jesus and a religious leader   3.1

One night Nicodemus, a leading Jew and a Pharisee, came to see Jesus.

"Master," he began, "we realize that you are a teacher who has come from God. Obviously no one could show the signs that you show unless God were with him."

"Believe me," returned Jesus, "a man cannot even see the kingdom of God without being born again."

"And how can a man who's getting old possibly be born?" replied Nicodemus. "How can he go back into his mother's womb and be born a second time?"

"I assure you," said Jesus, "that unless a man is born from water and from spirit he cannot enter the kingdom of God. Flesh gives birth to flesh and spirit gives birth to spirit: you must not be surprised that I told you that all of you must be born again. The wind blows where it likes, you can hear the sound of it but you have no idea where it comes from and where it goes. Nor can you tell how a man is born by the wind of the Spirit."

"How on earth can things like this happen?" replied Nicodemus.

"So you are a teacher of Israel," said Jesus, "and you do not recognize such things? I assure you that we are talking about something we really know and we are witnessing to something we have actually observed, yet men like you will not accept our evidence. Yet if I have spoken to you about things which happen on this earth and you will not believe me, what chance is there that you will believe me if I tell you about what happens in Heaven? No one has ever been up to Heaven except the Son of Man who came down from Heaven. The Son of Man must be lifted above the heads of men—as Moses lifted up that serpent in the desert—so that any man who believes in him may have eternal life. For God loved the world so much that he gave his only Son so that everyone who believes in him should not be lost, but should have eternal life. You must understand that God has not sent his Son into the world to pass sentence upon it, but to save it—through him. Any man who believes in him is not judged at all. It is the one who will not believe who stands already condemned, because he will not believe in the character of God's only Son. This *is* the judgment—that light has entered the world and men have preferred darkness to light because their deeds are evil. Anybody who does wrong hates the light and keeps away from it, for fear his deeds may be exposed. But anybody who is living by the truth will come to the light to make it plain that all he has done has been done through God."

Jesus and John again   3.22

After this Jesus went into the country of Judaea with his disciples and stayed there with them while the work of baptism was being carried on. John, too, was in Aenon near Salim, baptizing people because there was plenty of water in that district and they were still coming to him for baptism. (John, of course, had not yet been put in prison.)

This led to a question arising between John's disciples and one of the Jews about the whole matter of being cleansed. They approached John and said to him, "Master, look, the man who was with you on the other side of the Jordan, the one you testified to, is now baptizing and everybody is coming to him!"

"A man can receive nothing at all," replied John, "unless it is given him from Heaven. You yourselves can witness that I said, 'I am not Christ but I have been sent as his forerunner.' It is the bridegroom who possesses the bride, yet the bridegroom's friend who merely stands and listens to him can be overjoyed to hear the bridegroom's voice. That is why my happiness is now complete. He must grow greater and greater and I less and less.

"The one who comes from above is naturally above everybody. The one who arises from the earth belongs to the earth and speaks from the earth. The one who comes from Heaven is above all others and he bears witness to what he has seen and heard—yet no one is accepting his testimony. Yet if a man does accept it, he is acknowledging the fact that God is true. For the one whom God sent speaks the authentic words of God—and there can be no measuring of the Spirit given to *him*! The Father loves the Son and has put everything into his hand. The man who believes in the Son has eternal life. The man who refuses to believe in the Son will not see life; he lives under the anger of God."

Jesus meets a Samaritan woman   4.1

Now, when the Lord found that the Pharisees had heard that "Jesus is making and baptizing more disciples than John"—although, in fact, it was not Jesus who did the baptizing but his disciples—he left Judaea and went off again to Galilee, which meant his passing through Samaria. There he came to a little town called Sychar, which is near the historic plot of land that Jacob gave to his son, Joseph, and "Jacob's Spring" was there. Jesus, tired with the journey, sat down beside it, just as he was. The time was about midday. Presently, a Samaritan woman arrived to draw some water.

"Please give me a drink," Jesus said to her, for his disciples had gone away to the town to buy food. The Samaritan woman said to him, "How can you, a Jew, ask for a drink from me, a woman of Samaria?" (For Jews have no dealings with Samaritans.)

"If you knew what God can give," Jesus replied, "and if you knew who it is that said to you, 'Give me a drink,' I think you would have asked him, and he would have given you living water!"

"Sir," said the woman, "you have nothing to draw water with and this well is deep—where can you get your living water? Are you a greater man than our ancestor, Jacob, who gave us this well, and drank here himself with his family, and his cattle?"

Jesus said to her, "Everyone who drinks this water will be thirsty again. But whoever drinks the water I will give him will never be thirsty again. For my gift will become a spring in the man himself, welling up into eternal life."

The woman said, "Sir, give me this water, so that I may stop being thirsty—and not have to come here to draw water any more!"

"Go and call your husband and then come back here," said Jesus to her.

"I haven't got a husband!" the woman answered.

"You are quite right in saying, 'I haven't got a husband,' " replied Jesus, "for you have had five husbands and the man you have now is not your husband at all. Yes, you spoke the simple truth when you said that."

"Sir," said the woman again, "I can see that you are a prophet! Now our ancestors worshiped on this hillside, but you Jews say that Jerusalem is the place where men ought to worship—"

"Believe me," returned Jesus, "the time is coming when worshiping the Father will not be a matter of 'on this hillside' or 'in Jerusalem.' Nowadays you are worshiping with your eyes shut. We Jews are worshiping with our eyes open, for the salvation of mankind is to come from our race. Yet the time is coming, yes, and has already come, when true worshipers will worship the Father in spirit and in reality. Indeed, the Father looks for men who will worship him like that. God is Spirit, and those who worship him can only worship in spirit and in reality."

"Of course I know that Messiah is coming," returned the woman, "you know, the one who is called Christ. When he comes he will make everything plain to us."

"I am Christ, speaking to you now," said Jesus.

At this point his disciples arrived, and were very surprised to find him talking to a woman, but none of them asked, "What do you want?" or "What are you talking to her about?" So the woman left her water pot behind and went into the town and began to say to the people, "Come out and see the man who told me everything I've ever done! Can this be 'Christ'?" So they left the town and started to come to Jesus.

Meanwhile the disciples were begging him, "Master, do eat something."

To which Jesus replied, "I have food to eat that you know nothing about."

This, of course, made the disciples ask each other, "Do you think anyone has brought him any food?"

Jesus said to them: "My food is doing the will of him who sent me and finishing the work he has given me. Don't you say, 'Four months more and then comes the harvest'? But I tell you to open your eyes and look at the fields—they are gleaming white, all ready for the harvest! The reaper is already being rewarded and getting in a harvest for eternal life, so that both sower and reaper may be glad together. For in this harvest the old saying comes true, 'One man sows and another reaps.' I have sent you to reap a harvest for which you never labored; other men have worked hard and you have reaped the result of their labors."

Many of the Samaritans who came out of that town believed in him through the woman's testimony—"He told me everything I've ever done." And when they arrived they begged him to stay with them. He did stay there two days, and far more believed in him because of what he himself said. As they told the woman: "We don't believe any longer now because of what you said. We have heard him with our own ears. We know now that this must be the man who will save the world!"

Jesus, in Cana again, heals in response to faith   4.43

After the two days were over, Jesus left and went away to Galilee. (For Jesus himself testified that a prophet enjoys no honor in his own country.) And on his arrival the people received him with open arms. For they had seen all that he had done in Jerusalem during the festival, since they had themselves been present. So Jesus came again to Cana in Galilee, the place where he made the water into wine. At Capernaum there was an official whose son was very ill. When he heard that Jesus had left Judaea and had arrived in Galilee, he went off to see him and begged him to come down and heal his son, who was by this time at the point of death.

Jesus said to him, "I suppose you will never believe unless you see signs and wonders!"

"Sir," returned the official, "please come down before my boy dies!"

"You can go home," returned Jesus, "your son is alive and well."

And the man believed what Jesus had said to him and went on his way.

On the journey back his servants met him with the report, "Your son is alive and well." So he asked them at what time he had begun to recover, and they replied, "The fever left him yesterday at one o'clock in the afternoon." Then the father knew that this must have happened at the very moment when Jesus had said to him, "Your son is alive and well." And he and his whole household believed in Jesus. This, then, was the second sign that Jesus gave on his return from Judaea to Galilee.

Jesus heals in Jerusalem   5.1

Some time later came one of the Jewish feast days and Jesus went up to Jerusalem. There is in Jerusalem near the sheep gate a pool surrounded by five arches, which has the Hebrew name of Bethzatha. Under these arches a great many sick people were in the habit of lying; some of them were blind, some lame, and some had withered limbs. (They used to wait there for the "moving of the water," for at certain times an angel used to come down into the pool and disturb the water, and then the first person who stepped into the water after the disturbance would be healed of whatever he was suffering from.) One particular man had been there ill for thirty-eight years. When Jesus saw him lying there on his back —knowing that he had been like that for a long time, he said to him, "Do you want to get well again?"

"Sir," replied the sick man, "I just haven't got anybody to put me into the pool when the water is all stirred up. While I'm trying to get there somebody else gets down into it first."

"Get up," said Jesus, "pick up your bed and walk!"

At once the man recovered, picked up his bed and walked.

This happened on a Sabbath day, which made the Jews keep on telling the man who had been healed, "It's the Sabbath, you know; it's not right for you to carry your bed."

"The man who made me well," he replied, "was the one who told me, 'Pick up your bed and walk.' "

Then they asked him, "And who is the man who told you to do that?"

But the one who had been healed had no idea who it was, for Jesus had slipped away in the dense crowd. Later Jesus found him in the Temple and said to him, "Look: you are a fit man now. Do not sin again or something worse might happen to you!"

Then the man went off and informed the Jews that the one who had made him well was Jesus. It was because Jesus did such things on the Sabbath day that the Jews persecuted him. But Jesus' answer to them was this, "My Father is still at work and therefore I work as well."

This remark made the Jews all the more determined to kill him, because not only did he break the Sabbath but he referred to God as his own Father, so putting himself on equal terms with God.

Jesus makes his tremendous claim   5.19

Jesus said to them: "I assure you that the Son can do nothing of his own accord, but what he sees the Father doing. What the Son does is always modeled on what the Father does, for the Father loves the Son and shows him everything that he does himself. Yes, and he will show him even greater things than these to fill you with wonder. For just as the Father raises the dead and makes them live, so does the Son give life to any man he chooses. The Father is no man's judge: he has put judgment entirely into the Son's hands so that all men may honor the Son equally with the Father. The man who does not honor the Son does not honor the Father who sent him. I solemnly assure you that the man who hears what I have to say and believes in the one who has sent me has eternal life.

He does not have to face judgment; he has already passed from death into life. Yes, I assure you that a time is coming, in fact has already come, when the dead will hear the voice of the Son of God and when they have heard it they will live! For just as the Father has life in himself, so by the Father's gift the Son also has life in himself. And he has given him authority to judge because he is Son of Man. No, do not be surprised— the time is coming when all those who are dead and buried will hear his voice and out they will come—those who have done right will rise again to life, but those who have done wrong will rise to face judgment!

"By myself I can do nothing. As I hear, I judge, and my judgment is true because I do not live to please myself but to do the will of the Father who sent me. You may say that I am bearing witness about myself, that therefore what I say about myself has no value, but I would remind you that there is one who witnesses about me and I know that his witness about me is absolutely true. You sent to John, and he testified to the truth. Not that it is man's testimony that I accept—I only tell you this to help you to be saved. John certainly was a lamp that burned and shone, and for a time you were willing to enjoy the light that he gave. But I have a higher testimony than John's. The work that the Father gave me to complete, yes, these very actions which I do are my witness that the Father has sent me. This is how the Father who sent me has given his own personal testimony to me.

"Now you have never at any time heard what he says or seen what he is like. Nor do you really believe his word in your hearts, for you refuse to believe the man whom he has sent. You pore over the scriptures, for you imagine that you will find eternal life in them. And all the time they give their testimony to me! But you are not willing to come to me to have real life! Men's approval or disapproval means nothing to me, but I can tell that you have none of the love of God in your hearts. I have come in the name of my Father and you will not accept me. Yet if another man comes simply in his own name, you will accept him. How on earth can you believe while you are for ever looking for one another's approval and not for the glory that comes from the one God? There is no need for you to think that I have come to accuse you before the Father. You already have an accuser—Moses, in whom you put all your confidence! For if you really believed Moses, you would be bound to believe me; for it was about me that he wrote. But if you do not believe what he wrote, how can you believe what I say?"

Jesus shows his power over material things   6.1

After this, Jesus crossed the Lake of Galilee (or Tiberias), and a great crowd followed him because they had seen the signs which he gave in his dealings with the sick. But Jesus went up the hillside and sat down there with his disciples. The Passover, the Jewish festival, was near. So Jesus, raising his eyes and seeing a great crowd on their way toward him, said to Philip, "Where can we buy food for these people to eat?" (He said this to test Philip, for he himself knew what he was going to do.)

"Ten dollars' worth of bread would not be enough for them," Philip replied, "even if they had only a little each."

Then Andrew, Simon Peter's brother, another disciple, put in, "There is a boy here who has five small barley loaves and a couple of fish, but what's the good of that for such a crowd?"

Then Jesus said, "Get the people to sit down."

There was plenty of grass there, and the men, some five thousand of them, sat down. Then Jesus took the loaves, gave thanks for them and distributed them to the people sitting on the grass, and he distributed the fish in the same way, giving them as much as they wanted. When they had eaten enough, Jesus said to his disciples, "Collect the pieces that are left over so that nothing is wasted."

So they did as he suggested and filled twelve baskets with the broken pieces of the five barley loaves, which were left over after the people had eaten! When the men saw this sign of Jesus' power, they kept saying, "This certainly is the Prophet who was to come into the world!"

Then Jesus, realizing that they were going to carry him off and make him their king, retired once more to the hillside quite alone.

In the evening his disciples went down to the lake, embarked on the boat and made their way across the lake to Capernaum. Darkness had already fallen and Jesus had not returned to them. A strong wind sprang up and the water grew very rough. When they had rowed about three or four miles, they saw Jesus walking on the water and coming toward the boat, and they were terrified. But he spoke to them, "Don't be afraid: it is I myself."

So they gladly took him aboard, and at once the boat reached the shore they were making for.

Jesus teaches about the true bread   6.22

The following day, the crowd, who had remained on the other side of the lake, noticed that only the one boat had been there, and that Jesus had not embarked on it with his disciples, but that they had in fact gone off by themselves. Some other small boats from Tiberias had landed quite near the place where they had eaten the food and the Lord had given thanks. When the crowd realized that neither Jesus nor the disciples were there any longer, they themselves got into the boats and went off to Capernaum to look for Jesus. When they had found him on the other side of the lake, they said to him, "Master, when did you come here?"

"Believe me," replied Jesus, "you are looking for me now not because you saw my signs but because you ate that food and had all you wanted. You should not work for the food which does not last but for that food which lasts on into eternal life. This is the food the Son of Man will give you, and he is the one who bears the stamp of God the Father."

This made them ask him, "What must we do to carry out the work of God?"

"The work of God for you," replied Jesus, "is to believe in the one whom he has sent to you."

Then they asked him, "Then what sign can you give us that will make us believe in you? What work are you doing? Our forefathers ate manna in the desert just as the scripture says,

He gave them bread out of Heaven to eat."

To which Jesus replied, "Yes, but what matters is not that Moses *gave you* bread from Heaven but that my Father *is giving you* the true bread from Heaven. For the bread of God which comes down from Heaven gives life to the world."

This made them say to him, "Lord, please give us this bread, always!"

Then Jesus said to them: "I myself am the bread of life. The man who comes to me will never be hungry and the man who believes in me will never again be thirsty. Yet I have told you that you have seen me and do not believe. Everything that my Father gives me will come to me and I will never refuse anyone who comes to me. For I have come down from Heaven, not to do what I want, but to do the will of him who sent me. The will of him who sent me is that I should not lose anything of what he has given me, but should raise it up when the last day comes. And this is the will of the one who sent me, that everyone who sees the Son and trusts him should have eternal life, and I will raise him up when the last day comes."

At this, the Jews began grumbling at him because he said, "I am the bread which came down from Heaven," remarking, "Is not this Jesus, the son of Joseph, whose parents we know? How can he say that 'I have come down from Heaven'?"

So Jesus answered them: "Do not grumble among yourselves. Nobody comes to me unless he is drawn to me by the Father who sent me, and I will raise him up when the last day comes. In the Prophets it is written—

And they shall all be taught of God,

and this means that everybody who has heard the Father's voice and learned from him will come to me. Not that anyone has ever seen the Father except the one who comes from God —he has seen the Father. I assure you that the man who trusts in him has eternal life already. I myself am the bread of life. Your forefathers ate manna in the desert, *and they died*. This is bread that comes down from Heaven, so that a man may eat it and not die. I myself am the living bread which came down from Heaven, and if anyone eats this bread he will live for ever. The bread which I will give is my body and I shall give it for the life of the world."

This led to a fierce argument among the Jews, some of them saying, "How can this man give us his body to eat?"

So Jesus said to them: "Unless you do eat the body of the Son of Man and drink his blood, you are not really living at all. The man who eats my flesh and drinks my blood has eternal life and I will raise him up when the last day comes. For my body is real food and my blood is real drink. The man who eats my body and drinks my blood shares my life and I share his. Just as the living Father sent me and I am alive because of the Father, so the man who lives on me will live because of me. *This* is the bread which came down from Heaven! It is not like the manna which your forefathers used to eat, *and died*. The man who eats this bread will live for ever."

Jesus said all these things while teaching in the synagogue at Capernaum. Many of his disciples heard him say these things, and commented, "This is hard teaching indeed; who could accept that?"

Then Jesus, knowing intuitively that his disciples were complaining about what he had just said, went on: "Is this too much for you? Then what would happen if you were to see the Son of Man going up to the place where he was before? It is the Spirit which gives life. The flesh will not help you. The things which I have told you are spiritual and are life. But some of you will not believe me."

For Jesus knew from the beginning which of his followers did not trust him and who was the man who would betray him. Then he added, "This is why I said to you, 'No one can come to me unless my Father puts it into his heart to come.'"

As a consequence of this, many of his disciples withdrew and no longer followed him. So Jesus said to the twelve, "And are you too wanting to go away?"

"Lord," answered Simon Peter, "who else should we go to? Your words have the ring of eternal life! And we believe and are convinced that you are the holy one of God."

Jesus replied, "Did I not choose you twelve—and one of you has the devil in his heart?"

He was speaking of Judas, the son of Simon Iscariot, one of the twelve, who was planning to betray him.

Jesus delays his arrival at the festival   7.1

After this, Jesus moved about in Galilee but decided not to do so in Judaea since the Jews were planning to take his life. A Jewish festival, "The feast of the tabernacles," was approaching, and his brothers said to him, "You ought to leave here and go to Judaea so that your disciples can see what you are doing, for nobody works in secret if he wants to be known publicly. If you are going to do things like this, let the world see what you are doing." For not even his brothers had any faith in him. Jesus replied by saying: "It is not yet the right time for me, but any time is right for you. You see, it is impossible for you to arouse the world's hatred, but I provoke hatred because I show the world how evil its deeds really are. No, you go up to the festival; I shall not go up now, for it is not yet time for me to go." And after these remarks he remained where he was in Galilee.

Later, after his brothers had gone up to the festival, he went up himself, not openly but as though he did not want to be seen. Consequently, the Jews kept looking for him at the festival and asking, "Where is that man?" And there was an undercurrent of discussion about him among the crowds. Some would say, "He is a good man," others maintained that he was not, but that he was "misleading the people." Nobody, however, spoke openly about him for fear of the Jews.

Jesus openly declares his authority   7.14

But at the very height of the festival, Jesus went up to the Temple and began teaching. The Jews were amazed and remarked, "How does this man know all this—he has never been taught?"

Jesus replied to them: "My teaching is not really mine but comes from the one who sent me. If anyone wants to do God's will, he will know whether my teaching is from God or whether I merely speak on my own authority. A man who speaks on his own authority has an eye for his own reputation. But the man who is considering the glory of God who sent him is a true man. There can be no dishonesty about him.

"Did not Moses give you the Law? Yet not a single one of you obeys the Law. Why are you trying to kill me?"

The crowd answered: "You must be mad! Who is trying to kill you?"

Jesus answered them: "I have done one thing and you are all amazed at it. Moses gave you circumcision (not that it came from Moses originally but from your forefathers), and you will circumcise a man even on the Sabbath. If a man receives the cutting of circumcision on the Sabbath to avoid breaking the Law of Moses, why should you be angry with me because I have made a man's body perfectly whole on the Sabbath? You must not judge by the appearance of things but by the reality!"

Some of the people of Jerusalem, hearing him talk like this, were saying: "Isn't this the man whom they are trying to kill? It's amazing—he talks quite openly and they haven't a word to say to him. Surely our rulers haven't decided that this really is Christ! But then, we know this man and where he comes

from—when Christ comes, no one will know where he comes
from."

Jesus makes more unique claims   7.28

Then Jesus, in the middle of his teaching, called out in the
Temple: "So you know me and know where I have come from?
But I have not come of my own accord; I am sent by one who
is true and you do not know him! I do know him, because I
come from him and he has sent me here."

Then they attempted to arrest him, but actually no one laid
a finger on him because the right moment had not yet come.
Many of the crowd believed in him and kept on saying,
"When Christ comes, is he going to show greater signs than
this man?"

The Pharisees heard the crowd whispering these things about
him, and they and the chief priests sent officers to arrest him.
Then Jesus said: "I shall be with you only a little while longer
and then I am going to him who sent me. You will look for me
then but you will never find me. You cannot come where I shall
be."

This made the Jews say to one another: "Where is he going
to hide himself so that we cannot find him? Surely he's not going
to our refugees among the Greeks to teach Greeks? What
does he mean when he says, 'You will look for me and you
will never find me' and 'You cannot come where I shall be'?"

Then, on the last day, the climax of the festival, Jesus stood
up and cried out: "If any man is thirsty, he can come to me and
drink! The man who believes in me, as the scripture said, will
have rivers of living water flowing from his inmost heart."
(Here he was speaking about the Spirit which those who
believe in him would receive. The Holy Spirit had not yet been
given because Jesus had not yet been glorified.) When they
heard these words, some of the people were saying, "This
really is the Prophet." Others said, "This is Christ!" But some
said: "And does Christ come from Galilee? Don't the scriptures

say that Christ will be descended from David, and will come from Bethlehem, the village where David lived?"

So the people were in two minds about him—some of them wanted to arrest him, but so far no one laid hands on him.

Then the officers returned to the Pharisees and chief priests, who said to them, "Why haven't you brought him?"

"No man ever spoke like that!" they replied.

"Has he pulled the wool over your eyes, too?" retorted the Pharisees. "Have any of the authorities or any of the Pharisees believed in him? But this crowd, who know nothing about the Law, is damned anyway!"

One of their number, Nicodemus (the one who had previously been to see Jesus), remarked to them, "But surely our Law does not condemn the accused without hearing what he has to say, and finding out what he has done?"

"Are you a Galilean, too?" they answered him. "Look where you will—you won't find that any prophet comes out of Galilee!"

So they broke up their meeting and went home, while Jesus went off to the Mount of Olives.

Jesus deflates the rigorists   8.2

Early next morning he returned to the Temple and the entire crowd came to him. So he sat down and began to teach them. But the scribes and Pharisees brought in to him a woman who had been caught in adultery. They made her stand in front, and then said to him, "Now, master, this woman has been caught in adultery, in the very act. According to the Law, Moses commanded us to stone such women to death. Now, what do you say about her?"

They said this to test him, so that they might have some good grounds for an accusation. But Jesus stooped down and began to write with his finger in the dust on the ground. But as they persisted in their questioning, he straightened himself up and said to them, "Let the one among you who has never sinned throw the first stone at her." Then he stooped down again and continued writing with his finger on the ground. And when they heard what he said, they were convicted by their own consciences and went out, one by one, beginning with the eldest until they had all gone.

Jesus was left alone, with the woman still standing where they had put her. So he stood up and said to her, "Where are they all—did no one condemn you?"

And she said, "No one, sir."

"Neither do I condemn you," said Jesus to her. "Go home and do not sin again."

Jesus' bold claims—about himself—and his Father   8.12

Later, Jesus spoke to the people again and said: "I am the light of the world. The man who follows me will never walk in the dark but will live his life in the light."

This made the Pharisees say to him, "You are testifying to yourself—your evidence is not valid."

Jesus answered: "Even if I am testifying to myself, my evidence is valid, for I know where I have come from and I know where I am going. But as for you, you have no idea where I come from or where I am going. You are judging by human standards, but I am not judging anyone. Yet, if I should judge, my decision would be just, for I am not alone—the Father who sent me is with me. In your Law, it is stated that the witness of two persons is valid. I am one testifying to myself and the second witness to me is the Father who sent me."

"And where is this father of yours?" they replied.

"You do not know my Father," returned Jesus, "any more than you know me: if you had known me you would have known him."

Jesus made these statements while he was teaching in the Temple treasury. Yet no one arrested him, for his time had not yet come.

Later, Jesus spoke to them again and said: "I am going

away and you will try to find me, but you will die in your sins. You cannot come where I am going."

This made the Jews say: "Is he going to kill himself, then? Is *that* why he says, 'You cannot come where I am going'?"

"The difference between us," Jesus said to them, "is that you come from below and I am from above. You belong to this world but I do not. That is why I told you you will die in your sins. For unless you believe that I am who I am, you will die in your sins."

Then they said, "*Who are you?*"

"I am what I have told you I was from the beginning," replied Jesus. "There is much in you that I could speak about and condemn. But he who sent me is true, and I am only speaking to this world what I myself have heard from him."

They did not realize that he was talking to them about the Father. So Jesus resumed: "When you have lifted up the Son of Man, then you will realize that I am who I say I am, and that I do nothing on my own authority but speak simply as my Father has taught me. The one who sent me is with me now: the Father has never left me alone, for I always do what pleases him." And even while he said these words, many people believed in him.

Jesus speaks of personal freedom   8.31

So Jesus said to the Jews who believed in him: "If you are faithful to what I have said, you are truly my disciples. And you will know the truth and the truth will set you free!"

"But we are descendants of Abraham," they replied, "and we have never in our lives been any man's slaves. How can you say to us, 'You will be set free'?"

Jesus returned: "Believe me when I tell you that every man who commits sin is a slave. For a slave is no permanent part of a household, but a son is. If the Son, then, sets you free, you are really free! I know that you are descended from Abraham, but some of you are looking for a way to kill me because you can't bear my words. I am telling you what I have seen in the presence of my Father, and you are doing what you have seen in the presence of your father."

"Our father is Abraham!" they retorted.

"If you were the children of Abraham, you would do the sort of things Abraham did. But in fact, at this moment, you are looking for a way to kill me, simply because I am a man who has told you the truth that I have heard from God. Abraham would never have done that. No, you are doing your father's work."

"We are not illegitimate!" they retorted. "We have one Father—God."

"If God were really your Father," replied Jesus, "you would have loved me. For I came from God; and I am here. I did not come of my own accord—he sent me, and I am here. Why do you not understand my words? It is because you cannot hear what I am saying. Your father is the devil, and what you are wanting to do is what your father longs to do. He always was a murderer, and has never dealt with the truth, since the truth will have nothing to do with him. Whenever he tells a lie, he speaks in character, for he is a liar and the father of lies. And it is because I speak the truth that you will not believe me. Which of you can prove me guilty of sin? If I am speaking the truth, why is it that you do not believe me? The man who is born of God can hear the words of God, and the reason why you cannot hear the words of God is simply this, that you are not the sons of God."

"How right we are," retorted the Jews, "in calling you a Samaritan, and mad at that!"

"No," replied Jesus, "I am not mad. I am honoring my Father, and you are trying to dishonor me. But I am not concerned with my own glory: there is one whose concern it is, and he is the true judge. Believe me when I tell you that if anybody accepts my words, he will never see death at all."

"Now we know that you're mad," replied the Jews. "Why,

Abraham died and the prophets, too, and yet you say, 'If a man accepts my words, he will never experience death!' Are you greater than our father, Abraham? He died, and so did the prophets—who are you making yourself out to be?"

"If I were trying to glorify myself," returned Jesus, "such glory would be worthless. But it is my Father who glorifies me, the very one who you say is your God—though you have never known him. But I know him, and if I said I did not know him, I should be as much a liar as you are! But I do know him and I am faithful to what he says. As for your father, Abraham, his great joy was that he would see my coming. Now he has seen it and he is overjoyed."

"Look," said the Jews to him, "you are not fifty yet—and has Abraham seen you?"

"I tell you in solemn truth," returned Jesus, "before there was an Abraham, I AM!"

At this, they picked up stones to hurl at him, but Jesus disappeared and made his way out of the Temple.

Jesus and blindness, physical and spiritual   9.1

Later, as Jesus walked along he saw a man who had been blind from birth.

"Master, whose sin caused this man's blindness," asked the disciples, "his own or his parents'?"

"He was not born blind because of his own sin or that of his parents," returned Jesus, "but to show the power of God at work in him. We must carry on the work of him who sent me while the daylight lasts. Night is coming, when no one can work. I am the world's light as long as I am in it."

Having said this, he spat on the ground and made a sort of clay with the saliva. This he applied to the man's eyes and said, "Go and wash in the pool of Siloam." (Siloam means "one who has been sent.") So the man went off and washed and came home with his sight restored.

His neighbors and the people who had often seen him

before as a beggar remarked, "Isn't this the man who used to sit and beg?"

"Yes, that's the one," said some.

Others said, "No, but he's very like him."

But he himself said, "I'm the man, all right!"

"Then how was your blindness cured?" they asked.

"The man called Jesus made some clay and smeared it on my eyes," he replied, "and then he said, 'Go to Siloam and wash.' So off I went and washed—and that's how I got my sight!"

"Where is he now?" they asked.

"I don't know," he returned.

So they brought the man who had once been blind before the Pharisees. (It should be noted that Jesus made the clay and restored his sight on a Sabbath day.) The Pharisees asked the question all over again as to how he had become able to see.

"He put clay on my eyes; I washed it off, now I can see—that's all," he replied.

Some of the Pharisees commented, "This man cannot be from God since he does not observe the Sabbath."

"But how can a sinner give such wonderful signs as these?" others demurred. And they were in two minds about him. Finally, they asked the blind man again: "And what do *you* say about him? You're the one whose sight was restored."

"I believe he is a prophet," he replied.

The Jews did not really believe that the man had been blind and then had become able to see, until they had summoned his parents and asked them: "Is this your son who you say was born blind? How does it happen that he can now see?"

"We know that this is our son, and we know that he was born blind," returned his parents, "but how he can see now, or who made him able to see, we have no idea. Why don't you ask him? He is a grown-up man; he can speak for himself."

His parents said this because they were afraid of the Jews who had already agreed that anybody who admitted that

Christ had done this thing should be excommunicated. It was this fear which made his parents say, "Ask him, he is a grown-up man."

So, once again they summoned the man who had been born blind and said to him: "You should give God the glory for what has happened to you. We know that this man is a sinner."

"Whether he is a sinner or not, I couldn't tell, but one thing I am sure of," the man replied, "I used to be blind; now I can see!"

"But what did he *do* to you—how did he make you see?" they continued.

"I've told you before," he replied. "Weren't you listening? Why do you want to hear it all over again? Are you wanting to be his disciples too?"

At this, they turned on him furiously.

"You're the one who is his disciple! We are disciples of Moses. We know that God spoke to Moses, but as for this man, we don't even know where he came from."

"Now here's the extraordinary thing," he retorted, "you don't know where he came from and yet he gave me the gift of sight. Everybody knows that God does not listen to sinners. It is the man who has a proper respect for God and does what God wants him to do—he's the one God listens to. Why, since the world began, nobody's ever heard of a man who was born blind being given his sight. If this man did not come from God, he couldn't do such a thing!"

"You misbegotten wretch!" they flung back at him. "Are you trying to teach *us*?" And they threw him out.

Jesus heard that they had expelled him and when he had found him, he said, "Do you believe in the Son of Man?"

"And who is he, sir?" the man replied. "Tell me, so that I can believe in him."

"You have seen him," replied Jesus. "It is the one who is talking to you now."

"Lord, I do believe," he said, and worshiped him.

Then Jesus said, "My coming into this world is itself a judgment—those who cannot see have their eyes opened and those who think they can see become blind."

Some of the Pharisees near him overheard this and said, "So we're blind, too, are we?"

"If you were blind," returned Jesus, "nobody could blame you, but, as you insist 'We can see,' your guilt remains."

Jesus declares himself the true shepherd of men   10.1

Then Jesus said: "Believe me when I tell you that anyone who does not enter the sheepfold through the door, but climbs in by some other way, is a thief and a rogue. It is the shepherd of the flock who goes in by the door. It is to him the doorkeeper opens the door and it is his voice that the sheep recognize. He calls his own sheep by name and leads them out of the fold, and when he has driven all his own flock outside, he goes in front of them himself, and the sheep follow him because they know his voice. They will never follow a stranger—indeed, they will run away from him, for they do not recognize strange voices."

Jesus gave them this illustration, but they did not grasp the point of what he was saying to them. So Jesus said to them once more: "I do assure you that I myself am the door for the sheep. All who have gone before me are like thieves and rogues, but the sheep did not listen to them. I am the door. If a man goes in through me, he will be safe and sound; he can come in and out and find his food. The thief comes with the sole intention of stealing and killing and destroying, but I came to bring them life, and far more life than before. I am the good shepherd. The good shepherd will give his life for the sake of his sheep. But the hired man, who is not the shepherd, and does not own the sheep, will see the wolf coming, desert the sheep and run away. And the wolf will attack the flock and send them flying. The hired man runs away because he is only a hired man and has no interest in the sheep. I am the good shepherd, and I know those that are mine and my sheep know me, just as the Father knows me and I know the Father. And

I am giving my life for the sake of the sheep.

"And I have other sheep who do not belong to this fold. I must lead these also, and they will hear my voice. So there will be one flock and one shepherd. This is the reason why the Father loves me—that I lay down my life, and I lay it down to take it up again! No one is taking it from me, but I lay it down of my own free will. I have the power to lay it down and I have the power to take it up again. This is an order that I have received from my Father."

Jesus plainly declares who he is   10.19

Once again, the Jews were in two minds about him because of these words, many of them remarking: "The devil's in him and he's insane. Why do you listen to him?"

But others were saying, "This is not the sort of thing a devil-possessed man would say! Can a devil make a blind man see?"

Then came the dedication festival at Jerusalem. It was wintertime and Jesus was walking about inside the Temple in Solomon's cloisters. So the Jews closed in on him and said: "How much longer are you going to keep us in suspense? If you really are Christ, tell us so straight out!"

"I have told you," replied Jesus, "and you do not believe it. What I have done in my Father's name is sufficient to prove my claim, but you do not believe because you are not my sheep. My sheep recognize my voice and I know who they are. They follow me and I give them eternal life. They will never die and no one can snatch them out of my hand. My Father, who has given them to me, is greater than all. And no one can tear anything out of the Father's hand. I and the Father are one."

Again the Jews reached for stones to stone him to death but Jesus answered them, "I have shown you many good things from the Father—for which of these do you intend to stone me?"

"We're not going to stone you for any good things," replied the Jews, "but for blasphemy: because you, who are only a man, are making yourself out to be God."

"Is it not written in your own Law," replied Jesus, " 'I have said ye are gods'? And if he called those men 'gods' to whom the word of God came (and the scripture cannot be broken), can you say to the one whom the Father has consecrated and sent into the world, 'You are blaspheming' because I said, 'I am the Son of God'? If I fail to do what my Father does, then do not believe me. But if I do, even though you have no faith in me personally, then believe in the things that I do. Then you may come to know and realize that the Father is in me and I am in the Father."

And again they tried to arrest him, but he moved out of their reach.

Then Jesus went off again across the Jordan to the place where John had first baptized and there he stayed. A great many people came to him, and said, "John never gave us any sign but all that he said about this man was true."

And in that place many believed in him.

Jesus shows his power over death   11.1

Now there was a man by the name of Lazarus who became seriously ill. He lived in Bethany, the village where Mary and her sister Martha lived. (Lazarus was the brother of the Mary who poured perfume upon the Lord and wiped his feet with her hair.) So the sisters sent word to Jesus: "Lord, your friend is very ill."

When Jesus received the message, he said, "This illness is not meant to end in death; it is going to bring glory to God— for it will show the glory of the Son of God."

Now Jesus loved Martha and her sister and Lazarus. So when he heard of Lazarus' illness he stayed where he was two days longer. Only then did he say to the disciples, "Let us go back into Judaea."

"Master!" returned the disciples, "only a few days ago, the Jews were trying to stone you to death—are you going there again?"

"There are twelve hours of daylight every day, are there not?" replied Jesus. "If a man walks in the daytime, he does not stumble, for he has the daylight to see by. But if he walks at night he stumbles, because he cannot see where he is going."

Jesus spoke these words; then after a pause he said to them, "Our friend Lazarus has fallen asleep, but I am going to wake him up."

At this, his disciples said, "Lord, if he has fallen asleep, he will be all right."

Actually Jesus had spoken about his death, but they thought that he was speaking about falling into natural sleep. This made Jesus tell them quite plainly: "Lazarus has died, and I am glad that I was not there—for your sakes, that you may learn to believe. And now, let us go to him."

Thomas (known as the twin) then said to his fellow disciples, "Come on, then, let us all go and die with him!"

When Jesus arrived, he found that Lazarus had already been in the grave four days. Now Bethany is quite near Jerusalem, rather less than two miles away, and a good many of the Jews had come out to see Martha and Mary to offer them sympathy over their brother's death. When Martha heard that Jesus was on his way, she went out and met him, while Mary stayed in the house.

"If only you had been here, Lord," said Martha, "my brother would never have died. And I know that, even now, God will give you whatever you ask from him."

"Your brother will rise again," Jesus replied to her.

"I know," said Martha, "that he will rise again in the resurrection at the last day."

"I myself am the resurrection and the life," Jesus told her. "The man who believes in me will live even though he dies, and anyone who is alive and believes in me will never die at all. Can you believe that?"

"Yes, Lord," replied Martha. "I do believe that you are Christ, the Son of God, the one who was to come into the world." Saying this she went away and called Mary her sister, whispering, "The master's here and is asking for you." When Mary heard this she sprang to her feet and went to him. Now Jesus had not yet arrived at the village itself, but was still where Martha had met him. So when the Jews who had been condoling with Mary in the house saw her get up quickly and go out, they followed her, imagining that she was going to the grave to weep there.

When Mary met Jesus, she looked at him and then fell down at his feet. "If only you had been here, Lord," she said, "my brother would never have died."

When Jesus saw Mary weep and noticed the tears of the Jews who came with her, he was deeply moved and visibly distressed.

"Where have you put him?" he asked.

"Lord, come and see," they replied, and at this Jesus himself wept.

"Look how much he loved him!" remarked the Jews, though some of them asked, "Could he not have kept this man from dying if he could open that blind man's eyes?"

Jesus was again deeply moved at these words, and went on to the grave. It was a cave, and a stone lay in front of it.

"Take away the stone," said Jesus.

"But, Lord," said Martha, the dead man's sister, "he has been dead four days. By this time he will be decaying. . . ."

"Did I not tell you," replied Jesus, "that if you believed, you would see the wonder of what God can do?"

Then they took the stone away, and Jesus raised his eyes and said, "Father, I thank you that you have heard me. I know that you always hear me, but I have said this for the sake of these people standing here so that they may believe that you have sent me."

And when he had said this, he called out in a loud voice, "Lazarus, come out!"

And the dead man came out, his hands and feet bound with graveclothes and his face muffled with a handkerchief.

"Now unbind him," Jesus told them, "and let him go home."

Jesus' miracle leads to deadly hostility 11.45

After this many of the Jews who had accompanied Mary and observed what Jesus did believed in him. But some of them went off to the Pharisees and told them what Jesus had done. Consequently, the Pharisees and chief priests summoned the council and said: "What can we do? This man obviously shows many remarkable signs. If we let him go on doing this sort of thing we shall have everybody believing in him. Then we shall have the Romans coming and that will be the end of our holy place and our very existence as a nation!"

But one of them, Caiaphas, who was High Priest that year, addressed the meeting: "You plainly don't understand what is involved here. You do not realize that it would be a good thing for us if one man should die for the sake of the people—instead of the whole nation being destroyed." (He did not make this remark on his own initiative but, since he was High Priest that year, he was in fact inspired to say that Jesus was going to die for the nation's sake—and in fact not for that nation only, but to bring together into one family all the children of God scattered throughout the world.) From that day, then, they planned to kill him. As a consequence Jesus made no further public appearance among the Jews but went away to the countryside on the edge of the desert, and stayed with his disciples in a town called Ephraim. The Jewish Passover was approaching, and many people went up from the country to Jerusalem before the actual Passover, to go through a ceremonial cleansing. They were looking for Jesus there and kept saying to one another as they stood in the Temple, "What do you think? Surely he won't come to the festival?"

It should be understood that the chief priests and the Pharisees had issued an order that anyone who knew of Jesus' whereabouts should tell them, so that they could arrest him.

An act of love as the end approaches   12.1

Six days before the Passover, Jesus came to Bethany, the village of Lazarus whom he had raised from the dead. They gave a supper for him there, and Martha waited on the party while Lazarus took his place at table with Jesus. Then Mary took a whole pound of very expensive perfume and anointed Jesus' feet and then wiped them with her hair. The entire house was filled with the fragrance of the perfume. But one of his disciples, Judas Iscariot (the man who was going to betray Jesus), burst out: "Why on earth wasn't this perfume sold? It's worth thirty dollars, which could have been given to the poor!"

He said this, not because he cared about the poor, but because he was dishonest, and when he was in charge of the purse used to help himself from the contents.

• But Jesus replied to this outburst: "Let her alone, let her keep this for the day of my burial. You have the poor with you always—you will not always have me!"

The large crowd of Jews discovered that he was there and came to the scene—not only because of Jesus but to catch sight of Lazarus, the man whom he had raised from the dead. Then the chief priests planned to kill Lazarus as well, because he was the reason for many of the Jews' going away and putting their faith in Jesus.

Jesus experiences a temporary triumph   12.12

The next day, the great crowd who had come to the festival heard that Jesus was coming into Jerusalem, and went out to meet him with palm branches in their hands, shouting, "God save him! God bless the man who comes in the name of the Lord, God bless the king of Israel!"

For Jesus had found a young ass and was seated upon it, just as the scripture foretold—

Fear not, daughter of Zion: behold, thy king cometh, sitting on an ass's colt.

(The disciples did not realize the significance of what was happening at the time, but when Jesus was glorified, then they recollected that these things had been written about him and that they had carried them out for him.)

The people who had been with him, when he had summoned Lazarus from the grave and raised him from the dead, were continually talking about him. This accounts for the crowd who went out to meet him, for they had heard that he had given this sign. Seeing all this, the Pharisees remarked to one another, "You see?—There's nothing one can do! The whole world is running after him."

Among those who had come up to worship at the festival were some Greeks. They approached Philip (whose home town was Bethsaida in Galilee) with the request, "Sir, we want to see Jesus."

Philip went and told Andrew, and Andrew went with Philip and told Jesus.

Jesus told them: "The time has come for the Son of Man to be glorified. I tell you truly that unless a grain of wheat falls into the earth and dies, it remains a single grain of wheat; but if it dies, it brings a good harvest. The man who loves his own life will destroy it, and the man who hates his life in this world will preserve it for eternal life. If a man wants to enter my service, he must follow my way; and where I am, my servant will also be. And my Father will honor every man who enters my service.

"Now comes my hour of heartbreak, and what can I say, 'Father, save me from this hour'? No, it was for this very purpose that I came to this hour. 'Father, honor your own name!' "

At this there came a voice from Heaven, "I have honored it and I will honor it again!"

When the crowd of bystanders heard this, they said it thundered, but some of them said, "An angel spoke to him."

Then Jesus said: "That voice came for your sake, not for mine. Now is the time for the judgment of this world to begin, and now will the spirit that rules this world be driven out. As for me, if I am lifted up from the earth, I will draw all men to myself." (He said this to show the kind of death he was going to die.)

Then the crowd said: "We have heard from the Law that Christ lives for ever. How can you say that the Son of Man must be 'lifted up'? Who is this Son of Man?"

At this, Jesus said to them: "You have the light with you only a little while longer. Go on while the light is good, before the darkness comes down upon you. For the man who walks in the dark has no idea where he is going. You must believe in the light while you have the light, that you may become the sons of light."

Jesus said all these things, and then went away, out of their sight. But though he had given so many signs, yet they did not believe in him, so that the prophecy of Isaiah was fulfilled, when he said,

> Lord, who hath believed our report?
> And to whom hath the arm of the Lord been revealed?

Thus, they could not believe, for Isaiah said again—

> He hath blinded their eyes, and he hardened their heart:
> Lest they should see with their eyes, and perceive with their
>   heart,
> And should turn,
> And I should heal them.

Isaiah said these things because he saw the glory of Christ, and spoke about him. Nevertheless, many even of the authorities did believe in him. But they would not admit it for fear of the Pharisees, in case they should be excommunicated. They were more concerned to have the approval of men than to have the approval of God.

But later, Jesus cried aloud: "Every man who believes in me is believing in the one who sent me: and every man who sees me is seeing the one who sent me. I have come into the world as light, so that no one who believes in me need remain in the

dark. Yet, if anyone hears my sayings and does not keep them,
I do not judge him—for I did not come to judge the world but
to save it. Every man who rejects me and will not accept my
sayings has a judge—at the last day, the very words that I
have spoken will be his judge. For I have not spoken on my
own authority: the Father who sent me has commanded me
what to say and what to speak. And I know that what he commands means eternal life. All that I say I speak only in accordance with what the Father has told me."

Jesus teaches his disciples humility   13.1

Before the festival of the Passover began, Jesus realized
that the time had come for him to leave this world and
return to the Father. He had loved those who were his own in
this world and he loved them to the end. By suppertime, the
devil had already put the thought of betraying Jesus into the
mind of Judas Iscariot, Simon's son. Jesus, with the full knowledge that the Father had put everything into his hands and
that he had come from God and was going to God, rose from
the supper table, took off his outer clothes, picked up a towel
and fastened it round his waist. Then he poured water into the
basin and began to wash the disciples' feet and to dry them
with the towel around his waist.

So he came to Simon Peter, who said to him, "Lord, are you
going to wash my feet?"

"You do not realize now what I am doing," replied Jesus,
"but later on you will understand."

Then Peter said to him, "You must never wash my feet!"

"Unless you let me wash you, Peter," replied Jesus, "you
cannot share my lot."

"Then," returned Simon Peter, "please—not just my feet but
my hands and my face as well!"

"The man who has bathed," returned Jesus, "only needs to
wash his feet to be clean all over. And you are clean—though
not all of you."

(For Jesus knew his betrayer and that is why he said, "though not all of you.")

When Jesus had washed their feet and put on his clothes, he sat down again and spoke to them, "Do you realize what I have just done to you? You call me 'teacher' and 'Lord' and you are quite right, for I am your teacher and your Lord. But if I, your teacher and Lord, have washed your feet, you must be ready to wash one another's feet. I have given you this as an example so that you may do as I have done. Believe me, the servant is not greater than his master and the messenger is not greater than the man who sent him. Once you have realized these things, you will find your happiness in doing them.

Jesus foretells his betrayal   13.18

"I am not speaking about all of you—I know the men I have chosen. But let this scripture be fulfilled—

He that eateth my bread lifted up his heel against me.

From now onward, I shall tell you about things before they happen, so that when they do happen you may believe that I am the one I claim to be. I tell you truly that anyone who accepts my messenger will be accepting me, and anyone who accepts me will be accepting the one who sent me."

After Jesus had said this, he was clearly in anguish of soul, and he added solemnly,

"I tell you plainly, one of you is going to betray me."

At this the disciples stared at one another, completely mystified as to whom he could mean. And it happened that one of them, whom Jesus loved, was sitting very close to him. So Simon Peter nodded to this man and said, "Tell us whom he means."

He simply leaned forward on Jesus' shoulder, and asked, "Lord, who is it?"

And Jesus answered, "It is the one I am going to give this piece of bread to, after I have dipped it in the dish."

Then he took a piece of bread, dipped it in the dish and

gave it to Simon's son, Judas Iscariot. After he had taken the piece of bread, Satan entered his heart. Then Jesus said to him, "Be quick about your business!"

No one else at table knew what he meant in telling him this. Indeed, some of them thought that, since Judas had charge of the purse, Jesus was telling him to buy what they needed for the festival, or that he should give something to the poor. So Judas took the piece of bread and went out quickly—into the night.

When he had gone, Jesus spoke: "Now comes the glory of the Son of Man, and the glory of God in him! If God is glorified through him then God will glorify the Son of Man—and that without delay. Oh, my children, I am with you such a short time! You will look for me, and I have to tell you as I told the Jews, 'Where I am going, you cannot follow.' Now I am giving you a new command—love one another. Just as I have loved you, you must love one another. This is how all men will know that you are my disciples, because you have such love for one another."

Simon Peter said to him, "Lord, where are you going?"

"I am going," replied Jesus, "where you cannot follow me now, though you will follow me later."

"Lord, why can't I follow you now?" said Peter. "I would lay down my life for you!"

"Would you lay down your life for me?" replied Jesus. "Believe me, you will disown me three times before the cock crows!

Jesus reveals spiritual truths   14.1

"**Y**ou must not let yourselves be distressed—you must hold on to your faith in God and to your faith in me. There are many rooms in my Father's House. If there were not, should I have told you that I am going away to prepare a place for you? It is true that I am going away to prepare a place for you, but it is just as true that I am coming again to welcome you into my own home, so that you may be where I

am. You know where I am going and you know the road I am
going to take."

"Lord," Thomas remonstrated, "we do not know where
you're going, and how can we know what road you're going
to take?"

"I myself am the road," replied Jesus, "and the truth and
the life. No one approaches the Father except through me.
If you had known who I am, you would have known my Father.
From now on, you do know him and you have seen him."

Jesus explains his relationship with the Father   14.8

Then Philip said to him, "Show us the Father, Lord, and we
shall be satisfied."

"Have I been such a long time with you," returned Jesus,
"without your really knowing me, Philip? The man who has
seen me has seen the Father. How can you say, 'Show us the
Father'? Do you not believe that I am in the Father and the
Father is in me? The very words I say to you are not my own.
It is the Father who lives in me who carries out his work through
me. Do you believe me when I say that I am in the Father and
the Father is in me? But if you cannot, then believe me because
of what you see me do. I assure you that the man who believes
in me will do the same things that I have done, yes, and he will
do even greater things than these, for I am going away to the
Father. Whatever you ask the Father in my name, I will do—
that the Son may bring glory to the Father. And if you ask me
anything in my name, I will grant it.

Jesus promises the Spirit   14.15

"If you really love me, you will keep the commandments I
have given you and I shall ask the Father to give you someone
else to stand by you, to be with you always. I mean the Spirit
of truth, whom the world cannot accept, for it can neither see
nor recognize that Spirit. But you recognize him, for he is with
you now and will be in your hearts. I am not going to leave
you alone in the world—I am coming to you. In a very little

while, the world will see me no more but you will see me, because I am really alive and you will be alive too. When that day comes, you will realize that I am in my Father, that you are in me, and I am in you.

"Every man who knows my commandments and obeys them is the man who really loves me, and every man who really loves me will himself be loved by my Father, and I too will love him and make myself known to him."

Then Judas (not Iscariot) said, "Lord, how is it that you are going to make yourself known to us but not to the world?"

And to this Jesus replied: "When a man loves me, he follows my teaching. Then my Father will love him, and we will come to that man and make our home within him. The man who does not really love me will not follow my teaching. Indeed, what you are hearing from me now is not really my saying, but comes from the Father who sent me.

"I have said all this while I am still with you. But the one who is coming to stand by you, the Holy Spirit whom the Father will send in my name, will be your teacher and will bring to your minds all that I have said to you.

"I leave behind with you—peace; I give you my own peace and my gift is nothing like the peace of this world. You must not be distressed and you must not be daunted. You have heard me say, 'I am going away and I am coming back to you.' If you really loved me, you would be glad because I am going to my Father, for my Father is greater than I. And I have told you of it now, before it happens, so that when it does happen your faith in me will not be shaken. I shall not be able to talk much longer to you, for the spirit that rules this world is coming very close. He has no hold over me, but I go on my way to show the world that I love the Father and do what he sent me to do. . . . Get up now! Let us leave this place.

Jesus teaches union with himself 15.1

"I am the real vine; my Father is the vinedresser. He removes any of my branches which are not bearing fruit and he prunes every branch that does bear fruit to increase its yield. Now, you have already been pruned by my words. You must go on growing in me and I will grow in you. For just as the branch cannot bear any fruit unless it shares the life of the vine, so you can produce nothing unless you go on growing in me. I am the vine itself; you are the branches. It is the man who shares my life and whose life I share who proves fruitful. For the plain fact is that apart from me you can do nothing at all. The man who does not share my life is like a branch that is broken off and withers away. He becomes just like the dry sticks that men pick up and use for firewood. But if you live your life in me, and my words live in your hearts, you can ask for whatever you like and it will come true for you. This is how my Father will be glorified—in your becoming fruitful and being my disciples.

"I have loved you just as the Father has loved me. You must go on living in my love. If you keep my commandments you will live in my love just as I have kept my Father's commandments and live in his love. I have told you this so that you can share my joy, and that your happiness may be complete. This is my commandment: that you love one another as I have loved you. There is no greater love than this—that a man should lay down his life for his friends. You are my friends if you do what I tell you to do. I shall not call you servants any longer, for a servant does not share his master's confidence. No, I call you friends, now, because I have told you everything that I have heard from the Father.

"It is not that you have chosen me; but it is I who have chosen you. I have appointed you to go and bear fruit that will be lasting; so that whatever you ask the Father in my name, he will give it to you.

Jesus speaks of the world's hatred   15.17

"This I command you, love one another! If the world hates you, you know that it hated me first. If you belonged to the world, the world would love its own. But because you do not belong to the world and I have chosen you out of it, the world will hate you. Do you remember what I said to you, 'The servant is not greater than his master'? If they have persecuted me, they will persecute you as well, but if they have followed my teaching, they will also follow yours. They will do all these things to you as my disciples because they do not know the one who sent me. If I had not come and spoken to them, they would not have been guilty of sin, but now they have no excuse for their sin. The man who hates me, hates my Father as well. If I had not done among them things that no other man has ever done, they would not have been guilty of sin, but as it is they have seen and they have hated both me and my Father. Yet this only fulfills what is written in their Law—

They hated me without a cause.

But when the helper comes, that is, the Spirit of truth, who comes from the Father and whom I myself will send to you from the Father, he will speak plainly about me. And you yourselves will also speak plainly about me, for you have been with me from the first.

Jesus speaks of the future without his bodily presence   16.1

"I am telling you this now so that your faith in me may not be shaken. They will excommunicate you from their synagogues. Yes, the time is coming when a man who kills you will think he is thereby serving God! They will act like this because they have never had any true knowledge of the Father or of me, but I have told you all this so that when the time comes for it to happen you may remember that I told you about it. I have not spoken like this to you before, because I have been with you; but now the time has come for me to go away to the one who sent me. None of you asks me, 'Where are you going?' That is because you are so distressed at what I have told you. Yet I am telling you the simple truth when I assure you that it is a good thing for you that I should go away. For if I did not go away, the divine helper would not come to you. But if I go, then I will send him to you. When he comes, he will convince the world of the meaning of sin, of true goodness and of judgment. He will expose their sin because they do not believe in me; he will reveal true goodness for I am going away to the Father and you will see me no longer; and he will show them the meaning of judgment, for the spirit which rules this world will have been judged.

"I have much more to tell you but you cannot bear it now. Yet when that one I have spoken to you about comes—the Spirit of truth—he will guide you into everything that is true. For he will not be speaking of his own accord but exactly as he hears, and he will inform you about what is to come. He will bring glory to me, for he will draw on my truth and reveal it to you. Whatever the Father possesses is also mine; that is why I tell you that he will draw on my truth and will show it to you.

The disciples are puzzled: Jesus explains   16.16

"In a little while you will not see me any longer, and again, in a little while you will see me."

At this some of his disciples remarked to each other, "What is this that he tells us now, 'A little while and you will not see me, and again, in a little while you will see me' and 'for I am going away to the Father'? What is this 'little while' that he talks about?" they were saying. "We simply do not know what he means!"

Jesus knew that they wanted to ask him what he meant, so he said to them: "Are you trying to find out from each other what I meant when I said, 'In a little while you will not see me, and again, in a little while you will see me'? I tell you truly that you are going to be both sad and sorry while the world is glad. Yes, you will be deeply distressed, but your pain will turn into joy. When a woman gives birth to a child, she certainly knows pain when her time comes. Yet as soon as she has given birth to the child, she no longer remembers her agony for joy that a man has been born into the world. Now you are going through pain, but I shall see you again and your hearts will thrill with joy—the joy that no one can take away from you—and on that day you will not ask me any questions.

"I assure you that whatever you ask the Father he will give you in my name. Up to now you have asked nothing in my name; ask now, and you will receive, that your joy may be overflowing.

Jesus speaks further of the future   16.25

"I have been speaking to you in parables—but the time is coming to give up parables and tell you plainly about the Father. When that time comes, you will make your requests to him in my name, for I need make no promise to plead to the Father for you, for the Father himself loves you, because you have loved me and have believed that I came from God. Yes, I did come from the Father and I came into the world. Now I leave the world behind and return to the Father."

"Now you are speaking plainly," cried the disciples, "and are not using parables. Now we know that everything is known to you—no more questions are needed. This makes us sure that you did come from God."

"So you believe in me now?" replied Jesus. "The time is coming, indeed, it has already come, when you will be scattered, every one of you going home and leaving me alone. Yet I am not really alone, for the Father is with me. I have told you all this so that you may find your peace in me. You will find trouble in the world—but, never lose heart, I have conquered the world!"

Jesus' prayer for his disciples—present and future   17.1

When Jesus had said these words, he raised his eyes to Heaven and said: "Father, the hour has come. Glorify your Son now so that he may bring glory to you, for you have given him authority over all men to give eternal life to all that you have given to him. And this is eternal life, to know you, the only true God, and him whom you have sent—Jesus Christ.

"I have brought you honor upon earth, I have completed the task which you gave me to do. Now, Father, honor me in your own presence with the glory that I knew with you before the world was made. I have shown your self to the men whom you gave me from the world. They were your men and you gave them to me, and they have accepted your word. Now they realize that all that you have given me comes from you—and that every message that you gave me I have given them. They have accepted it all and have come to know in their hearts that I did come from you—they are convinced that you sent me.

"I am praying to you for them: I am not praying for the world but for the men whom you gave me, for they are yours—everything that is mine is yours and yours mine—and they have done me honor. Now I am no longer in the world, but they are in the world and I am returning to you. Holy Father, keep the men you gave me by your power that they may be one, as we are one. As long as I was with them, I kept them by the power that you gave me; I guarded them, and not one of them was destroyed, except the son of destruction—that the scripture might come true.

"And now I come to you and I say these things in the world that these men may find my joy completed in themselves. I have given them your word, and the world has hated them, for they are no more sons of the world than I am. I am not praying that you will take them out of the world but that you will keep them from the evil one. They are no more the sons of the world than I am—make them holy by the truth for your word is the truth. I have sent them to the world just as you sent me to the world and I consecrate myself for their sakes that they may be made holy by the truth.

"I am not praying only for these men but for all those who will believe in me through their message, that they may all be one. Just as you, Father, live in me and I live in you, I am asking that they may live in us, that the world may believe that you did send me. I have given them the honor that you gave me, that they may be one, as we are one—I in them and you in me, that they may grow complete into one, so that the world may realize that you sent me and have loved them as you loved me. Father, I want those whom you have given me to be with me where I am; I want them to see that glory which you have made mine—for you loved me before the world began. Father of goodness and truth, the world has not known you, but I have known you and these men now know that you have sent me. I have made your self known to them and I will continue to do so that the love which you have had for me may be in their hearts—and that I may be there also."

Jesus is arrested in the garden   **18.1**

When Jesus had spoken these words, he went out with his disciples across the Cedron valley to a place where there was a garden, and they went into it together. Judas who betrayed him knew the place, for Jesus often met his disciples there. So Judas fetched the guard and the officers which the chief priests and Pharisees had provided for him, and came to the place with torches and lanterns and weapons. Jesus, fully realizing all that was going to happen to him, went forward and said to them, "Who are you looking for?"

"Jesus of Nazareth," they answered.

"I am the man," said Jesus. (Judas who was betraying him was standing there with the others.)

When he said to them, "I am the man," they retreated and fell to the ground. So Jesus asked them again, "Who are you looking for?"

And again they said, "Jesus of Nazareth."

"I have told you that I am the man," replied Jesus. "If I am the man you are looking for, let these others go." (Thus fulfilling his previous words, "I have not lost one of those whom you gave me.")

At this, Simon Peter, who had a sword, drew it and slashed at the High Priest's servant, cutting off his right ear. (The servant's name was Malchus.) But Jesus said to Peter, "Put your sword back into its sheath. Am I not to drink the cup the Father has given me?"

Peter follows Jesus, only to deny him   18.12

Then the guard, with their captain and the Jewish officers, took hold of Jesus and tied his hands together, and led him off to Annas first, for he was father-in-law to Caiaphas, who was High Priest that year. Caiaphas was the man who advised the Jews, "that it would be a good thing that one man should die for the sake of the people." Behind Jesus followed Simon Peter, and one other disciple who was known personally to the High Priest. He went in with Jesus into the High Priest's courtyard, but Peter was left standing at the door outside. So this other disciple, who was acquainted with the High Priest, went out and spoke to the doorkeeper, and brought Peter inside. The young woman at the door remarked to Peter, "Are you one of this man's disciples, too?"

"No, I am not," retorted Peter.

In the courtyard, the servants and officers stood around a charcoal fire which they had made, for it was cold. They were warming themselves, and Peter stood there with them, keeping himself warm.

Meanwhile the High Priest interrogated Jesus about his disciples and about his own teaching.

"I have always spoken quite openly to the world," replied Jesus. "I have always taught in the synagogue or in the Temple where all Jews meet together, and I have said nothing in secret. Why do you question me? Why not question those who have heard me about what I said to them? Obviously they are the ones who know what I actually said."

As he said this, one of those present, an officer, slapped Jesus with his open hand, remarking, "Is that the way for you to answer the High Priest?"

"If I have said anything wrong," Jesus said to him, "you must give evidence about it, but if what I said was true why do you strike me?"

Then Annas sent him, with his hands still tied, to the High Priest, Caiaphas.

Peter's denial   18.25

In the meantime Simon Peter was still standing, keeping himself warm. Some of them said to him, "Surely you too are one of his disciples, aren't you?"

And he denied it and said, "No, I am not."

Then one of the High Priest's servants, a relation of the man whose ear Peter had cut off, remarked, "Didn't I see you in the garden with him?"

And again Peter denied it. And immediately the cock crew.

Jesus is taken before the Roman authority   18.28

Then they led Jesus from Caiaphas' presence into the palace. It was now early morning and the Jews themselves did not go into the palace, for fear that they would be contaminated and would not be able to eat the Passover. So Pilate walked out to them and said, "What is the charge that you are bringing against this man?"

"If he were not an evildoer, we should not have handed him over to you," they replied.

To which Pilate retorted, "Then take him yourselves and judge him according to your law."

"We are not allowed to put a man to death," replied the Jews (thus fulfilling Christ's prophecy of the method of his own death).

So Pilate went back into the palace and called Jesus to him. "Are you the king of the Jews?" he asked.

"Are you asking this of your own accord," replied Jesus, "or have other people spoken to you about me?"

"Do you think *I* am a Jew?" replied Pilate. "It's your people and your chief priests who handed you over to me. What have you done, anyway?"

"My kingdom is not founded in this world—if it were, my servants would have fought to prevent my being handed over to the Jews. But in fact my kingdom is not founded on all this!"

"So you are a king, are you?" returned Pilate.

"Indeed I am a king," Jesus replied; "the reason for my birth and the reason for my coming into the world is to witness to the truth. Every man who loves truth recognizes my voice."

To which Pilate retorted, "What is 'truth'?" and went straight out again to the Jews and said:

"I find nothing criminal about him at all. But I have an arrangement with you to set one prisoner free at Passover time. Do you wish me then to set free for you the 'king of the Jews'?"

At this, they shouted out again, "No, not this man, but Barabbas!"

Barabbas was a bandit.

Pilate's vain efforts to save Jesus   19.1

Then Pilate took Jesus and had him flogged, and the soldiers twisted thorn twigs into a crown and put it on his head, threw a purple robe around him and kept coming into his presence, saying, "Hail, king of the Jews!" And then they slapped him with their open hands.

Then Pilate went outside again and said to them, "Look, I bring him out before you here, to show that I find nothing criminal about him at all."

And at this Jesus came outside too, wearing the thorn crown and the purple robe.

"Look," said Pilate, "here's the man!"

The sight of him made the chief priests and Jewish officials shout at the top of their voices, "Crucify! Crucify!"

"You take him and crucify him," retorted Pilate. "He's no criminal as far as I can see!"

The Jews answered him, "We have a Law, and according to that Law, he must die, for he made himself out to be Son of God!"

When Pilate heard them say this, he became much more uneasy, and returned to the palace again and spoke to Jesus, "Where do you come from?"

But Jesus gave him no reply. So Pilate said to him: "Won't you speak to me? Don't you realize that I have the power to set you free, and I have the power to have you crucified?"

"You have no power at all against me," replied Jesus, "except what was given to you from above. And for that reason the one who handed me over to you is even more guilty than you are."

From that moment Pilate tried hard to set him free, but the Jews were shouting: "If you set this man free, you are no friend of Caesar! Anyone who makes himself out to be a king is anti-Caesar!"

When Pilate heard this, he led Jesus outside and sat down upon the Judgment seat in the place called the Pavement (in Hebrew, Gabbatha). It was the preparation day of the Passover and it was now getting on toward midday. Pilate now said to the Jews, "Look, here's your king!"

At which they yelled, "Take him away, take him away, crucify him!"

"Am I to crucify your king?" Pilate asked them.

"Caesar is our king and no one else," replied the chief priests. And at this Pilate handed Jesus over to them for crucifixion.

The crucifixion   **19.17**

So they took Jesus and he went out carrying the cross himself, to a place called Skull Hill (in Hebrew, Golgotha). There
they crucified him, and two others, one on either side of him
with Jesus in the middle. Pilate had a placard written out and
put on the cross, reading, "JESUS OF NAZARETH, THE KING OF
THE JEWS." This placard was read by many of the Jews
because the place where Jesus was crucified was quite near
Jerusalem, and it was written in Hebrew as well as in Latin and
Greek. So the chief priests said to Pilate, "You should not
write 'The King of the Jews,' but 'This man said, I am King of
the Jews.' "

To which Pilate retorted, "Indeed? What I have written, I
have written."

When the soldiers had crucified Jesus, they divided his
clothes between them, taking a quarter-share each. There
remained his shirt, which was seamless—woven in one piece
from the top to the bottom. So they said to each other, "Don't
let us tear it; let's draw lots and see who gets it."

This happened to fulfill the scripture which says—

They parted my garments among them,
And upon my vesture did they cast lots.

Jesus provides for his mother from the cross   19.25

While the soldiers were doing this, Jesus' mother was standing near the cross with her sister, and with them Mary, the wife of Clopas, and Mary of Magdala. Jesus saw his mother and the disciple whom he loved standing by her side, and said to her, "Look, there is your son!" And then he said to the disciple, "And there is your mother!"

And from that time the disciple took Mary into his own home.

After this, Jesus realizing that everything was now completed, said (fulfilling the saying of scripture), "I am thirsty."

There was a bowl of sour wine standing there. So they soaked a sponge in the wine, put it on a spear, and pushed it up toward his mouth. When Jesus had taken it, he cried, "It is finished!" His head fell forward, and he died.

The body of Jesus is removed   19.31

As it was the day of preparation for the Passover, the Jews
wanted to avoid the bodies being left on the crosses over the
Sabbath (for that was a particularly important Sabbath), and
they requested Pilate to have the men's legs broken and the
bodies removed. So the soldiers went and broke the legs of
the first man and of the other who was crucified with Jesus.
But when they came to him, they saw that he was dead already
and they did not break his legs. But one of the soldiers pierced
his side with a spear, and at once there was an outrush of
blood and water. And the man who saw this is our witness: his
evidence is true. (He is certain that he is speaking the truth, so
that you may believe as well.) For this happened to fulfill the
scripture,

A bone of him shall not be broken.

And again another scripture says—

They shall look on him whom they pierced.

After it was all over, Joseph (who came from Arimathaea
and was a disciple of Jesus, though secretly for fear of the
Jews), requested Pilate that he might take away Jesus' body,
and Pilate gave him permission. So he came and took his
body down. Nicodemus also, the man who had come to him
at the beginning by night, arrived bringing a mixture of myrrh
and aloes, weighing about a hundred pounds. So they took
his body and wound it round with linen strips with the spices,
according to the Jewish custom of preparing a body for burial.
In the place where he was crucified, there was a garden con-
taining a new tomb in which nobody had yet been laid.
Because it was the preparation day and because the tomb
was conveniently near, they laid Jesus in this tomb.

The first day of the week: the risen Lord 20.1

But on the first day of the week, Mary of Magdala arrived at the tomb, very early in the morning, while it was still dark, and noticed that the stone had been taken away from the tomb. At this she ran, found Simon Peter and the other disciple whom Jesus loved, and told them, "They have taken the Lord out of the tomb and we don't know where they have put him."

Peter and the other disciple set off at once for the tomb, the two of them running together. The other disciple ran faster than Peter and was the first to arrive at the tomb. He stooped and looked inside and noticed the linen cloths lying there but did not go in himself. Hard on his heels came Simon Peter and went straight into the tomb. He noticed that the linen cloths were lying there, and that the handkerchief, which had been round Jesus' head, was not lying with the linen cloths but was rolled up by itself, a little way apart. Then the other disciple, who was the first to arrive at the tomb, came inside as well, saw what had happened and believed. (They did not yet understand the scripture which said that he must rise from the dead.) So the disciples went back again to their homes.

But Mary stood just outside the tomb, and she was crying. And as she cried, she looked into the tomb and saw two angels in white who sat, one at the head and the other at the foot of the place where the body of Jesus had lain.

The angels spoke to her. "Why are you crying?" they asked.

"Because they have taken away my Lord, and I don't know where they have put him!" she said.

Then she turned and noticed Jesus standing there, without realizing that it was Jesus.

"Why are you crying?" said Jesus to her. "Who are you looking for?"

She, supposing that he was the gardener, said, "Oh, sir, if you have carried him away, please tell me where you have put him and I will take him away."

Jesus said to her, "Mary!"

At this she turned right round and said to him, in Hebrew, "Master!"

"No!" said Jesus, "do not hold me now. I have not yet gone up to the Father. Go and tell my brothers that I am going up to my Father, and your Father, to my God and your God."

And Mary of Magdala went off to the disciples, with the news, "I have seen the Lord!" and she told them what he had said to her.

In the evening of that first day of the week, the disciples had met together with the doors locked for fear of the Jews. Jesus came and stood right in the middle of them and said, "Peace be with you!"

Then he showed them his hands and his side, and when they saw the Lord the disciples were overjoyed.

Jesus said to them again: "Yes, peace be with you! Just as the Father sent me, so I am going to send you."

And then he breathed upon them and said, "Receive holy spirit.* If you forgive any men's sins, they are forgiven, and if you hold them unforgiven, they are unforgiven."

*Lit., "receive holy spirit." Historically the Holy Spirit was not given until Pentecost.

The risen Jesus and Thomas   20.24

But one of the twelve, Thomas (called the twin), was not with them when Jesus came. The other disciples kept on telling him, "We have seen the Lord," but he replied, "Unless I see in his own hands the mark of the nails, and put my finger where the nails were, and put my hand into his side, I will never believe!"

Just over a week later, the disciples were indoors again and Thomas was with them. The doors were shut, but Jesus came and stood in the middle of them and said, "Peace be with you!"

Then he said to Thomas, "Put your finger here—look, here are my hands. Take your hand and put it in my side. You must not doubt, but believe."

"My Lord and my God!" cried Thomas.

"Is it because you have seen me that you believe?" Jesus said to him. "Happy are those who have never seen me and yet have believed!"

Jesus gave a great many other signs in the presence of his disciples which are not recorded in this book. But these have been written so that you may believe that Jesus is Christ, the Son of God, and that in that faith you may have life as his disciples.

The risen Jesus and Peter   21.1

Later on, Jesus showed himself again to his disciples on the shore of Lake Tiberias, and he did it in this way. Simon Peter, Thomas (called the twin), Nathanael from Cana of Galilee, the sons of Zebedee and two other disciples were together, when Simon Peter said,

"I'm going fishing."

"All right," they replied, "we'll go with you."

So they went out and got into the boat and during the night caught nothing at all. But just as dawn began to break, Jesus stood there on the beach, although the disciples had no idea that it was Jesus.

"Have you caught anything, lads?" Jesus called out to them.

"No," they replied.

"Throw the net on the right side of the boat," said Jesus, "and you'll have a catch."

So they threw out the net and found that they were now not strong enough to pull it in because it was so full of fish! At this, the disciple that Jesus loved said to Peter, "It is the Lord!"

Hearing this, Peter slipped on his clothes, for he had been naked, and plunged into the sea. The other disciples followed in the boat, for they were only about a hundred yards from the shore, dragging in the net full of fish. When they had landed, they saw that a charcoal fire was burning, with a fish placed on it, and some bread. Jesus said to them, "Bring me some of the fish you've just caught."

So Simon Peter got into the boat and hauled the net ashore full of large fish, one hundred and fifty-three altogether. But in spite of the large number the net was not torn.

Then Jesus said to them, "Come and have your breakfast."

None of the disciples dared to ask him who he was; they knew it was the Lord.

Jesus went and took the bread and gave it to them and gave them all fish as well. This is already the third time that

Jesus showed himself to his disciples after his resurrection from the dead.

When they had finished breakfast Jesus said to Simon Peter, "Simon, son of John, do you love me more than these others?"

"Yes, Lord," he replied, "you know that I am your friend."

"Then feed my lambs," returned Jesus. Then he said for the second time,

"Simon, son of John, do you love me?"

"Yes, Lord," returned Peter. "You know that I am your friend."

"Then care for my sheep," replied Jesus. Then for the third time, Jesus spoke to him and said,

"Simon, son of John, are you my friend?"

Peter was deeply hurt because Jesus' third question to him was "Are you my friend?" and he said: "Lord, you know everything. You know that I am your friend!"

"Then feed my sheep," Jesus said to him. "I tell you truly, Peter, that when you were younger, you used to dress yourself and go where you liked, but when you are an old man, you are going to stretch out your hands and someone else will dress you and take you where you do not want to go."

(He said this to show the kind of death by which Peter was going to honor God.)

Then Jesus said to him, "You must follow me."

Then Peter turned round and noticed the disciple whom Jesus loved following behind them. (He was the one who had his head on Jesus' shoulder at supper and had asked, "Lord, who is the one who is going to betray you?") So he said, "Yes, Lord, but what about him?"

"If it is my wish," returned Jesus, "for him to stay until I come, is that your business, Peter? You must follow me."

This gave rise to the saying among the brothers that this disciple would not die. Yet, of course, Jesus did not say, "He will not die," but simply, "If it is my wish for him to stay until I come, is that your business?"

All the above was written by an eyewitness 21.24

Now it is this same disciple who is hereby giving his testimony to these things and has written them down. We know that his witness is reliable. Of course, there are many other things which Jesus did, and I suppose that if each one were written down in detail, there would not be room in the whole world for all the books that would have to be written.

THE ACTS OF
THE APOSTLES

Introduction   1.1

My dear Theophilus,
      In my first book I gave you some account of all that
Jesus began to do and teach until the time of his ascension.
Before he ascended he gave his instructions, through the Holy
Spirit, to the special messengers of his choice. For after his
suffering he showed himself alive to them in many convincing
ways, and appeared to them repeatedly over a period of
forty days talking with them about the affairs of the kingdom
of God.

Jesus' parting words before his ascension   1.4

On one occasion, while he was eating a meal with them,
he emphasized that they were not to leave Jerusalem, but to
wait for the Father's promise.

"You have already heard me speak about this," he said,
"for John used to baptize with water, but before many days
are passed you will be baptized with the Holy Spirit."

This naturally brought them all together, and they asked
him,

"Lord, is this the time when you are going to restore the
kingdom to Israel?"

To this he replied,

"You cannot know times and dates which have been fixed by the Father's sole authority. But you are to be given power when the Holy Spirit has come to you. You will be witnesses to me, not only in Jerusalem, not only throughout Judaea, not only in Samaria, but to the very ends of the earth!"

When he had said these words he was lifted up before their eyes till a cloud hid him from their sight. While they were still gazing up into the sky as he went, suddenly two men dressed in white stood beside them and said,

"Men of Galilee, why are you standing here looking up into the sky? This very Jesus who has been taken up from you into Heaven will come back in just the same way as you have seen him go."

At this they returned to Jerusalem from the Mount of Olives which is near the city, only a Sabbath day's journey away. On entering Jerusalem they went straight to the upstairs room where they had been staying. There were Peter, John, James, Andrew, Philip, Thomas, Bartholomew, Matthew, James the son of Alphaeus, Simon the patriot, and Judas the son of James. By common consent all these men, together with the women who had followed Jesus, Mary his mother, as well as his brothers, devoted themselves to prayer.

Judas' place is filled   1.15

It was during this period that Peter stood up among the brothers—there were about a hundred and twenty present at the time—and said,

"My brothers, the prophecy of scripture given through the Holy Spirit by the lips of David concerning Judas was bound to come true. He was the man who acted as guide to those who arrested Jesus, though he was one of our number and he had a share in this ministry of ours."

(This man had bought a piece of land with the proceeds of his infamy, but his body swelled up and his intestines burst. This fact became well known to all the residents of Jerusalem so that the piece of land came to be called in their language Akeldama, which means "the field of blood.")

"Now it is written in the book of psalms of such a man:

Let his habitation be made desolate,
And let no man dwell therein:

and

His office let another take.

"It becomes necessary then that whoever joins us must be someone who has been in our company during the whole time that the Lord Jesus lived his life with us, from the beginning when John baptized him until the day when He was taken up from us. This man must be an eyewitness with us to the resurrection of Jesus."

Two men were put forward, Joseph called Barsabas who was also called Justus, and Matthias. Then they prayed,

"Thou, Lord, who knowest the hearts of all men, show us which of these two thou hast chosen to accept that apostle's ministry which Judas forfeited to go where he belonged."

Then they drew lots for these men, and the lot fell to Matthias, and thereafter he was considered equally an apostle with the eleven.

The first Pentecost for the young Church   2.1

Then when the actual day of Pentecost came they were all assembled together. Suddenly there was a sound from heaven like the rushing of a violent wind, and it filled the whole house where they were seated. Before their eyes appeared tongues like flames, which separated off and settled above the head of each one of them. They were all filled with the Holy Spirit and began to speak in different languages as the Spirit gave them power to proclaim his message.

The Church's first impact on devout Jews   2.5

Now there were staying in Jerusalem Jews of deep faith from every nation of the world. When they heard this sound a crowd quickly collected and were completely bewildered because each one of them heard these men speaking in his own language. They were absolutely amazed and said in their astonishment,

"Listen, surely all these speakers are Galileans? Then how does it happen that every single one of us can hear the particular language he has known from a child? There are Parthians, Medes and Elamites; there are men whose homes are in Mesopotamia, in Judaea and Cappadocia, Pontus, Asia, Phrygia, Pamphylia, Egypt, and the parts of Africa near Cyrene, as well as visitors from Rome! There are Jews and proselytes, men from Crete and men from Arabia, yet we can all hear these men speaking of the magnificence of God in our native language."

Everyone was utterly amazed and did not know what to make of it. Indeed they kept saying to each other,

"What on earth can this mean?"

But there were others who laughed mockingly and said,

"These fellows have drunk too much new wine!"

Peter explains the fulfillment of God's promise   2.14

Then Peter, with the eleven standing by him, raised his voice and addressed them:

"Fellow Jews, and all who are living now in Jerusalem, listen carefully to what I say while I explain to you what has happened! These men are not drunk as you suppose—it is after all only nine o'clock in the morning of this great feast day. No, this is something which was predicted by the prophet Joel,

And it shall be in the last days, saith God,
I will pour forth of my Spirit upon all flesh:
And your sons and your daughters shall prophesy,
And your young men shall see visions,
And your old men shall dream dreams:
Yea and on my servants and on my handmaidens in those
    days
Will I pour forth of my Spirit; and they shall prophesy.
And I will shew wonders in the heaven above,
And signs on the earth beneath;
Blood, and fire, and vapor of smoke:
The sun shall be turned into darkness,
And the moon into blood,
Before the day of the Lord come,
That great and notable day:
And it shall be, that whosoever shall call on the name of
    the Lord shall be saved.

"Men of Israel, I beg of you to listen to my words. Jesus of Nazareth was a man proved to you by God himself through the works of power, the miracles and the signs which God showed through him here amongst you—as you very well know. This man, who was put into your power by the predetermined plan and foreknowledge of God, you nailed up and murdered, and you used for your purpose men without the Law! But God would not allow the bitter pains of death to touch him. He raised him to life again—and indeed there was nothing by which death could hold such a man. When David speaks about him he says,

> I beheld the Lord always before my face;
> For he is on my right hand, that I should not be moved:
> Therefore my heart was glad, and my tongue rejoiced;
> Moreover my flesh also shall dwell in hope:
> Because thou wilt not leave my soul in Hades,
> Neither wilt thou give thy holy one to see corruption.
> Thou madest known unto me the ways of life;
> Thou shalt make me full of gladness with thy countenance.

"Men and brother Jews, I can surely speak freely to you about the patriarch David. There is no doubt that he died and was buried, and his grave is here among us to this day. But while he was alive he was a prophet. He knew that God had given him a most solemn promise that he would place one of his descendants upon his throne. He foresaw the resurrection of Christ, and it is this of which he is speaking. Christ was not deserted in death and his body was never destroyed. *Christ is the man Jesus, whom God raised up—a fact of which all of us are eyewitnesses!* He has been raised to the right hand of God; he has received from the Father and poured out upon us the promised Holy Spirit—*that* is what you now see and hear! David never ascended to Heaven, but he certainly said,

> The Lord said unto my *Lord,*
> Sit thou on my right hand,
> Till I make thine enemies the footstool of thy feet.

"Now therefore the whole nation of Israel must know beyond the shadow of a doubt that this Jesus, whom you crucified, God has declared to be both Lord and Christ."

The reaction to Peter's speech   2.37

When they heard this they were cut to the quick, and they cried to Peter and the other apostles,

"Men and fellow Jews, what shall we do now?"

Peter told them,

"You must repent and every one of you must be baptized in the name of Jesus Christ, so that you may have your sins forgiven and receive the gift of the Holy Spirit. For this great promise is for you and your children—yes, and for all who are far away, for as many as the Lord our God shall call to himself!"

Peter said much more than this as he gave his testimony and implored them, saying,

"Save yourselves from this perverted generation!"

The first large-scale conversion   2.14

Then those who welcomed his message were baptized, and on that day alone about three thousand souls were added to the number of disciples. They continued steadily learning the teaching of the apostles, and joined in their fellowship, in the breaking of bread, and in prayer.

Everyone felt a deep sense of awe while many miracles and signs took place through the apostles. All the believers shared everything in common; they sold their possessions and goods and divided the proceeds among the fellowship according to individual need. Day after day they met by common consent in the Temple; they broke bread together in their homes, sharing meals with simple joy. They praised God continually and all the people respected them. Every day the Lord added to their number those who were finding salvation.

A public miracle and its explanation   3.1

One afternoon Peter and John were on their way to the Temple for the three o'clock hour of prayer. A man who had been lame from birth was being carried along in the crowd, for it was the daily practice to put him down at what was known as the Beautiful Gate of the Temple, so that he could beg from the people as they went in. As this man saw Peter and John just about to enter he asked them to give him something. Peter looked intently at the man and so did John.

Then Peter said,

"Look straight at us!"

The man looked at them expectantly, hoping that they would give him something.

"If you are expecting silver or gold," Peter said to him, "I have neither, but what I have I will certainly give you. In the name of Jesus Christ of Nazareth, *walk!*"

Then he took him by the right hand and helped him up. At once his feet and ankle bones were strengthened, and he positively jumped to his feet, stood, and then walked. Then he went with them into the Temple, where he walked about, leaping and praising God. Everyone noticed him as he walked and praised God and recognized him as the same beggar who used to sit at the Beautiful Gate, and they were all overcome with wonder and sheer astonishment at what had happened to him. Then while the man himself still clung to Peter and John all the people in their excitement ran together and crowded round them in Solomon's Porch. When Peter saw this he spoke to the crowd.

"Men of Israel, why are you so surprised at this, and why are you staring at us as though we had made this man walk through some power or piety of our own? It is the God of Abraham and Isaac and Jacob, the God of our fathers, who has done this thing to honor his servant Jesus—the man whom you betrayed and denied in the presence of Pilate, even when he had decided to let him go. But you disowned the holy and righteous one, and begged to be granted instead a man who was a murderer! You killed the prince of life, but God raised him from the dead—a fact of which we are eyewitnesses. It is the name of this same Jesus, it is faith in that name, which has cured this man whom you see and recognize. Yes, it was faith in Christ which gave this man perfect health and strength in full view of you all.

Peter explains ancient prophecy   **3.17**

"Now of course I know, my brothers, that you had no idea

what you were doing any more than your leaders had. But God had foretold through all his prophets that his Christ must suffer and this was how his words came true. Now you must repent and turn to God so that your sins may be wiped out, that time after time your souls may know the refreshment that comes from the presence of God. Then he will send you Jesus, your long-heralded Christ, although for the time he must remain in Heaven until that universal restoration of which God spoke in ancient times through all his holy prophets. For Moses said,

> A prophet shall the Lord God raise up unto you from among your brethren, like unto me; to him shall ye hearken in all things whatsoever he shall speak unto you. And it shall be that every soul, which shall not hearken to that prophet, shall be utterly destroyed from among the people.

Indeed, all the prophets from Samuel onwards who have spoken at all have foretold these days. You are the sons of the prophets and heirs of the agreement which God made with our fathers when he said to Abraham, 'Through your children shall all the families of the earth be blessed.' It was to you first that God sent his servant after he had raised him up to bring you great blessing by turning every one of you away from his evil ways."

The first clash with Jewish authorities   4.1

While they were still talking to the people the priests, the captain of the temple guard and the Sadducees moved toward them, thoroughly incensed that they should be teaching the people and should assure them that the resurrection of the dead had been proved through the rising of Jesus. So they arrested them and, since it was now evening, kept them in custody until the next day. Nevertheless, many of those who had heard what they said believed, and the number of men alone rose to about five thousand.

Peter's boldness at formal questioning   4.5

Next day the leading members of the council, the elders and scribes met in Jerusalem with Annas the High Priest, Caiaphas, John, Alexander, and the whole of the High Priest's family. They had the apostles brought in to stand before them and they asked them formally,

"By what power and in whose name have you done this thing?"

At this Peter, filled with the Holy Spirit, spoke to them,

"Leaders of the people and elders, if we are being called in question today over the matter of a kindness done to a helpless man and as to how he was healed, it is high time that all of you and the whole people of Israel knew that it was done in the name of Jesus Christ of Nazareth! He is the one whom you crucified but whom God raised from the dead, and it is by his power that this man at our side stands in your presence perfectly well. He is the 'stone which you builders rejected, which has now become the head of the corner.' In no one else can salvation be found. For in all the world no other name has been given to men but this, and it is by this name that we must be saved!"

The embarrassment of the authorities   4.13

When they saw the complete assurance of Peter and John, who were obviously uneducated and untrained men, they were staggered. They recognized them as men who had been with Jesus, yet since they could see the man who had been cured standing beside them, they could find no effective reply. All they could do was to order them out of the Sanhedrin and hold a conference among themselves.

"What are we going to do with these men?" they said to each other. "It is evident to everyone living in Jerusalem that an extraordinary miracle has taken place through them, and that is something we cannot deny. Nevertheless, to prevent such a thing spreading further among the people, let us warn them that if they say anything more to anyone in his name it will be at their peril."

So they called them in and ordered them bluntly not to speak or teach a single further word about the name of Jesus. But Peter and John gave them this reply:

"Whether it is right in the eyes of God for us to listen to what you say rather than to what he says, you must decide; for we cannot help speaking about what we have actually seen and heard!"

After further threats they let them go. They could not think of any way of punishing them because of the attitude of the people. Everybody was thanking God for what had happened —that this miracle of healing had taken place in a man who was more than forty years old.

The united prayer of the young Church—   4.23

After their release the apostles went back to their friends and reported to them what the chief priests and elders had said to them. When they heard it they raised their voices to God in united prayer and said,

"Almighty Lord, thou art the one who hast made the heaven and the earth, the sea and all that is in them. It was thou who didst speak by the Holy Spirit through the lips of our forefather David thy servant in the words:

Why did the gentiles rage,
And the peoples imagine vain things?
The kings of the earth set themselves in array,
And the rulers were gathered together,
Against the Lord, and against his anointed:

For indeed in this city the rulers have gathered together against thy holy servant, Jesus, thine anointed—yes, Herod and Pontius Pilate, the gentiles and the peoples of Israel have gathered together to carry out what thine hand and will had planned to happen. And now, O Lord, observe their threats and give thy servants courage to speak thy word fearlessly, while thou dost stretch out thine hand to heal, and cause signs and wonders to be performed in the name of thy holy servant Jesus."

When they had prayed their meeting-place was shaken; they were all filled with the Holy Spirit and spoke the Word of God fearlessly.

—and their close fellowship   4.32

Among the large number who had become believers there was complete agreement of heart and soul. Not one of them claimed any of his possessions as his own but everything was common property to all. The apostles continued to give their witness to the resurrection of the Lord Jesus with great force, and a wonderful spirit of generosity pervaded the whole fellowship. Indeed, there was not a single person in need among them, for those who owned land or property would sell it and bring the proceeds of the sales and place it at the apostles' feet. They distributed to each one according to his need.

Generosity and covetousness   4.36

It was at this time that Barnabas (the name, meaning son of comfort, given by the apostles to Joseph, a Levite from Cyprus) sold his farm and put the proceeds at the apostles' disposal.

But there was a man named Ananias who, with his wife Sapphira, had sold a piece of property but, with her full knowledge, reserved part of the price for himself. He brought the remainder to put at the apostles' disposal. But Peter said to him,

"Ananias, why has Satan so filled your mind that you could cheat the Holy Spirit and keep back for yourself part of the price of the land? Before the land was sold it was yours, and after the sale the disposal of the price you received was entirely in your hands, wasn't it? Then whatever made you think of such a thing as this? You have not lied to men, but to God!"

As soon as Ananias heard these words he collapsed and died. All who were within earshot were appalled at this incident. The young men got to their feet and after wrapping up his body carried him out and buried him.

About three hours later it happened that his wife came in not knowing what had taken place. Peter spoke directly to her,

"Tell me, did you sell your land for so much?"

"Yes," she replied, "that was it."

Then Peter said to her,

"How could you two have agreed to put the Spirit of the Lord to such a test? Listen, you can hear the footsteps of the men who have just buried your husband coming back through the door, and they will carry you out as well!"

Immediately she collapsed at Peter's feet and died. When the young men came into the room they found her a dead woman, and they carried her out and buried her by the side of her husband. At this happening a deep sense of awe swept over the whole Church and indeed over all those who heard about it.

The young Church takes its stand in the Temple— 5.12b

By common consent they all used to meet now in Solomon's Porch. But as far as the others were concerned no one dared to associate with them, even though their general popularity was very great. Yet more and more believers in the Lord joined them, both men and women in really large numbers.

—and miraculous power radiates from it   5.15

Many signs and wonders were now happening among the people through the apostles' ministry. In consequence people would bring out their sick into the streets and lay them down on stretchers or beds, so that as Peter came by at least his shadow might fall upon some of them. In addition a large crowd collected from the cities round about Jerusalem, bringing with them their sick and all those who were suffering from evil spirits. And they were all cured.

Furious opposition reduced to impotence

All this roused the High Priest and his allies the Sadducean party, and in a fury of jealousy they had the apostles arrested and put into the common jail. But during the night an angel of the Lord opened the prison doors and led them out, saying,

"Go and stand and speak in the Temple. Tell the people all about this new life!"

After receiving these instructions they entered the Temple about daybreak, and began to teach. When the High Priest arrived he and his supporters summoned the Sanhedrin and indeed the whole senate of the people of Israel. Then he sent to the jail to have the apostles brought in. But when the officers arrived at the prison they could not find them there. They came back and reported,

"We found the prison securely locked and the guards standing on duty at the doors, but when we opened up we found no one inside."

When the captain of the Temple guard and the chief priests heard this report they were completely mystified at the apostles' disappearance and wondered what further developments there would be. However, someone arrived and reported to them,

"Why, the men you put in jail are standing in the Temple teaching the people!"

Then the captain went out with his men and fetched them. They dared not use any violence, however, for the people might have stoned them. So they brought them in and made them stand before the Sanhedrin. The High Priest called for an explanation.

"We gave you the strictest possible orders," he said to them, "not to give any teaching in this name. And look what has happened—you have filled Jerusalem with your teaching, and what is more you are determined to fasten the guilt of that man's death upon us!"

The apostles speak the unpalatable truth   5.29

Then Peter and the apostles answered him,

"It is our duty to obey the orders of God rather than the orders of men. It was the God of our fathers who raised up Jesus, whom you murdered by hanging him on a cross of wood. God has raised this man to his own right hand as prince and savior, to bring repentance and the forgiveness of sins to Israel. What is more, we are witnesses to these matters, and so is the Holy Spirit which God gives to those who obey his commands."

Calm counsel temporarily prevails   5.33

When the members of the council heard these words they were so furious that they wanted to kill them. But one man stood up in the assembly, a Pharisee by the name of Gamaliel, a teacher of the Law who was held in great respect by the people, and gave orders for the apostles to be taken outside for a few minutes. Then he addressed the assembly:

"Men of Israel, be very careful of what action you intend to take against these men! Remember that some time ago a man called Theudas made himself conspicuous by claiming to be someone or other, and he had a following of four hundred men. He was killed, all his followers were dispersed, and the movement came to nothing. Then later, in the days of the census, that man Judas from Galilee appeared and enticed many of the people to follow him. But he too died and his whole following melted away. My advice to you now therefore is to let these men alone; leave them to themselves. For if this teaching or movement is merely human it will collapse of its own accord. But if it should be from God you cannot defeat them, and you might actually find yourselves to be fighting against God!"

They accepted his advice and called in the apostles. They had them beaten and after commanding them not to speak in the name of Jesus they let them go. So the apostles went out from the presence of the Sanhedrin full of joy that they had been considered worthy to bear humiliation for the sake of the name. Then day after day in the Temple and in people's houses they continued to teach unceasingly and to proclaim the good news of Jesus Christ.

The first deacons are chosen   6.1

About this time, when the number of disciples was continually increasing, the Greeks complained that in the daily distribution of food the Hebrew widows were being given preferential treatment. The twelve summoned the whole body of the disciples together, and said,

"It is not right that we should have to neglect preaching the Word of God in order to look after the accounts. You, our brothers, must look round and pick out from your number seven men of good reputation who are both practical and spiritually-minded and we will put them in charge of this matter. Then we shall devote ourselves wholeheartedly to prayer and the ministry of the Word."

This brief speech met with unanimous approval and they chose Stephen, a man full of faith and the Holy Spirit, Philip, Prochorus, Nicanor, Timon, Parmenas, and Nicolas of Antioch who had previously been a convert to the Jewish faith. They brought these men before the apostles, and they, after prayer, laid their hands upon them.

So the Word of God gained more and more ground. The number of disciples in Jerusalem very greatly increased, while a considerable proportion of the priesthood accepted the faith.

The attack on the new deacon, Stephen   6.8

Stephen, full of grace and spiritual power, continued to perform miracles and remarkable signs among the people. However, members of a Jewish synagogue known as the Libertines, together with some from the synagogues of Cyrene and Alexandria, as well as some men from Cilicia and Asia, tried debating with Stephen, but found themselves quite unable to stand up against either his practical wisdom or the spiritual force with which he spoke. In desperation they bribed men to allege, "We have heard this man making blasphemous statements against Moses and against God." At the same time they worked upon the feelings of the people, the elders and the scribes. Then they suddenly confronted Stephen, seized him and marched him off before the Sanhedrin. There they brought forward false witnesses to say, "This man's speeches are one long attack against this holy place and the Law. We have heard him say that Jesus of Nazareth will destroy this place and change the customs which Moses handed down to us." All who sat there in the Sanhedrin looked intently at Stephen, and as they looked his face appeared to them like the face of an angel.

Stephen makes his defense from Israel's history: 7.1
The time of Abraham

Then the High Priest said,
  "Is this statement true?"
And Stephen answered,
  "My brothers and my fathers, listen to me. Our glorious God appeared to our forefather Abraham while he was in Mesopotamia before he ever came to live in Haran, and said to him, 'Get thee out of thy land and from thy kindred, and come into a land which I shall shew thee.' That was how he came to leave the land of the Chaldeans and settle in Haran. And it was from there after his father's death that God moved him into this very land where you are living today. Yet God gave him no part of it as an inheritance, not a foot that he could call his own, and yet promised that it should eventually belong to him and his descendants—even though at the time he had no descendant at all. And this is the way in which God spoke to him: he told him that his descendants should live as strangers in a foreign land where they would become slaves and be ill treated for four hundred years, 'And the nation to which they shall be in bondage will I judge, said God; and after that shall they come forth, and serve me in this place.'
  "Further, he gave him the agreement of circumcision, so that when Abraham became the father of Isaac he circumcised him on the eighth day.

Stephen's defense: the patriarchs   7.8b

"Isaac became the father of Jacob, and Jacob the father of the twelve patriarchs. Then the patriarchs in their jealousy of Joseph sold him as a slave into Egypt. But God was with him and saved him from all his troubles and gave him favor and wisdom in the eyes of Pharaoh the king of Egypt. Pharaoh made him governor of Egypt and put him in charge of his own entire household.

"Then came the famine over all the land of Egypt and Canaan which caused great suffering, and our forefathers could find no food. But when Jacob heard that there was corn in Egypt he sent our forefathers out of their own country for the first time. It was on their second visit that Joseph was recognized by his brothers, and his ancestry became plain to Pharaoh. Then Joseph sent and invited to come and live with him his father and all his kinsmen, seventy-five people in all. So Jacob came down to Egypt and both he and our fathers ended their days there. After their death they were carried back into Shechem and laid in the tomb which Abraham had bought with silver from the sons of Hamor, in Shechem.

"But as the time drew near for the fulfillment of the promise which God had made to Abraham, our people grew more and more numerous in Egypt. Finally another king came to the Egyptian throne who knew nothing of Joseph. This man cleverly victimized our race. He treated our forefathers abominably, forcing them to expose their infant children so that the race should die out.

Stephen's defense: God's providence and Moses   7.20

"It was at this very time that Moses was born. He was a child of remarkable beauty, and for three months he was brought up in his father's house, and then when the time came for him to be abandoned Pharaoh's daughter adopted him and brought him up as her own son. So Moses was trained in all the wisdom of the Egyptians, and became not only an excellent speaker but a man of action as well.

Moses' first abortive attempt at rescue   7.23

"Now when he was turned forty the thought came into his mind that he should go and visit his own brothers, the sons of Israel. He saw one of them being unjustly treated, went to the rescue and paid rough justice for the man who had been ill treated by striking down the Egyptian. He fully imagined that his brothers would understand that God was using him to rescue them. But they did not understand. Indeed, on the very next day he came upon two of them who were quarreling and urged them to make peace, saying, 'Men, you are brothers. What good can come from your injuring each other?' But the man who was wronging his neighbor pushed Moses aside, saying, 'Who made you a ruler and judge over us? Do you want to kill me as you killed that Egyptian yesterday?' At that retort Moses fled and lived as an exile in the land of Midian, where he became the father of two sons.

Moses hears the voice of God   7.30

"It was forty years later in the desert of Mount Sinai that an angel appeared to him in the flames of a burning bush, and the sight filled Moses with wonder. As he approached to look at it more closely the voice of the Lord spoke to him, saying, 'I am the God of thy fathers, the God of Abraham, and the God of Isaac, and the God of Jacob.' Then Moses trembled and was afraid to look any more. But the Lord spoke to him and said, *'Loose the shoes from thy feet: for the place whereon thou standest is holy ground. I have surely seen the affliction of my people which is in Egypt, and have heard their groaning, and I am come down to deliver them: and now come, I will send thee into Egypt.'*

But Israel rejects Moses   7.35

"So this same Moses whom they had rejected in the words, 'Who appointed you a ruler and judge?' God sent to be both ruler and deliverer with the help of the angel who had appeared to him in the bush. This is the man who showed wonders and signs in Egypt and in the Red Sea, the man who led them out of Egypt and was their leader in the desert for forty years. He was Moses, the man who said to the sons of Israel, *'A prophet shall God raise up unto you from among your brethren, like unto me.'* In that church in the desert this was the man who was the mediator between the angel who used to talk with him on Mount Sinai and our fathers. This was the man who received words, living words, which were to be given to you; and this was the man to whom our forefathers turned a deaf ear! They disregarded him, and in their hearts hankered after Egypt. They said to Aaron, 'Make us gods to go before us. For as for this Moses who led us out of Egypt, we do not know what has become of him.' In those days they even made a calf, and offered sacrifices to their idol. They rejoiced in the work of their own hands. So God turned away from them and left them to worship the Host of Heaven, as it is written in the book of the prophets,

> Did ye offer unto me slain beasts and sacrifices
> Forty years in the wilderness, O house of Israel?
> And ye took up the tabernacle of Moloch,
> And the star of the god Rephan,
> The figures which ye made to worship them:
> And I will carry you away beyond Babylon.

God's privileges to Israel   7.44

"There in the desert our forefathers possessed the Tabernacle of witness made according to the pattern which Moses saw when God instructed him to build it. This Tabernacle was handed down to our forefathers, and they brought it here when the Gentiles were defeated under Joshua, for God drove them out as our ancestors advanced. Here it stayed until the time of David. David won the approval of God and prayed that he might find a habitation for the God of Jacob, even though it was not he but Solomon who actually built a house for him. Yet of course the most high does not live in man-made houses. As the prophet says,

> The heaven is my throne,
> And the earth the footstool of my feet:
> What manner of house will ye build me? saith the Lord:
> Or what is the place of my rest?
> Did not my hand make all these things?

Yet Israel is blind and disobedient   7.51

"You obstinate people, heathen in your thinking, heathen in the way you are listening to me now! It is always the same— you never fail to resist the Holy Spirit! Just as your fathers did, so are you doing now. Can you name a single prophet whom your fathers did not persecute? They killed the men who long ago foretold the coming of the just one, and now in our own day you have become his betrayers and his murderers. You are the men who have received the Law of God miraculously, by the hand of angels, *and you are the men who have disobeyed it!*"

The truth arouses murderous fury   7.54

These words stung them to fury and they ground their teeth at him in rage. Stephen, filled through all his being with the Holy Spirit, looked steadily up into Heaven. He saw the glory of God, and Jesus himself standing at his right hand.

"Look!" he exclaimed, "the heavens are opened and I can see the Son of Man standing at God's right hand!"

At this they put their fingers in their ears. Yelling with fury, as one man they made a rush at him and hustled him out of the city and stoned him. The witnesses* of the execution flung their clothes at the feet of a young man by the name of Saul.

So they stoned Stephen while he called upon God, and said, "Jesus, Lord, receive my spirit!"

Then, on his knees, he cried in ringing tones,

"Lord, forgive them for this sin."

And with these words he fell into the sleep of death, while Saul gave silent assent to his execution.

Widespread persecution follows Stephen's death   8.1b

On that very day a great storm of persecution burst upon the Church in Jerusalem. All Church members except the apostles were scattered over the countryside of Judaea and Samaria. While reverent men buried Stephen and mourned deeply over him, Saul harassed the Church bitterly. He would go from house to house, drag out both men and women and have them committed to prison. Those who were dispersed by this action went throughout the country, preaching the good news of the message as they went. Philip, for instance, went down to the city of Samaria and preached Christ to the people there. His words met with a ready and sympathetic response from the large crowds who listened to him and saw the miracles which he performed. With loud cries evil spirits came out of those who had been possessed by them; and many paralyzed and lame people were cured. As a result there was great rejoicing in that city.

*In Jewish Law the "witnesses" were also the executioners.

A magician believes in Christ   8.9

But there was a man named Simon in the city who had been practicing magic for some time and mystifying the people of Samaria. He pretended that he was somebody great and everyone from the lowest to the highest was fascinated by him. Indeed, they used to say, "This man must be that great power of God." He had influenced them for a long time, astounding them by his magical practices. But when they had come to believe Philip as he proclaimed to them the good news of the kingdom of God and of the name of Jesus Christ, men and women alike were baptized. Even Simon himself became a believer and after his baptism attached himself closely to Philip. As he saw the signs and remarkable demonstrations of power which took place, he lived in a state of constant wonder.

God confirms Samaria's acceptance of the gospel   8.14

When the apostles in Jerusalem heard that Samaria had accepted the Word of God, they sent Peter and John down to them. When these two had arrived they prayed for the Samaritans that they might receive the Holy Spirit for as yet he had not fallen upon any of them. They were living simply as men and women who had been baptized in the name of the Lord Jesus. So then and there they laid their hands on them and they received the Holy Spirit.

Simon's monstrous suggestion is sternly rebuked   8.18

When Simon saw how the Spirit was given through the apostles' laying their hands upon people he offered them money with the words,

"Give me this power too, so that if I were to put my hands on anyone he could receive the Holy Spirit."

But Peter said to him,

"To hell with you and your money!* How dare you think you could buy the gift of God? You can have no share or place in this ministry, for your heart is not honest before God. All you can do now is to repent of this wickedness of yours and pray earnestly to God that the evil intention of your heart may be forgiven. For I can see inside you, and I see a man bitter with jealousy and bound with his own sin!"

*These words are exactly what the Greek means. It is a pity that their real meaning is obscured by modern slang usage.

To this Simon answered,

"Please pray to the Lord for me that none of these things that you have spoken about may come upon me!"

When Peter and John had given their clear witness and spoken the Word of the Lord, they returned to Jerusalem, preaching the good news to many Samaritan villages as they went.

Philip is given a unique opportunity   8.26

But an angel of the Lord said to Philip,

"Get up and go south down the road which runs from Jerusalem to Gaza, out in the desert."

Philip arose and began his journey. At this very moment an Ethiopian eunuch, a minister and in fact the treasurer to Candace, queen of the Ethiopians, was on his way home after coming to Jerusalem to worship. He was sitting in his carriage

reading the prophet Isaiah. The Spirit said to Philip,
    "Approach this carriage, and keep close to it."
    Then as Philip ran forward he heard the man reading the
prophet Isaiah, and he said,
    "Do you understand what you are reading?"
    And he replied,
    "How can I unless I have someone to guide me?"
    And he invited Philip to get up and sit by his side. The
passage of scripture he was reading was this:

He was led as a sheep to the slaughter;
And as a lamb before his shearer is dumb,
So he openeth not his mouth:
In his humiliation his judgment was taken away:
His generation who shall declare?
For his life is taken from the earth.

    The eunuch turned to Philip and said,
    "Tell me, I beg you, about whom is the prophet saying this—
is he speaking about himself or about someone else?"
    Then Philip began, and using this scripture as a starting
point, he told the eunuch the good news about Jesus. As they
proceeded along the road they came to some water, and the
eunuch said,
    "Look, here is some water; is there any reason why I should
not be baptized now?"
    And he gave orders for the carriage to stop. Then both of
them went down to the water and Philip baptized the eunuch.
When they came up out of the water the Spirit of the Lord
took Philip away suddenly and the eunuch saw no more of
him, but proceeded on his journey with a heart full of joy.
Philip found himself at Azotus and as he passed through the
countryside he went on telling the good news in all the cities
until he came to Caesarea.

The crisis for Saul   9.1

But Saul, still breathing murderous threats against the disciples of the Lord, went to the High Priest and begged him for letters to the synagogues in Damascus, so that if he should find there any followers of the Way, whether men or women, he could bring them back to Jerusalem as prisoners.

But on his journey, as he neared Damascus, a light from Heaven suddenly blazed around him, and he fell to the ground. Then he heard a voice speaking to him,

"Saul, Saul, why are you persecuting me?"

"Who are you, Lord?" he asked.

"I am Jesus whom you are persecuting," was the reply. "But now stand up and go into the city and there you will be told what you must do."

His companions on the journey stood there speechless, for they had heard the voice but could see no one. Saul got up from the ground, but when he opened his eyes he could see nothing. So they took him by the hand and led him into Damascus. There he remained sightless for three days, and during that time he had nothing either to eat or drink.

God's preparation for the converted Saul   9.10

Now in Damascus there was a disciple by the name of Ananias. The Lord spoke to this man in a dream, calling him by his name.

"I am here, Lord," he replied.

Then the Lord said to him,

"Get up and go down to the street called Straight and inquire at the house of Judas for a man named Saul from Tarsus. At this moment he is praying and he sees in his mind's eye a man by the name of Ananias coming into the house, and placing his hands upon him to restore his sight."

But Ananias replied,

"Lord, I have heard on all hands about this man and how much harm he has done to your holy people in Jerusalem! Why even now he holds powers from the chief priests to arrest all who call upon your name."

But the Lord said to him,

"Go on your way, for this man is my chosen instrument to bear my name before the gentiles and their kings, as well as to the sons of Israel. Indeed, I myself will show him what he must suffer for the sake of my name."

Then Ananias set out and went to the house, and there he laid his hands upon Saul, and said,

"Saul, brother, the Lord has sent me—Jesus who appeared to you on your journey here—so that you may recover your sight and be filled with the Holy Spirit."

Immediately something like scales fell from Saul's eyes, and he could see again. He got to his feet and was baptized. Then he took some food and regained his strength.

Saul's conversion astounds the disciples   9.19b

Saul stayed with the disciples in Damascus for some time. Without delay he proclaimed Jesus in the synagogues declaring that he is the Son of God. All his hearers were staggered and kept saying,

"Isn't this the man who so bitterly persecuted those who called on the name in Jerusalem, and came down here with the sole object of taking back all such people as prisoners before the chief priests?"

But Saul went on from strength to strength, reducing to confusion the Jews who lived at Damascus by proving beyond doubt that this man is Christ.

The long revenge on the "renegade" begins   9.23

After some time the Jews made a plot to kill Saul, but news of this came to his ears. Although in their murderous scheme the Jews watched the gates day and night for him, Saul's disciples took him one night and let him down through an opening in the wall by lowering him in a basket.

At Jerusalem Saul is suspect: Barnabas conciliates   9.26

When Saul reached Jerusalem he tried to join the disciples. But they were all afraid of him, finding it impossible to believe that he was a disciple. Barnabas, however, took him by the hand and introduced him to the apostles, and explained to them how he had seen the Lord on his journey, and how the Lord had spoken to him. He further explained how Saul had spoken in Damascus with the utmost boldness in the name of Jesus. After that Saul joined with them in all their activities in Jerusalem, preaching fearlessly in the name of the Lord. He used to talk and argue with the Greek-speaking Jews, but they made several attempts on his life. When the brothers realized this they took him down to Caesarea and sent him off to Tarsus.

A time of peace   9.31

The whole Church throughout Judaea, Galilee and Samaria now enjoyed a period of peace. It became established and as it went forward in reverence for the Lord and in the strengthening presence of the Holy Spirit, continued to grow in numbers.

Peter heals at Lydda   9.32

Now it happened that Peter, in the course of traveling about among them all, came down to God's people living at Lydda. There he found a man called Aeneas who had been bedridden for eight years through paralysis. Peter said to him,

"Aeneas, Jesus Christ heals you! Get up and make your bed."

He got to his feet at once. And all those who lived in Lydda and Sharon saw him and turned to the Lord.

—and again at Joppa   **9.36**

Then there was a woman in Joppa, a disciple called Tabitha, whose name in Greek was Dorcas (meaning Gazelle). She was a woman whose whole life was full of good and kindly actions, but in those days she became seriously ill and died. So when they had washed her body they laid her in an upper room. Now Lydda is quite near Joppa, and when the disciples heard that Peter was in Lydda, they sent two men to him and begged him,

"Please come to us without delay."

Peter got up and went back with them, and when he arrived in Joppa they took him to the room upstairs. All the widows stood around him with tears in their eyes, holding out for him to see the dresses and cloaks which Dorcas used to make for them while she was with them. But Peter put them all outside the room and knelt down and prayed. Then he turned to the body and said,

"Tabitha, get up!"

She opened her eyes, and as soon as she saw Peter she sat up. He took her by the hand, helped her to her feet, and then called out to the believers and widows and presented her to them alive. This became known throughout the whole of Joppa and many believed in the Lord. Peter himself remained there for some time, staying with a tanner called Simon.

God speaks to a good-living gentile   **10.1**

There was a man in Caesarea by the name of Cornelius, a centurion in what was called the Italian regiment. He was a deeply religious man who reverenced God, as did all his household. He made many charitable gifts to the people and was a real man of prayer. About three o'clock one afternoon he saw perfectly clearly in a dream an angel of God coming into his room, approaching him, and saying,

"Cornelius!"

He stared at the angel in terror, and said,

"What is it, Lord?"

The angel replied,

"Your prayers and your deeds of charity have gone up to Heaven and are remembered before God. Now send men to Joppa for a man called Simon, who is also known as Peter. He is staying as a guest with another Simon, a tanner, whose house is down by the sea."

When the angel who had spoken to him had gone, Cornelius called out for two of his house servants and a devout soldier, who was one of his personal attendants. He told them the whole story and then sent them off to Joppa.

Peter's startling vision   10.9

Next day, while these men were still on their journey and approaching the city, Peter went up about midday on to the flat roof of the house to pray. He became very hungry and longed for something to eat. But while the meal was being prepared he fell into a trance and saw the heavens open and something like a great sheet descending upon the earth, let down by its four corners. In it were all kinds of animals, reptiles and birds. Then came a voice which said to him,

"Get up, Peter, kill and eat!"

But Peter said,

"Never, Lord! For not once in all my life have I ever eaten anything common or unclean."

Then the voice spoke to him a second time,

"You must not call what God has cleansed common."

This happened three times, and then the thing was gone, taken back into heaven.

The meaning of the vision becomes apparent   10.17

While Peter was still puzzling about the meaning of the vision which he had just seen, the men sent by Cornelius had arrived asking for the house of Simon. They were in fact standing at the very doorway of the house calling out to inquire if Simon, surnamed Peter, were lodging there. Peter was still thinking deeply about the vision when the Spirit said to him,

"Three men are here looking for you. Get up and go downstairs. Go with them without any misgiving, for I myself have sent them."

So Peter went down to the men and said,

"I am the man you are looking for; what brings you here?" They replied,

"Cornelius the centurion, a good-living and God-fearing man, whose character can be vouched for by the whole Jewish people, was commanded by a holy angel to send for you to come to his house, and to listen to your message."

Then Peter invited them in and entertained them.

Peter, obeying the Spirit, disobeys Jewish Law   10.23b

On the next day he got up and set out with them, accompanied by some of the brothers from Joppa, arriving at Caesarea on the day after that. Cornelius was expecting them and had invited together all his relations and intimate friends. As Peter entered the house Cornelius met him by falling on his knees before him and worshiping him. But Peter roused him with the words,

"Stand up, I am a human being too!"

Then Peter went right into the house in deep conversation with Cornelius and found that a large number of people had assembled. Then he spoke to them,

"You all know that it is forbidden for a man who is a Jew to associate with, or even visit, a man of another nation. But God has shown me plainly that no man must be called 'common' or 'unclean.' That is why I came here when I was sent for without raising any objection. Now I want to know what made you send for me."

Then Cornelius replied,

"Three days ago, about this time, I was observing the afternoon hour of prayer in my house, when suddenly a man in shining clothes stood before me and said, 'Cornelius, your prayer has been heard and your charitable gifts have been remembered before God. Now you must send to Joppa and

invite here a man called Simon whose surname is Peter. He is
staying in the house of a tanner by the name of Simon, down
by the sea.' So I sent to you without delay and you have been
most kind in coming. Now we are all here in the presence of
God to listen to everything that the Lord has commanded you
to say."

Peter's momentous discovery 10.34

Then Peter began to speak,

"In solemn truth I can see now that God is no respecter of
persons, but that in every nation the man who reverences him
and does what is right is acceptable to him! He has sent his
message to the sons of Israel by giving us the good news of
peace through Jesus Christ—he is the Lord of us all. You must
know the story of Jesus of Nazareth—why, it has spread
through the whole of Judaea, beginning from Galilee after

the baptism that John proclaimed. You must have heard how God anointed him with the power of the Holy Spirit, of how he went about doing good and healing all who suffered from the devil's power—because God was with him. Now we are eyewitnesses of everything that he did, both in the Judaean country and in Jerusalem itself, and yet they murdered him by hanging him on a cross. But on the third day God raised that same Jesus and let him be clearly seen, not indeed by the whole people, but by witnesses whom God had previously chosen. We are those witnesses, we who ate and drank with him after he had risen from the dead! Moreover, we are the men whom he commanded to preach to the people and bear fearless witness to the fact that he is the one appointed by God to be the judge of both the living and the dead. It is to him that all the prophets bear witness, that every man who believes in him may receive forgiveness of sins through his name."

The Holy Spirit confirms Peter's action   10.44

While Peter was still speaking these words the Holy Spirit fell upon all who were listening to his message. The Jewish believers who had come with Peter were absolutely amazed that the gift of the Holy Spirit was being poured out on gentiles also; for they heard them speaking in foreign tongues and glorifying God.

Then Peter exclaimed,

"Could anyone refuse water or object to these men being baptized—men who have received the Holy Spirit just as we did ourselves?"

And he gave orders for them to be baptized in the name of Jesus Christ. Afterwards they asked him to stay with them for some days.

The Church's disquiet at Peter's action   11.1

Now the apostles and the brothers who were in Judaea heard that the gentiles also had received God's message. So when Peter next visited Jerusalem the circumcision party were full of criticism, saying to him, "You actually went in and shared a meal with uncircumcised men!"

Peter's explanation 11.4

But Peter began to explain how the situation had actually arisen.

"I was in the city of Joppa praying," he said, "and while completely unconscious of my surroundings I saw a vision— something like a great sheet coming down toward me, let down from heaven by its four corners. It came right down to me and when I looked at it closely I saw animals and wild beasts, reptiles and birds. Then I heard a voice say to me, 'Get up, Peter, kill and eat.' But I said, 'Never, Lord, for nothing common or unclean has ever passed my lips.' But the voice from Heaven spoke a second time and said, 'You must not call what God has cleansed common!' This happened three times, and then the whole thing was drawn up again into heaven. The extraordinary thing is that at that very moment three men arrived at the house where we were staying, sent to me personally from Caesarea. The Spirit told me to go with these men without any misgiving. And these six of our brothers accompanied me and we went into the man's house. He told us how he had seen the angel standing in his house, saying, 'Send to Joppa and bring Simon, surnamed Peter. He will give you a message which will save both you and your whole household.' While I was beginning to tell them this message the Holy Spirit fell upon them just as on us at the beginning. There came into my mind the words of our Lord when he said, 'John indeed baptized with water, but you will be baptized with the Holy Spirit.' If then God gave them exactly the same gift as he gave to us when we believed on the Lord Jesus Christ, who was I to think that I could hinder the working of God?"

The flexibility of the young Church   11.18

When they heard this they had no further objection to raise. And they praised God, saying,

"Then obviously God has given to the gentiles as well the gift of repentance which leads to life."

Persecution has spread the gospel   11.19

Now those who had been dispersed by the persecution which arose over Stephen traveled as far as Phoenicia, Cyprus and Antioch, giving the message as they went to Jews only. However, among their number were natives of Cyprus and Cyrene, and these men, on their arrival at Antioch, proclaimed their message to the Greeks as well, telling them the good news of the Lord Jesus. The hand of the Lord was with them, and a great number believed and turned to the Lord. News of these things came to the ears of the church in Jerusalem and they sent Barnabas to Antioch. When he arrived and saw this working of God's grace, he was delighted. He urged them all to be resolute in their faithfulness to the Lord, for he was a good man, full of the Holy Spirit and of faith. So it happened that a considerable number of people became followers of the Lord.

Believers are called "Christians" for the first time 11.25

Then Barnabas went to Tarsus to find Saul. When he found him he brought him up to Antioch. Then for a whole year they met together with the church and taught a large crowd. It was in Antioch that the disciples were first given the name of "Christians."

The young Church and famine relief   11.27

During this period some prophets came down from Jerusalem to Antioch. One of them by the name of Agabus stood up and foretold by the Spirit that there was to be a great famine throughout the world. (This actually happened in the days of Claudius.) The disciples determined to send relief to the brothers in Judaea, each contributing as he was able. This they did, sending their contribution to the elders there personally through Barnabas and Saul.

Herod kills James and imprisons Peter   12.1

It was at this time that King Herod laid violent hands on some of the church members. James, John's brother, he executed with the sword, and when he found this action pleased the Jews he went on to arrest Peter as well. It was during the days of unleavened bread that he actually made the arrest. He put Peter in prison with no less than four platoons of soldiers to guard him, intending to bring him out to the people after the Passover. So Peter was closely guarded in the prison, while the church prayed to God earnestly on his behalf.

Peter's miraculous rescue   12.6

On the very night that Herod was planning to bring him out, Peter was asleep between two soldiers, chained with double chains, while guards maintained a strict watch in the doorway of the prison. Suddenly an angel of the Lord appeared, and light shone in the cell. He tapped Peter on the side and woke him up, saying, "Get up quickly." His chains fell away from his hands and the angel said to him, "Fasten your belt and put on your sandals." And he did so. Then the angel continued, "Wrap your cloak round you and follow me." So Peter followed him out, not knowing whether what the angel was doing were real—indeed he felt he must be taking part in a vision. So they passed right through the first and second guardpoints and came to the iron gate that led out into the city. This opened for them of its own accord, and they went out and had passed along one street when the angel suddenly vanished from Peter's sight. Then Peter came to himself and said aloud, "Now I know for certain that the Lord has sent his angel to rescue me from the power of Herod and from all that the Jewish people are expecting." As the truth broke upon him he went to the house of Mary, the mother of John surnamed Mark, where many were gathered together in prayer. As he knocked at the door a young maid called Rhoda came to answer it, but on recognizing Peter's voice failed to open the door from sheer joy. Instead she ran inside and reported that Peter was standing on the doorstep. At this they said to her,

"You must be mad!"

But she insisted that it was true. Then they said,

"Then it is his angel."

But Peter continued to stand there knocking on the door, and when they opened it and recognized him they were simply amazed. Peter, however, made a gesture to them to stop talking while he explained to them how the Lord had brought him out of prison. Then he said,

"Go and tell James and the other brothers what has happened."

After this he left them and went on to another place.

Peter's escape infuriates Herod   12.18

But when morning came there was a great commotion among the soldiers as to what could have happened to Peter. When Herod had had a search put out for him without success, he cross-examined the guards and then ordered their execution. Then he left Judaea and went down to Caesarea and stayed there.

But Herod dies a terrible death   12.20

Now Herod was very angry with the people of Tyre and Sidon. They approached him in a body and after winning over Blastus the king's chamberlain, they begged him for peace. They were forced to do this because their country's food supply was dependent on the king's dominions. So on an appointed day Herod put on his royal robes, took his seat on the public throne and made a speech to them. At this the people kept shouting, "This is a god speaking, not a mere man!" Immediately an angel of the Lord struck him down because he did not give God the glory. And in fearful internal agony he died.

The message continues to spread 12.24

But the Word of the Lord continued to gain ground and increase its influence. Barnabas and Saul returned from Jerusalem when they had completed their mission there, bringing with them John whose surname was Mark.

Saul and Barnabas are called to a special task 13.1

Now there were in the church at Antioch both prophets and teachers—Barnabas, for example, Simeon surnamed Niger, Lucius the Cyrenian, Manaen the foster brother of the governor Herod, and Saul. While they were worshiping the Lord and fasting, the Holy Spirit spoke to them, saying,

"Set Barnabas and Saul apart for me for a task to which I have called them."

At this, after further fasting and prayer, they laid their hands on them and set them free for this work. So these two, sent at the Holy Spirit's command, went down to Seleucia and from there they sailed off to Cyprus. On their arrival at Salamis they began to proclaim God's message in the Jewish synagogues, having John as their assistant. As they made their way through the island as far as Paphos they came across a man named Bar-Jesus, a Jew who was both a false prophet and a magician. This man was attached to Sergius Paulus, the proconsul, who was himself a man of intelligence. He sent for Barnabas and Saul as he was anxious to hear God's message. But Elymas the magician (for that is the translation of his name) opposed them, doing his best to dissuade the proconsul from accepting the faith. Then Saul (who is also called Paul), filled with the Holy Spirit, eyed him closely and said,

"You son of the devil, you enemy of all true goodness, you monster of trickery and evil, is it not high time you gave up trying to pervert the truth of the Lord? Now listen, the Lord himself will touch you, for some time you will not see the light of the sun—you will be blind!"

Immediately a mist and then an utter blackness came over his eyes, and he went round trying to find someone to lead him by the hand. When the proconsul saw what had happened he believed, for he was shaken to the core at the Lord's teaching.

Saul (now Paul) comes to Antioch in Pisidia   13.13

Then Paul and his companions set sail from Paphos and went to Perga in Pamphylia. There John left them and turned back to Jerusalem, but they continued their journey through Perga to the Antioch in Pisidia. They went to the synagogue on the Sabbath day and took their seats. After the reading of the Law and Prophets, the leaders of the synagogue sent to them with a message,

"Men and brothers, if you have any message of encouragement for the people, by all means speak."

Paul shows the Jews where their history leads   13.16

So Paul stood up, and motioning with his hand, began:

"Men of Israel and all of you who fear God, listen to me. The God of this people Israel chose our fathers and prospered the people even while they were exiles in the land of Egypt. Then he lifted up his arm and led them out of that land. Yes, and he bore with them for forty years in the desert. He destroyed seven nations in the land of Canaan before he gave them that land as their inheritance for some four hundred and fifty years. After that he gave them judges until the time of the prophet Samuel. Then when they begged for a king God gave them Saul the son of Kish, a man of the tribe of Benjamin, to be their king for forty years. After he had deposed him he raised David to the throne, a man of whom God himself bore testimony in the words, 'I have found David, the son of Jesse, a man after my own heart, who shall do all my will.' From the descendants of this man, according to his promise, God has brought Jesus to Israel to be their savior. John came before him to prepare his way preaching the baptism of repentance for all the people of Israel. Indeed, as John reached the end of his time he said these words: 'What do you think I am?

I am not he. But know this, someone comes after me whose shoelace I am not fit to untie!'

Now the message is urgent and contemporary   13.26

"Men and brothers, sons of the race of Abraham, and all among you who fear God, it is to us that this message of salvation has now been sent! For the people of Jerusalem and their rulers refused to recognize him and to understand the voice of the prophets which are read every Sabbath day—even though in condemning him they fulfilled these very prophecies! For though they found no cause for putting him to death, they begged Pilate to have him executed. And when they had completed everything that was written about him, they took him down from the cross and laid him in a tomb. But God raised him from the dead. For many days he was seen by those who had come up from Galilee to Jerusalem with him, and these men are now his witnesses to the people. And as for us we tell you the good news that the promise made to our forefathers has come true—that, in raising up Jesus, God has fulfilled it for us their children. This is endorsed in the second psalm: '*Thou art my son, this day have I begotten thee.*' And as for the fact of God's raising him from the dead, never to return to corruption, he has spoken in these words: '*I will give you the sure mercies of David.*' And then going further he says in another psalm: '*Thou shalt not suffer thine holy one to see corruption.*' For David, remember, after he had served God's purpose in his own generation fell asleep and was laid with his ancestors. He did in fact 'see corruption,' but this man whom God raised never saw corruption! It is therefore imperative, men and brothers, that every one of you should realize that forgiveness of sins is proclaimed to you through this man. And through faith in him a man is absolved from all those things from which the Law of Moses could never set him free. Take care then that this saying of the prophets should never apply to you:

Behold, ye despisers, and wonder, and perish;
For I work a work in your days,
A work which ye shall in no wise believe, if
   one declare it unto you."

Paul succeeds in arousing deep interest—   13.42

As they were going out the people kept on asking them to
say all this again on the following Sabbath. After the meeting
of the synagogue broke up, many of the Jews and devout
proselytes followed Paul and Barnabas who spoke personally
to them and urged them to put their trust in the grace of God.

—but a week later he meets bitter opposition   13.44

On the next Sabbath almost the entire population of the
city assembled to hear the message of God, but when the
Jews saw the crowds they were filled with jealousy and con-
tradicted what Paul was saying, covering him with abuse. At
this Paul and Barnabas did not mince their words but said,

"We felt it our duty to speak the message of God to you
first, but since you spurn it and evidently do not think yourselves fit for eternal life, watch us now as we turn to the
gentiles! Indeed the Lord has commanded us to do so in the
words:

I have set thee for a light of the gentiles,
That thou shouldest be for salvation unto the uttermost part
   of the earth."

When the gentiles heard this they were delighted and
thanked God for his message. All those who were destined
for eternal life believed, and the Word of the Lord spread
over the whole country. But the Jews worked upon the feelings
of religious and respectable women and some of the leading
citizens, and succeeded in starting a persecution against Paul
and Barnabas, and expelled them from the district. But they
on their part simply shook off the dust from their feet in protest

and went on to Iconium. And the disciples continued to be full
of joy and the Holy Spirit.

Jewish behavior repeats itself   14.1

Much the same thing happened at Iconium. On their
arrival they went to the Jewish synagogue and spoke
with such conviction that a very large number of both Jews
and Greeks believed. But the unbelieving Jews stirred up the
feelings of the gentiles and poisoned their minds against the
brothers. So they remained there for a long time and spoke
fearlessly for the Lord, who made it plain that they were
proclaiming the Word of his grace, by allowing them to perform signs and miracles. But the great mass of the people of
the city were divided in their opinions, some taking the side
of the Jews, and some that of the apostles. But when a hostile
movement arose from both gentiles and Jews in collaboration
with the authorities to insult and stone them, they got to know
about it, fled to the Lycaonian cities of Lystra and Derbe, and
the surrounding countryside—and from there they continued
to proclaim the gospel.

A miracle in a completely pagan city   14.8

Now it happened one day at Lystra that a man was sitting
who had no power in his feet. He had in fact been lame from
birth and had never been able to walk. He was listening to
Paul as he spoke, and Paul, looking him straight in the eye and
seeing that he had the faith to be made well, said in a loud
voice,

"Stand straight up on your feet!"

And he sprang to his feet and walked. When the crowd saw
what Paul had done they shouted in the Lycaonian language,

"The gods have come down to us in human form!"

They began to call Barnabas Jupiter, and Paul Mercury,
since he was the chief speaker. What is more, the high priest
of Jupiter whose temple was at the gateway of the city,
brought garlanded oxen to the gates and wanted to offer

sacrifice with the people. But when the apostles, Barnabas and Paul, heard of their intention they tore their clothes and rushed into the crowd, crying at the top of their voices,

"Men, men, why are you doing these things? We are only human beings with feelings just like yours! We are here to tell you good news—that you should turn from these meaningless things to the living God! He is the one who made heaven and earth, the sea and all that is in them. In generations gone by he allowed all nations to go on in their own ways—not that he left men without evidence of himself. For he had shown kindnesses to you; he has sent you rain from heaven and fruitful seasons, giving you food and happiness to your hearts' content."

Yet even with these words they only just succeeded in restraining the crowd from making sacrifices to them.

Paul is dogged by his Jewish enemies   14.19

Then some Jews arrived from Antioch and Iconium and after turning the minds of the people against Paul they stoned him and dragged him out of the city thinking he was dead. But while the disciples were gathered in a circle round him, Paul got up and walked back into the city. And the very next day he went out with Barnabas to Derbe, and when they had preached the gospel to that city and made many disciples, they turned back to Lystra, Iconium and Antioch. They put fresh heart into the disciples there, urging them to stand firm in the faith, and reminding them that it is "*through many tribulations that we must enter into the kingdom of God.*" They appointed elders for them in each church, and with prayer and fasting commended these men to the Lord in whom they had believed. Then they crossed Pisidia and arrived in Pamphylia. They proclaimed their message in Perga and then went down to Attalia. From there they sailed back to Antioch (in Syria) where they had first been commended to the grace of God for the task which they had now completed. When they arrived there they called the church together and reported

to them how greatly God had worked with them and how he had opened the door of faith for the gentiles. And here at Antioch they spent a considerable time with the disciples.

The opposition from reactionaries   15.1

Then some men came down from Judaea and began to teach the brothers, saying, "unless you are circumcised according to the custom of Moses you cannot be saved." Naturally this caused a serious upset among them and much earnest discussion followed with Paul and Barnabas. Finally it was agreed that Paul and Barnabas should go up to Jerusalem with some of their own people to confer with the apostles and elders about the whole question.

The church sent them off on their journey and as they went through Phoenicia and Samaria they told the story of the conversion of the gentiles and all the brothers were overjoyed to hear about it. On their arrival at Jerusalem they were welcomed by the church, by the apostles and elders, and they reported how greatly God had worked with them. But some members of the Pharisees' party who had become believers stood up and declared that it was absolutely essential that these men be told that they must be circumcised and observe the Law of Moses.

Peter declares that God is doing something new   15.6

The apostles and elders met to consider this matter. After an exhaustive inquiry Peter stood up and addressed them in these words:

"Men and brothers, you know that from the earliest days God chose me as the one from whose lips the gentiles should hear the Word and should believe it. Moreover, God who knows men's inmost thoughts had plainly shown that this is so, for when he had cleansed their hearts through their faith he gave the Holy Spirit to the gentiles exactly as he did to us. Why then must you now strain the patience of God by trying to put on the shoulders of these disciples a burden which neither our fathers nor we were able to bear? Surely the fact is that it is by the grace of the Lord Jesus that we are saved by faith, just as they are!"

These words produced absolute silence, and they listened to Barnabas and Paul while they gave a detailed account of the signs and wonders which God had worked through them among the gentiles.

James expresses the feeling of the meeting   15.13

Silence again followed their words and then James made this reply:

"Men and brothers, listen to me. Symeon has shown how in the first place God chose a people from among the nations who should bear his name. This is in full agreement with what the prophets wrote, as in this scripture:

After these things I will return,
And I will build again the tabernacle of David, which is
    fallen;
And I will build again the ruins thereof,
And I will set it up:
That the residue of men may seek after the Lord,
And all the gentiles, upon whom my name is called,
Saith the Lord who maketh these things known from the
    beginning of the world.

"I am firmly of the opinion that we should not put any additional obstacles before any gentiles who are turning toward God. Instead, I think we should write to them telling them to avoid anything polluted by idols, sexual immorality, eating the meat of strangled animals, or tasting blood. For after all, for many generations now Moses has had his preachers in every city and has been read aloud in the synagogues every Sabbath day."

The Church's deputation: the message   **15.22**
to gentile Christians

Then the apostles, the elders and the whole Church agreed
to choose representatives and send them to Antioch with Paul
and Barnabas. Their names were Judas, surnamed Barsabas,
and Silas, both leading men of the brotherhood. They carried
with them a letter bearing this message: "The apostles and
elders who are your brothers send their greetings to the
brothers who are gentiles in Antioch, Syria and Cilicia. Since
we have heard that some of our number have caused you deep
distress and have unsettled your minds by giving you a message
which certainly did not originate from us, we are unanimously
agreed to send you chosen representatives with our well loved
Barnabas and Paul—men who have risked their lives for the
name of our Lord Jesus Christ. So we have sent you Judas and
Silas who will give you the same message personally by word
of mouth. For it has seemed right to the Holy Spirit and to us
to lay no further burden upon you except what is absolutely
essential, namely, that you avoid what has been sacrificed to
idols, tasting blood, eating the meat of what has been
strangled, and sexual immorality. Keep yourselves clear of
these things and you will make good progress. Farewell."

The message is received with delight   **15.30**

So this party, sent off by the Church, went down to Antioch
and after gathering the congregation together, handed over
the letter to them. And they, when they read it, were delighted
with the encouragement it gave them. Judas and Silas were
themselves both inspired preachers and greatly encouraged
and strengthened the brothers by many talks to them. Then,
after spending some time there, the brothers sent them back in
peace to those who had commissioned them. Paul and Barnabas
however stayed on in Antioch teaching and preaching the
gospel of the Word of the Lord in company with many others.

Paul and Barnabas flatly disagree   15.36
but the work prospers

Some days later Paul spoke to Barnabas,

"Now let us go back and visit the brothers in every city where we have proclaimed the Word of the Lord to see how they are."

Barnabas wanted to take John, surnamed Mark, as their companion. But Paul disapproved of taking with them a man who had deserted them in Pamphylia and was not prepared to go on with them in their work. There was a sharp clash of opinion, so much so that they went their separate ways, Barnabas taking Mark and sailing to Cyprus, while Paul chose Silas and set out on his journey, commended to the grace of the Lord by the brothers as he did so. He traveled through Syria and Cilicia and strengthened the churches.

Paul chooses Timothy as companion   16.1

He also went to Derbe and Lystra. At Lystra there was a disciple by the name of Timothy whose mother was a Jewish Christian, though his father was a Greek. Timothy was held in high regard by the brothers at Lystra and Iconium, and Paul wanted to take him on as his companion. Everybody knew that his father was a Greek, and Paul therefore had him circumcised because of the attitude of the Jews in these places. As they went on their way through the cities they passed on to them for their observance the decisions which had been reached by the apostles and elders in Jerusalem. Consequently the churches grew stronger and stronger in the faith and their numbers increased daily.

Paul and Silas find their journey divinely directed   16.6

They made their way through Phrygia and Galatia, but the Holy Spirit prevented them from speaking God's message in Asia. When they came to Mysia they tried to enter Bithynia, but again the Spirit of Jesus would not allow them. So they passed by Mysia and came down to Troas, where one night

Paul had a vision of a Macedonian man standing and appealing to him in the words: "Come over to Macedonia and help us!" As soon as Paul had seen this vision we made every effort to get on to Macedonia, convinced that God had called us to give them the good news.

The gospel comes to Europe: a businesswoman   16.11
is converted

So we set sail from Troas and ran a straight course to Samothrace, and on the following day to Neapolis. From there we went to Philippi, a Roman garrison town and the chief city in that part of Macedonia. We spent some days in Philippi and on the Sabbath day we went out of the city gate to the riverside, where we supposed there was a place for prayer. There we sat down and spoke to the women who had assembled. One of our hearers was a woman named Lydia. (She came from Thyatira and was a dealer in purple-dyed cloth.) She was already a believer in God, and he opened her heart to accept Paul's words. When she and her household had been baptized she appealed to us, saying,

"If you are satisfied that I am a true believer in the Lord, then come down to my house and stay there."

And she insisted on our doing so.

Conflict with evil spirits and evil men   16.16

One day while we were going to the place of prayer we were met by a young girl who had a spirit of clairvoyance and brought her owners a good deal of profit by foretelling the future. She would follow Paul and the rest of us, crying out, "These men are servants of the most high God, and they are telling you the way of salvation." She continued this behavior for many days, and then Paul, in a burst of irritation, turned round and spoke to the spirit in her,

"I command you in the name of Jesus Christ to come out of her!"

And it came out immediately. But when the girl's owners saw

that their hope of making money out of her had disappeared, they seized Paul and Silas and dragged them before the authorities in the market square. There they brought them before the chief magistrates and said,

"These men are Jews and are causing a great disturbance in our city. They are proclaiming customs which it is illegal for us as Roman citizens to accept or practice."

At this the crowd joined in the attack, and the magistrates had them stripped and ordered them to be beaten with rods. Then, after giving them a severe beating, they threw them into prison, instructing the jailer to keep them safe. On receiving such strict orders, he hustled them into the inner jail and fastened their feet securely in the stocks.

The midnight deliverance: the jailer becomes   16.25
a Christian

But about midnight Paul and Silas were praying and singing hymns to God while the other prisoners were listening to them. Suddenly there was a great earthquake, big enough to shake the foundations of the prison. Immediately all the doors flew open and everyone's chains were unfastened. When the jailer woke and saw that the doors of the prison had been opened he drew his sword and was on the point of killing himself, for he imagined that all the prisoners had escaped. But Paul called out to him at the top of his voice,

"Don't hurt yourself—we are all here!"

Then the jailer called for lights, rushed in, and trembling all over, fell at the feet of Paul and Silas. He led them outside, and said,

"Sirs, what must I do to be saved?"

And they replied,

"Believe in the Lord Jesus and then you will be saved, you and your household."

Then they told him and all the members of his household the message of God. There and then in the middle of the night he took them aside and washed their wounds, and he himself and all his family were baptized without delay. Then he took them into his house and offered them food, he and his whole household overjoyed at finding faith in God.

Paul, in a strong position, makes   16.35
the authorities apologize

When morning came, the magistrates sent their constables with the message, "Let those men go." The jailer reported this message to Paul, saying,

"The magistrates have sent to have you released. So now you can leave this place and go on your way in peace."

But Paul said to the constables,

"They beat us publicly without any kind of trial; they threw us into prison despite the fact that we are Roman citizens. And now do they want to get rid of us in this underhand way? Oh no, let them come and take us out themselves!"

The constables reported this to the magistrates, who were thoroughly alarmed when they heard that they were Romans. So they came in person and apologized to them, and after taking them outside the prison, requested them to leave the city. But on leaving the prison Paul and Silas went to Lydia's house, and when they had seen the brothers and given them fresh courage, they took their leave.

Bitter opposition at Thessalonica—   17.1

Next they journeyed through Amphipolis and Apollonia and arrived at Thessalonica. Here there was a synagogue of the Jews which Paul entered, following his usual custom. On three Sabbath days he argued with them from the scriptures, explaining and quoting passages to prove the necessity for the death of Christ and his rising again from the dead. "This Jesus whom I am proclaiming to you," he concluded, "is God's Christ!" Some of them were convinced and threw in their lot with Paul and Silas, and they were joined by a great many believing Greeks and a considerable number of influential women. But the Jews, in a fury of jealousy, got hold of some of the unprincipled loungers of the market place, gathered a crowd together and set the city in an uproar. Then they attacked Jason's house in an attempt to bring Paul and Silas out before the people. When they could not find them they hustled Jason and some of the brothers before the civic authorities, shouting, "These are the men who have turned the world upside down and have now come here, and Jason has taken them into his house. What is more, all these men act against the decrees of Caesar, saying that there is another king called Jesus!" By these words the Jews succeeded in alarming both the people and the authorities, and they only released Jason and the others after binding them over to keep the peace.

### —followed by encouragement at Beroea		17.10

Without delay the brothers dispatched Paul and Silas off to Beroea that night. On their arrival there they went to the Jewish synagogue. The Jews proved more generous-minded than those in Thessalonica, for they accepted the message most eagerly and studied the scriptures every day to see if what they were now being told were true. Many of them became believers, as did a number of Greek women of social standing and quite a number of men. But when the Jews at Thessalonica found out that God's message had been proclaimed by Paul at Beroea as well, they came there too to cause trouble and spread alarm among the people. The brothers at Beroea then sent Paul off at once to make his way to the seacoast, but Silas and Timothy remained there. The men who accompanied Paul took him as far as Athens and returned with instructions for Silas and Timothy to rejoin Paul as soon as possible.

### Paul is irritated by the idols of Athens		17.16

Paul had some days to wait at Athens for Silas and Timothy to arrive, and while he was there his soul was exasperated beyond endurance at the sight of a city so completely idolatrous. He felt compelled to discuss the matter with the Jews in the synagogue as well as with God-fearing gentiles, and he even argued daily in the open market place with the passers-by. While he was speaking there some Epicurean and Stoic philosophers came across him, and some of them remarked,

"What is this cock sparrow trying to say?"

Others said,

"He seems to be trying to proclaim some more gods to us, and outlandish ones at that!"

For Paul was actually proclaiming "Jesus" and "the resurrection." So they got hold of him and conducted him to their council, the Areopagus. There they asked him,

"May we know what this new teaching of yours really is? You talk of matters which sound strange to our ears, and we should like to know what they mean." (For all the Athenians, and even foreign visitors to Athens, had an obsession for any novelty and would spend their whole time talking about or listening to anything new.)

Paul's speech to the "gentlemen of Athens"   17.22

So Paul got to his feet in the middle of their council, and began,

"Gentlemen of Athens, my own eyes tell me that you are in all respects an extremely religious people. For as I made my way here and looked at your shrines I particularly noticed one altar on which were inscribed the words, TO GOD THE UNKNOWN. It is this God whom you are worshiping in ignorance that I am here to proclaim to you! God who made the world and all that is in it, being Lord of both Heaven and earth, does not live in temples made by human hands, nor is he ministered to by human hands, as though he had need of anything—seeing that he is the one who gives to all men life and breath and everything else. From one forefather he has created every race of men to live over the face of the whole earth. He has determined the times of their existence and the limits of their habitation, so that they might search for God,

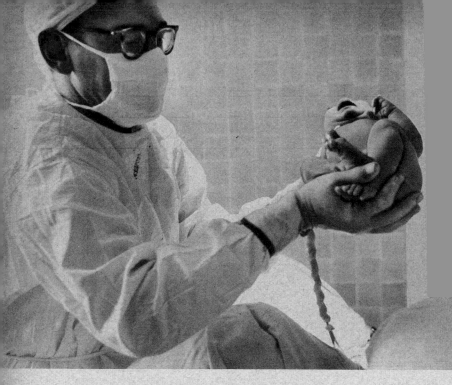

in the hope that they might feel for him and find him—yes, even though he is not far from any one of us. Indeed, it is in him that we live and move and have our being. Some of your own poets have endorsed this in the words, 'For we are indeed his children.' If then we are the children of God, we ought not to imagine God in terms of gold or silver or stone, contrived by human art or imagination. Now while it is true that God has overlooked the days of ignorance he now commands all men everywhere to repent. For he has fixed a day on which he will judge the whole world in justice by the standard of a man whom he has appointed. That this is so he has guaranteed to all men by raising this man from the dead."

But when his audience heard Paul talk about the resurrection from the dead some of them laughed outright, but others said,

"We should like to hear you speak again on this subject."

So with this mixed reception Paul retired from their assembly.

Yet some did in fact join him and accept the faith, including Dionysius a member of the Areopagus, a woman by the name of Damaris, and some others as well.

At Corinth Paul is yet again rejected by the Jews   18.1

Before long Paul left Athens and went on to Corinth where he found a Jew called Aquila, a native of Pontus. This man had recently come from Italy with his wife Priscilla, because Claudius had issued a decree that all Jews should leave Rome. He went to see them in their house and because they practiced the same trade as himself he stayed with them. They all worked together, for their trade was tent-making. Every Sabbath Paul used to speak in the synagogue trying to persuade both Jews and Greeks. By the time Silas and Timothy arrived from Macedonia Paul was completely absorbed in preaching the message, showing the Jews as clearly as he could that Jesus is Christ. However, when they turned against him and abused him he shook his garments at them, and said,

"Your blood be on your own heads! From now on I go with a perfectly clear conscience to the gentiles."

Then he left them and went to the house of a man called Titius Justus, a man who reverenced God and whose house was next door to the synagogue. Crispus, the leader of the synagogue, became a believer in the Lord, with all his household, and many of the Corinthians who heard the message believed and were baptized. Then one night the Lord spoke to Paul in a vision,

"Do not be afraid, but go on speaking and let no one silence you, for I myself am with you and no man shall lift a finger to harm you. There are many in this city who belong to me."

So Paul settled down there for eighteen months and taught them God's message.

Paul's enemies fail to impress the governor   18.12

Then, while Gallio was governor of Achaia, the Jews banded

together to attack Paul, and took him to court, saying,

"This man is perverting men's minds to make them worship God in a way that is contrary to the Law."

Paul was all ready to speak, but before he could utter a word Gallio said to the Jews,

"Listen, Jews! If this were a matter of some crime or wrong-doing I might reasonably be expected to put up with you. But since it is a question which concerns a word and names and your own Law, you must attend to it yourselves. I flatly refuse to be judge in these matters."

And he had them ejected from the court. Then they got hold of Sosthenes, the synagogue leader, and beat him in front of the courthouse. But Gallio remained completely unmoved.

Paul returns, and reports to Jerusalem and Antioch   18.18

Paul stayed for some time after this incident and then took leave of the brothers and sailed for Syria, taking Priscilla and Aquila with him. At Cenchrea he had his hair cut short, for he had taken a solemn vow. They all arrived at Ephesus and there Paul left Aquila and Priscilla, but he himself went into the synagogue and debated with the Jews. When they asked him to stay longer he refused, bidding them farewell with the words, "If it is God's will I will come back to you again." Then he set sail from Ephesus and went down to Caesarea. Here he disembarked and after paying his respects to the church in Jerusalem, he went down to Antioch. He spent some time there before he left and proceeded to visit systematically throughout Galatia and Phrygia, putting new heart into all the disciples as he went.

Apollos speaks powerfully at Ephesus and Corinth   18.24

Now a Jew called Apollos, a native of Alexandria and a gifted speaker, well versed in the scriptures, arrived at Ephesus. He had been instructed in the way of the Lord, and he spoke with burning zeal, teaching the facts about Jesus faithfully even though he knew only the baptism of John. This man began to speak with great boldness in the synagogue. But when Priscilla and Aquila heard him they took him aside and explained the way of God to him more accurately. Then as he wanted to cross into Achaia, the brothers gave him every encouragement and wrote a letter to the disciples there, asking them to make him welcome. On his arrival he proved a source of great strength to those who had believed through grace, for by his powerful arguments he publicly refuted the Jews, quoting from the scriptures to prove that Jesus is Christ.

Ephesus has its own Pentecost   19.1

While Apollos was in Corinth Paul journeyed through the upper parts of the country and arrived at Ephesus. There he discovered some disciples, and he asked them,

"Did you receive the Holy Spirit when you believed?"

"No," they replied, "we have never even heard that there is a Holy Spirit."

"Well then, how were you baptized?" asked Paul.

"We were baptized with John's baptism," they replied.

"John's baptism was a baptism to show a change of heart," Paul explained, "but he always told the people that they must believe in the one who should come after him, that is, in Jesus."

When these men heard this they were baptized in the name of the Lord Jesus, and then, when Paul had laid his hands on them, the Holy Spirit came upon them and they began to speak with tongues and the inspiration of prophets. (There were about twelve of them in all.)

Paul's two-year ministry at Ephesus   19.8

Then Paul made his way into the synagogue there and for three months he spoke with the utmost confidence, using both argument and persuasion as he talked of the kingdom of God. But when some of them hardened in their attitude toward the message and refused to believe it and, what is more, spoke offensively about the Way in public, Paul left them, and withdrew his disciples, and held daily discussions in the lecture hall of Tyrannus. He continued this practice for two years, so that all who lived in Asia, both Greeks and Jews, could hear the Lord's message. God gave most unusual demonstrations of power through Paul's hands, so much so that people took to the sick any handkerchiefs or clothing which had been in contact with his body, and they were cured of their diseases and their evil spirits left them.

The violence of evil and the power of "the name" 19.13

But there were some itinerant Jewish exorcists who attempted to invoke the name of the Lord Jesus when dealing with those who had evil spirits. They would say, "I command you in the name of Jesus whom Paul preaches." Seven brothers, sons of a chief priest called Sceva, were engaged in this practice on one occasion, when the evil spirit answered, "Jesus I know, and I am acquainted with Paul, but who on earth are you?" And the man in whom the evil spirit was living sprang at them and overpowered them all with such violence that they rushed out of that house wounded, with their clothes torn off their backs. This incident became known to all the Jews and Greeks who were living in Ephesus, and a great sense of awe came over them all, while the name of the Lord Jesus became highly respected. Many of those who had professed their faith began openly to admit their former practices. A number of those who had previously practiced magic collected their books and burned them publicly. (They estimated the value of these books and found it to be no less than ten thousand dollars.) In this way the Word of the Lord continued to grow irresistibly in power and influence.

Paul speaks of his plans   19.21

After these events Paul set his heart on going to Jerusalem by way of Macedonia and Achaia, remarking,

"After I have been there I must see Rome as well."

Then he dispatched to Macedonia two of his assistants, Timothy and Erastus, while he himself stayed for a while in Asia.

The silversmiths' riot at Ephesus 19.23

Now it happened about this time that a great commotion arose concerning the Way. A man by the name of Demetrius, a silversmith who made silver shrines for Diana, provided considerable business for his craftsmen. He gathered these men together with workers in similar trades, and spoke to them,

"Men," he said, "you all realize how our prosperity depends on this particular work. If you use your eyes and ears you also know that not only in Ephesus but practically throughout Asia this man Paul has succeeded in changing the minds of a great number of people by telling them that gods made by human hands are not gods at all. Now the danger is not only that this trade of ours might fall into disrepute, but also that the temple of the great goddess Diana herself might come to be lightly regarded. There is a further danger, that her actual majesty might be degraded, she whom the whole of Asia, and indeed the whole world, worships!"

When they heard this they were furiously angry, and shouted,

"Great is Diana of the Ephesians!"

Soon the whole city was in an uproar, and on a common impulse the people rushed into the theater dragging with them Gaius and Aristarchus, two Macedonians who were Paul's traveling companions. Paul himself wanted to go in among the crowd, but the disciples would not allow him. Moreover, some high-ranking officials who were Paul's friends sent to him begging him not to risk himself in the theater. Meanwhile some were shouting one thing and some another, and the whole assembly was at sixes and sevens, for most of them had no idea why they had come together at all. A man called Alexander whom the Jews put forward was pushed into the forefront of

the crowd, and there, after making a gesture with his hand, he tried to make a speech of defense to the people. But as soon as they realized that he was a Jew they shouted as one man for about two hours, "Great is Diana of the Ephesians!"

Public authority intervenes   19.35

But when the town clerk had finally quietened the crowd, he said,

"Gentlemen of Ephesus, who in the world could be ignorant of the fact that our city of Ephesus is temple guardian of the great Diana and of the image which fell down from Jupiter himself? These are undeniable facts and it is your plain duty to remain calm and do nothing which you might afterwards regret. For you have brought these men forward, though they are neither plunderers of the temple, nor have they uttered any blasphemy against our goddess. If Demetrius and his fellow craftsmen have a charge to bring against anyone, well, the courts are open and there are magistrates; let them take legal action. But if you require anything beyond that then it must be resolved in the regular assembly. For all of us are in danger of being charged with rioting over today's events—particularly as we have no real excuse to offer for this commotion."

And with these words he dismissed the assembly.

Paul departs on his second journey to Europe   20.1

A fter this disturbance had died down, Paul sent for the disciples and after speaking encouragingly said good-bye to them, and went on his way to Macedonia. As he made his journey through these districts he spoke many heartening words to the people and then went on to Greece, where he stayed for three months. Then when he was on the point of setting sail for Syria the Jews made a further plot against him and he decided to make his way back through Macedonia. His companions on the journey were Sopater a Beroean, the son of Pyrrhus; two Thessalonians, Aristarchus and Secundus; Gaius from Derbe, Timothy, and two Asians, Tychicus and Trophimus. This party proceeded to Troas to await us there, while we sailed from Philippi after the days of unleavened bread, and joined them five days later at Troas, where we spent a week.

Paul's enthusiasm leads to an accident   20.7

On the first day of the week, when we were assembled for the breaking of bread, Paul, since he intended to leave on the following day, began to speak to them and prolonged his address until almost midnight. There were a great many lamps burning in the upper room where we met, and a young man called Eutychus who was sitting on the window sill fell fast asleep as Paul's address became longer and longer. Finally, completely overcome by sleep, he fell to the ground from the third story and was picked up as dead. But Paul went down, bent over him and holding him gently in his arms, said,

"Don't be alarmed; he is still alive."

Then he went upstairs again and, when he had broken bread and eaten, continued a long earnest talk with them until daybreak, and so finally departed. As for the boy, they took him home alive, feeling immeasurably relieved.

We sail to Miletus 20.13

Meanwhile we had gone aboard the ship and sailed on ahead for Assos, intending to pick up Paul there, for that was the arrangement he had made, since he himself had planned to go overland. When he met us on our arrival at Assos we took him aboard and went on to Mitylene. We sailed from there and arrived off the coast of Chios the next day. On the day following we crossed to Samos, and the day after that we reached Miletus. For Paul had decided to sail past Ephesus with the idea of spending as little time as possible in Asia. He hoped, if it should prove possible, to reach Jerusalem in time for the day of Pentecost.

Paul's moving farewell message to the elders 20.17
of Ephesus

At Miletus he sent to Ephesus to summon the elders of the church. On their arrival he addressed them in these words:

"I am sure you know how I have lived among you ever since I first set foot in Asia. You know how I have served the Lord most humbly and what tears I have shed over the trials that have come to me through the plots of the Jews. You know I have never shrunk from telling you anything that was for your good, nor from teaching you in public or in your own homes. On the contrary I have most emphatically urged upon both Jews and Greeks repentance towards God and faith in our Lord Jesus. And now here I am, compelled by the Spirit to go to Jerusalem. I do not know what may happen to me there, except that the Holy Spirit warns me that imprisonment and persecution await me in every city that I visit. But frankly I do not consider my own life valuable to me so long as I can finish my course and complete the ministry which the Lord Jesus has given me in declaring the good news of the grace of God. Now I know well enough that not one of you among whom I have moved as I preached the kingdom of God will ever see my face again. That is why I must tell you solemnly today that my conscience is clear as far as any of you is concerned, for I have never shrunk from declaring to you the complete will of God. Now be on your guard for yourselves and for every flock of which the Holy Spirit has made you guardians—you are to be shepherds to the Church of God, which he won at the cost of his own blood. I know that after my departure savage wolves will come in among you without mercy for the flock. Yes, and even from among you men will arise speaking perversions of the truth, trying to draw away the disciples and make them followers of themselves. This is why I tell you to keep on the alert, remembering that for three years I never failed night and day to warn every one of you, even with tears in my eyes. Now I commend you to the Lord and to the message of his grace which can build you up and give you your place among all those who are consecrated to God. I have never coveted anybody's gold or silver or clothing. You know well enough that these hands of mine have provided for my own needs and for those of my companions. In everything I have shown you that by such hard work we must help the weak and must remember the words of the Lord Jesus when he said, 'To give is happier than to receive.' "

With these words he knelt down with them all and prayed. All of them were in tears, and throwing their arms round Paul's neck they kissed him affectionately. What saddened them most of all was his saying that they would never see his face again. And they went with him down to the ship.

The brothers at Tyre warn Paul not to go   21.1
to Jerusalem

When he had finally said farewell to them we set sail, running a straight course to Cos, and the next day we

went to Rhodes and from there to Patara. Here we found a
ship bound for Phoenicia, and we went aboard her and set
sail. After sighting Cyprus and leaving it on our left we sailed
for Syria and put in at Tyre, since that was where the ship
was to discharge her cargo. We sought out the disciples there
and stayed with them for a week. They felt led by the Spirit
again and again to warn Paul not to go up to Jerusalem. But
when our time was up we left them and continued our journey.
They all came out to see us off, bringing their wives and
children with them, accompanying us till we were outside the
city. Then kneeling down on the beach we prayed and said
good-bye to each other. Then we went aboard the ship, while
the disciples went back home. We sailed away from Tyre
and arrived at Ptolemais. We greeted the brothers there and
stayed with them for just one day. On the following day we
left and proceeded to Caesarea and there we went to stay
at the house of Philip the evangelist, one of the seven deacons.
He had four unmarried daughters, all of whom spoke by the
Spirit of God. During our stay there of several days a prophet
by the name of Agabus came down from Judaea. When he
came to see us he took Paul's girdle and used it to tie his own
hands and feet together, saying, "The Holy Spirit says this: the
man to whom this girdle belongs will be bound like this by the
Jews in Jerusalem and handed over to the gentiles!"

We all warn Paul, but he is immovable   21.12

When we heard him say this, we and the people there
begged Paul not to go up to Jerusalem. Then Paul answered us,
"What do you mean by unnerving me with all your tears? I
am perfectly prepared not only to be bound but to die in
Jerusalem for the sake of the name of the Lord Jesus."
Since he could not be dissuaded all we could do was to say,
"May the Lord's will be done," and hold our tongues.

Paul is warmly welcomed at first   21.15

After this we made our preparations and went up to Jeru-

salem. Some of the disciples from Caesarea accompanied us
and they brought us to the house of Mnason, a native of
Cyprus and one of the earliest disciples, with whom we were
going to stay. On our arrival at Jerusalem the brothers gave
us a very warm welcome. On the following day Paul went with
us to visit James, and all the elders were present. When he
had greeted them he gave them a detailed account of all
that God had done among the gentiles through his ministry,
and they, on hearing this account, glorified God. Then they
said to him,

"You know, brother, how many thousands there are among
the Jews who have become believers, and that every one of
these is a staunch upholder of the Law. They have been told
about you—that you teach all Jews who live among the
gentiles to disregard the Law of Moses, and tell them not to
circumcise their children nor observe the old customs. What will
happen now, for they are simply bound to hear that you have
arrived? Now why not follow this suggestion of ours? We
have four men here under a vow. Suppose you join them and
be purified with them, pay their expenses so that they may
have their hair cut short, and then everyone will know there
is no truth in the stories about you, but that you yourself observe
the Law. As for those gentiles who have believed, we have
sent them a letter with our decision that they should abstain
from what has been offered to idols, from blood and from
what has been strangled, and from sexual immorality."

But his enemies attempt to murder him   21.26

So Paul joined the four men and on the following day, after
being purified with them, went into the Temple to give notice
of the time when the period of purification would be finished
and an offering would be made on behalf of each one of them.
The seven days were almost over when the Jews from Asia
caught sight of Paul in the Temple. They stirred up the whole
crowd and seized him, shouting, "Men of Israel, help! This is
the man who is teaching everybody everywhere to despise

our people, our Law and this place. Why, he has even brought Greeks into the Temple and he has defiled this holy place!" For they had previously seen Trophimus the Ephesian with Paul in the city and they had concluded that Paul had brought him into the Temple. The whole city was stirred by this speech and a mob collected who seized Paul and dragged him outside the Temple, and the doors were slammed behind him.

Paul is rescued by Roman soldiers   21.31

They were trying to kill him when a report reached the ears of the colonel of the regiment that the whole of Jerusalem was in an uproar. Without a moment's delay he took soldiers and centurions and ran down to them. When they saw the colonel and the soldiers they stopped beating Paul. The colonel came up to Paul and arrested him and ordered him to be bound with two chains. Then he inquired who the man was and what he had been doing. Some of the crowd shouted one thing and some another, and since he could not be certain of the facts because of the shouting that was going on, the colonel ordered him to be brought to the barracks. When Paul got to the steps he was actually carried by the soldiers because of the violence of the mob. For the mass of the people followed, shouting, "Kill him!" Just as they were going to take him into the barracks Paul asked the colonel,

"May I say something to you?"

"So you know Greek, do you?" the colonel replied. "Aren't you that Egyptian who not long ago raised a riot and led those four thousand assassins into the desert?"

"I am a Jew," replied Paul. "I am a man of Tarsus, a citizen of that not insignificant city. I ask you to let me speak to the people."

Paul attempts to defend himself   21.40; 22.1

On being given permission Paul stood on the steps and made a gesture with his hand to the people. There was a deep hush as he began to speak to them in Hebrew.

"My brothers and my fathers, listen to what I have to say in my own defense."

As soon as they heard him addressing them in Hebrew the silence became intense.

"I myself am a Jew," Paul went on. "I was born in Tarsus in Cilicia, but I was brought up here in this city, I received my training at the feet of Gamaliel, and I was schooled in the strictest observance of our fathers' Law. I was as much on fire with zeal for God as you all are today. I am also the man who persecuted this Way to the death, arresting both men and women and throwing them into prison, as the High Priest and the whole council can readily testify. Indeed, it was after receiving letters from them to their brothers in Damascus that I was on my way to that city, intending to arrest any followers of the Way I could find there and bring them back to Jerusalem for .punishment. Then this happened to me. As I was on my journey and getting near to Damascus, about midday a great light from Heaven suddenly blazed around me. I fell to the ground, and I heard a voice saying to me, 'Saul, Saul, why are you persecuting me?' I replied, 'Who are you, Lord?' He said to me, 'I am Jesus of Nazareth whom you are persecuting.' My companions naturally saw the light, but they did not hear the voice of the one who was talking to me. 'What am I to do, Lord?' I asked. And the Lord told me, 'Get up and go to Damascus and there you will be told of all that has been determined for you to do.' I was blinded by the brightness of that light and my companions had to take me by the hand as we went on to Damascus. There, there was a man called Ananias, a reverent observer of the Law and a man highly respected by all the Jews who lived there. He came to visit me and as he stood by my side said, 'Saul, brother, you may see again!' At once I regained my sight and looked up at him. 'The God of our fathers,' he went on, 'has chosen you to know his will, to see the righteous one, to hear words from his own lips, so that you may become his witness before all men of what you have seen and heard. And now what are you waiting for?

Get up and be baptized! Be clean from your sins as you call on his name.'

Paul claims that God sent him to the gentiles   22.17

"Then it happened that after my return to Jerusalem, while I was at prayer in the Temple, unconscious of everything else, I saw him and he said to me, 'Make haste and leave Jerusalem at once, for they will not accept your testimony about me.' And I said, 'But, Lord, they know how I have been through all the synagogues imprisoning and beating all those who believe in you. They know also that when the blood of your martyr Stephen was shed I stood by, giving my approval —why, I was even holding in my arms the outer garments of those who killed him.' But he said to me, 'Go, for I will send you far away to the gentiles.' "

The consequence of Paul's speech   22.22

They had listened to him until he said this, but now they raised a great shout,

"Kill him, and rid the earth of such a man! He is not fit to live!"

As they were yelling and ripping their clothes and hurling dust into the air, the colonel gave orders to bring Paul into the barracks and directed that he should be examined by scourging, so that he might discover the reason for such an uproar against him. But when they had strapped him up, Paul spoke to the centurion standing by,

"Is it legal for you to flog a man who is a Roman citizen, and untried at that?"

On hearing this the centurion went in to the colonel and reported to him, saying,

"Do you realize what you were about to do? This man is a Roman citizen!"

Then the colonel himself came up to Paul and said,

"Tell me, are you a Roman citizen?"

And he said,

"Yes."

Whereupon the colonel replied,

"It cost me a good deal to get my citizenship."

"Ah," replied Paul, "but I was born a citizen."

Then those who had been about to examine him left hurriedly, while even the colonel himself was alarmed at discovering that Paul was a Roman and that he had had him bound.

Roman fair-mindedness   22.30

Next day the colonel, determined to get to the bottom of Paul's accusation by the Jews, released him and ordered the assembly of the chief priests and the whole Sanhedrin. Then he took Paul down and placed him in front of them.

Paul again attempts defense   23.1

Paul looked steadily at the Sanhedrin and spoke to them, "Men and brothers, I have lived my life with a perfectly clear conscience before God up to the present day—" Then Ananias the High Priest ordered those who were standing near to strike him on the mouth. At this Paul said to him,

"God will strike you, you whitewashed wall! How dare you sit there judging me by the Law and give orders for me to be struck, which is clean contrary to the Law?"

Those who stood by said,

"Do you mean to insult God's High Priest?"

But Paul said,

"My brothers, I did not know that he was the High Priest, for it is written:

Thou shalt not speak evil of a ruler of thy people."

Paul seizes his opportunity   23.6

Then Paul, realizing that part of the council were Sadducees and the other part Pharisees, raised his voice and said to them,

"I am a Pharisee, the son of Pharisees. It is for my hope in the resurrection of the dead that I am on trial!"

At these words an immediate tension arose between the

Pharisees and the Sadducees, and the meeting was divided. For the Sadducees claim that there is no resurrection and that there is neither angel nor spirit, while the Pharisees believe in all three. A great uproar ensued and some of the scribes of the Pharisees' party jumped to their feet and protested violently,

"We find nothing wrong with this man! Suppose some angel or spirit has really spoken to him?"

As the tension mounted the colonel began to fear that Paul would be torn to pieces between them. He therefore ordered his soldiers to come down and rescue him from them and bring him back to the barracks.

God's direct encouragement to Paul   23.11

That night the Lord stood by Paul, and said,

"Take heart! For as you have witnessed boldly for me in Jerusalem so you must give your witness for me in Rome."

Paul's acute danger   23.12

Early in the morning the Jews made a conspiracy and bound themselves by a solemn oath that they would neither eat nor drink until they had killed Paul. Over forty of them were involved in this plot, and they approached the chief priests and elders and said,

"We have bound ourselves by a solemn oath to let nothing pass our lips until we have killed Paul. Now you and the council must make it plain to the colonel that you want him to bring Paul down to you, suggesting that you want to examine his case more closely. We shall be standing by ready to kill him before he gets here."

Leakage of information leads to Paul's protection 23.16

However, Paul's nephew got wind of this plot and he came and found his way into the barracks and told Paul about it. Paul called one of the centurions and said,

"Take this young man to the colonel for he has something to

report to him."

So the centurion took him and brought him into the colonel's presence, and said,

"The prisoner Paul called me and requested that this young man should be brought to you as he has something to say to you."

The colonel took his hand and drew him aside (where they could not be overheard), and asked,

"What have you got to tell me?"

And he replied,

"The Jews have agreed to ask you to bring Paul down to the Sanhedrin tomorrow as though they were going to inquire more carefully into his case. But I beg you not to let them persuade you. For more than forty of them are waiting for him—they have sworn a solemn oath that they will neither eat nor drink until they have killed him. They are all ready at this moment—all they want now is for you to give the order."

At this the colonel dismissed the young man with the caution,

"Don't let a soul know that you have given me this information."

Then he summoned two of his centurions, and said,

"Get two hundred men ready to proceed to Caesarea, with seventy horsemen and two hundred spearmen, by nine o'clock tonight." (Mounts were also to be provided to carry Paul safely to Felix the governor.)

The Roman view of Paul's position   23.25

He further wrote a letter to Felix of which this is a copy:

"Claudius Lysias sends greeting to his excellency the governor Felix,

"This man had been seized by the Jews and was on the point of being murdered by them when I arrived with my troops and rescued him, since I had discovered that he was a Roman citizen. Wishing to find out what the accusation was that they were making against him, I had him brought down to their Sanhedrin. There I discovered he was being accused over questions of their law, and that there was no charge against him which deserved either death or imprisonment. Now, however, that I have received private information of a plot against his life, I have sent him to you without delay. At the same time I have notified his accusers that they must make their charges against him in your presence."

Paul is taken into protective custody   23.31

The soldiers, acting on their orders, took Paul and, riding through that night, brought him down to Antipatris. Next day they returned to the barracks, leaving the horsemen to accompany him further. They went into Caesarea and after delivering the letter to the governor, they handed Paul over to him. When the governor had read the letter he asked Paul what province he came from, and on learning that he came from Cilicia, he said,

"I will hear your case as soon as your accusers arrive."

Then he ordered him to be kept under guard in Herod's palace.

The "professional" puts the case against Paul   24.1

Five days later Ananias the High Priest came down himself with some of the elders and a lawyer by the name of Tertullus. They presented their case against Paul before the governor, and when Paul had been summoned, Tertullus began the prosecution in these words:

"We owe it to you personally, your excellency, that we enjoy lasting peace, and we know that it is due to your foresight that the nation enjoys improved conditions of living. At all times, and indeed everywhere, we acknowledge these things with the deepest gratitude. However—for I must not detain you too long—I beg you to give us a brief hearing with your customary kindness. The simple fact is that we have found this man a pestilential disturber of the peace among the Jews all over the world. He is a ringleader of the Nazareth sect, and he was on the point of desecrating the Temple when we overcame him. But you yourself will soon discover from the man himself all the facts about which we are accusing him."

Paul is given the chance to defend himself   24.9

While Tertullus was speaking the Jews kept joining in, asserting that these were the facts. Then Paul, at a nod from the governor, made his reply:

"I am well aware that you have been governor of this nation for many years, and I can therefore make my defense with every confidence. You can easily verify the fact that it is not more than twelve days ago that I went up to worship at Jerusalem. I was never found either arguing with anyone in the Temple or gathering a crowd, either in the synagogues or in the open air. These men are quite unable to prove the charges they are now making against me. I will freely admit to you, however, that I do worship the God of our fathers according to the Way which they call a heresy, although in fact I believe in the scriptural authority of both the Law and the Prophets. I have the same hope in God which they themselves hold, that there is to be a resurrection of both good men and bad. With this hope before me I do my utmost to live my whole life with a clear conscience before God and man.

Paul has nothing to hide   24.17

"It was in fact after several years' absence from Jerusalem that I came back to make charitable gifts to my own nation and to make my offerings. It was in the middle of these duties that they found me, a man purified in the Temple. There was no mob and there was no disturbance until these Jews from Asia came, who should in my opinion have come before you and made their accusation, if they had anything against me. Or else, let these men themselves speak out now and say what crime they found me guilty of when I stood before the Sanhedrin—unless it was that one sentence that I shouted as I stood among them. All I said was this, 'It is about the resurrection of the dead that I am on trial before you this day.'"

Felix defers decision   24.22

Then Felix, who was better acquainted with the Way than most people, adjourned the case and said,

"As soon as Colonel Lysias arrives I will give you my decision."

Then he gave orders to the centurion to keep Paul in custody, but to grant him reasonable liberty and allow any of his personal friends to look after his needs.

Felix plays for safety—and hopes   24.24
for personal gain

Some days later Felix arrived with his wife Drusilla, herself a Jewess, and sent for Paul, and heard what he had to say about faith in Christ Jesus. But while Paul was talking about goodness, self-control and the judgment that is to come, Felix became alarmed, and said,

"You may go for the present. When I find a convenient moment I will send for you again."

At the same time he nursed a secret hope that Paul would pay him money—which is why Paul was frequently summoned to come and talk with him. However, when two full years had passed, Felix was succeeded by Porcius Festus and, as he wanted to remain in favor with the Jews, he left Paul still a prisoner.

Felix's successor begins his duties with vigor—   25.1

Three days after Festus had taken over his province he went up from Caesarea to Jerusalem. The chief priests and elders of the Jews informed him of the case against Paul and begged him as a special favor to have Paul sent to Jerusalem. They themselves had already made a plot to kill him on the way. But Festus replied that Paul was in custody in Caesarea, and that he himself was going there shortly.

"What you must do," he told them, "is to provide some competent men of your own to go down with me and if there is anything wrong with the man they can present their charges against him."

Festus spent not more than eight or ten days among them at Jerusalem and then went down to Caesarea. On the day after his arrival he took his seat on the bench and ordered Paul to be brought in. As soon as he arrived the Jews from Jerusalem stood up on all sides of him, bringing forward many serious accusations which they were quite unable to substantiate. Paul, in his defense, maintained,

"I have committed no offense in any way against the Jewish Law, or against the Temple or against Caesar."

—but is afraid of antagonizing the Jews   25.9

But Festus, wishing to gain the goodwill of the Jews, spoke direct to Paul,

"Are you prepared to go up to Jerusalem and stand your trial over these matters in my presence there?"

But Paul replied,

"I am standing in Caesar's court and that is where I should be judged. I have done the Jews no harm, as you very well know. It comes to this: if I were a criminal and had committed some crime which deserved the death penalty, I should not try to evade sentence of death. But as in fact there is no truth in the accusations these men have made, I am not prepared to be used as a means of gaining their favor—*I appeal to Caesar!*"

Then Festus, after a conference with his advisers, replied to Paul,

"You have appealed to Caesar—then to Caesar you shall go!"

Festus outlines Paul's case to Agrippa   25.13

Some days later king Agrippa and Bernice arrived at Caesarea on a state visit to Festus. They prolonged their stay for some days, and this gave Festus an opportunity of laying Paul's case before the king.

"I have a man here," he said, "who was left a prisoner by Felix. When I was in Jerusalem the chief priests and Jewish elders made allegations against him and demanded his conviction! I told them that the Romans were not in the habit of giving anybody up to please anyone, until the accused had had the chance of facing his accusers personally and been given the opportunity of defending himself on the charges made against him. Since these Jews came back here with me, I wasted no time but on the very next day I took my seat on the bench and ordered the man to be brought in. But when his accusers got up to speak they did not charge him with any such crimes as I had anticipated. Their differences with him were about their own religion and concerning a certain Jesus who had died, but whom Paul claimed to be still alive. I did not feel qualified to investigate such matters and so I asked the man if he were willing to go to Jerusalem and stand his trial over these matters there. But when he appealed to have his case reserved for the decision of the emperor himself, I ordered him to be kept in custody until such time as I could send him to Caesar."

Then Agrippa said to Festus,

"I have been wanting to hear this man myself."

"Then you shall hear him tomorrow," replied Festus.

Festus formally explains the difficulty of Paul's case   25.23

When the next day came, Agrippa and Bernice proceeded to the audience chamber with great pomp and ceremony, with an escort of military officers and prominent townsmen. Festus ordered Paul to be brought in and then he spoke:

"King Agrippa and all of you who are present, you see here the man about whom the whole Jewish people both at Jerusalem and in this city have petitioned me. They din it into my ears that he ought not to live any longer, but I for my part discovered nothing that he has done which deserves the death penalty. And since he has appealed to Caesar, I have decided to send him to Rome. Frankly, I have nothing specific to write to the emperor about him, and I have therefore brought him forward before you all, and especially before you, King

Agrippa, so that from your examination of him there may emerge some charge which I may put in writing. For it seems ridiculous to me to send a prisoner before the emperor without indicating the charges against him."

Then Agrippa said to Paul,

"You have our permission to speak for yourself."

Paul repeats his story on a state occasion   26.1b

So Paul, with that characteristic gesture of the hand, began his defense:

"King Agrippa, in answering all the charges that the Jews have made against me, I must say how fortunate I consider myself to be in making my defense before you personally today. For I know that you are thoroughly familiar with all the customs and disputes that exist among the Jews. I therefore ask you to listen to me patiently.

"The fact that I lived from my youth upwards among my own people in Jerusalem is well known to all Jews. They have known all the time, and could witness to the fact if they wished, that I lived as a Pharisee according to the strictest sect of our religion. Even today I stand here on trial because of a hope that I hold in a promise that God made to our forefathers—a promise for which our twelve tribes serve God zealously day and night, hoping to see it fulfilled. It is about this hope, your majesty, that I am being accused by Jews! Why does it seem incredible to you all that God should raise the dead? I once thought it my duty to oppose with the utmost vigor the name of Jesus of Nazareth. Yes, that is what I did in Jerusalem, and I had many of God's people imprisoned on the authority of the chief priests, and when they were on trial for their lives I gave my vote against them. Many and many a time in all the synagogues I had them punished and I used to try and force them to deny their Lord. I was mad with fury against them, and I hounded them to distant cities. Once, your majesty, on my way to Damascus on this business, armed with the full authority and commission of the chief priests, at midday I saw a light from Heaven, far brighter than the sun, blazing about me and my fellow travelers. We all fell to the ground and I heard a voice saying to me in Hebrew, 'Saul, Saul, why are you persecuting me? It is not easy for you to kick against your own conscience.' 'Who are you, Lord?' I said. And the Lord said to me, 'I am Jesus whom you are persecuting. Now get up and stand on your feet for I have shown myself to you for a reason—you are chosen to be my servant and a witness of what you have seen of me today, and of other visions of myself which I will give you. I will keep you safe both from your own people and from the gentiles to whom I now send you. I send you to open their eyes, to turn them from darkness to light, from the power of Satan to God himself, so that they may know forgiveness of their sins and take their place with all those who are made holy by their faith in me.' After that, King Agrippa, I could not disobey the heavenly vision. But both in Damascus and in Jerusalem, through the whole of Judaea, and to the gentiles, I preached that men should repent and turn to God and live lives to prove their change of heart. This is why the Jews seized me in the Temple and tried to kill me. To this day I have received help from God himself, and I stand here as a witness to high and low, adding nothing to what the prophets and Moses foretold should take place, that is, that Christ should suffer, that he should be the first to rise from the dead, and so proclaim the message of light both to our people and to the gentiles!"

Festus concludes that Paul's enthusiasm is insanity 26.24

While he was thus defending himself Festus burst out, "You are raving, Paul! All your learning has driven you mad!" But Paul replied,

"I am not mad, your excellency. I speak nothing but the sober truth. The king knows of these matters, and I can speak freely before him. I cannot believe that any of these matters has escaped his notice, for it has been no hole-and-corner business. King Agrippa, do you believe the prophets? But I know that

you believe them."

"Much more of this, Paul," returned Agrippa, "and you will be making me a Christian!"

"Ah," replied Paul, "whether it means 'much more' or 'only a little,' I would to God that you and all who can hear me this day might stand where I stand—but without these chains!"

The Roman officials consider Paul innocent   26.30

Then the king rose to his feet and so did the governor and Bernice and those sitting with them, and when they had retired from the assembly they discussed the matter among themselves and agreed, "This man is doing nothing to deserve either death or imprisonment."

Agrippa remarked to Festus,

"He might easily have been discharged if he had not appealed to Caesar."

The last journey begins 27.1

As soon as it was decided that we should sail away to Italy, Paul and some other prisoners were turned over to a centurion named Julius, of the emperor's own regiment. We embarked on a ship hailing from Adramyttium, bound for the Asian ports, and set sail. Among our company was Aristarchus, a Macedonian from Thessalonica. On the following day we put in at Sidon, where Julius treated Paul most considerately by allowing him to visit his friends and accept their hospitality. From Sidon we put to sea again and sailed to leeward of Cyprus, since the wind was against us. Then, when we had crossed the gulf that lies off the coasts of Cilicia and Pamphylia, we arrived at Myra in Lycia. There the centurion found an Alexandrian ship bound for Italy and put us aboard her. For several days we beat slowly up to windward and only just succeeded in arriving off Cnidus. Then, since the wind was still blowing against us, we sailed under the lee of Crete, and rounded Cape Salmone. Coasting along with difficulty we came to a place called Fair Havens, near which is the city of Lasea. We had by now lost a great deal of time and sailing had already become dangerous as it was so late in the year.

Paul's warning is disregarded 27.9b

So Paul warned them, and said,

"Men, I can see that this voyage is likely to result in damage and considerable loss—not only to ship and cargo, but even of our own lives as well."

But Julius paid more attention to the helmsman and the captain than to Paul's words of warning. Moreover, since the harbor is unsuitable for a ship to winter in, the majority were in favor of setting sail again in the hope of reaching Phoenix and wintering there. Phoenix is a harbor in Crete, facing southwest and northwest. So, when a moderate breeze sprang up, thinking they had obtained just what they wanted, they weighed anchor and coasted along, hugging the shores of

Crete. But before long a terrific gale, which they called a northeaster, swept down upon us from the land. The ship was caught by it and since she could not be brought up into the wind we had to let her fall off and run before it. Then, running under the lee of a small island called Clauda, we managed with some difficulty to secure the ship's boat. After hoisting it aboard they used cables to brace the ship. To add to the difficulties they were afraid all the time of drifting on to the Syrtis banks, so they shortened sail and lay to, drifting. The next day, as we were still at the mercy of the violent storm, they began to throw cargo overboard. On the third day with their own hands they threw the ship's tackle over the side. Then, when for many days there was no glimpse of sun or stars and we were still in the grip of the gale, all hope of our being saved was given up.

Paul's practical courage and faith   27.21

Nobody had eaten for some time, when Paul came forward among the men and said,

"Men, you should have listened to me and not set sail from Crete and suffered this damage and loss. However, now I beg you to keep up your spirits for no one's life is going to be lost, though we shall lose the ship. I know this because last night, the angel of God to whom I belong, and whom I serve, stood by me and said, 'Have no fear, Paul! You must stand before Caesar. And God, as a mark of his favor toward you, has granted you the lives of those who are sailing with you.' Take courage then, men, for I believe God, and I am certain that everything will happen exactly as I have been told. But we shall have to run the ship ashore on some island."

At last we near land   27.27

On the fourteenth night of the storm, as we were drifting in the Adriatic, about midnight the sailors sensed that we were nearing land. Indeed, when they sounded they found twenty fathoms, and then after sailing on only a little way they

sounded again and found fifteen. So, for fear that we might
be hurled on the rocks, they threw out four anchors from the
stern and prayed for daylight. The sailors wanted to desert
the ship and they got as far as letting a boat down into the
sea, pretending that they were going to run out anchors from
the bow. But Paul said to the centurion and the soldiers,

"Unless these men stay aboard the ship there is no hope of
your being saved."

At this the soldiers cut the ropes of the boat and let her fall
away.

Paul's sturdy common sense 27.33

Then while everyone waited for the day to break Paul
urged them to take some food, saying,

"For two weeks now you've had no food—you haven't had
a bite while you've been on watch. Now take some food, I
beg you—you need it for your own well-being, for not a hair
of anyone's head will be lost."

When he had said this he took some bread and, after
thanking God before them all, he broke it and began to eat.
This raised everybody's spirits and they began to take food
themselves. There were about two hundred and seventy-six
of us all told aboard that ship. When they had eaten enough
they lightened the ship by throwing the grain over the side.

Land at last—but we lose the ship 27.39

When daylight came no one recognized the land. But they
made out a bay with a sandy shore where they planned to
beach the ship if they could. So they cut away the anchors and
left them in the sea, and at the same time cut the ropes which
held the steering oars. They then hoisted the foresail to catch
the wind and made for the beach. But they struck a shoal and
the ship ran aground. The bow stuck fast, while the stern began
to break up under the strain. The soldier's plan had been to
kill the prisoners in case any of them should try to swim to
shore and escape. But the centurion, in his desire to save Paul,

put a stop to this, and gave orders that all those who could swim should jump overboard first and get to land, while the rest should follow, some on planks and others on the wreckage of the ship. So it came true that everyone reached the shore in safety.

A small incident establishes Paul's reputation 28.1

After our escape we discovered that the island was called Melita. The natives treated us with uncommon kindness. Because of the driving rain and the cold they lit a fire and made us all welcome. Then when Paul had collected a large bundle of sticks and was about to put it on the fire, a viper driven out by the heat fastened itself on his hand. When the natives saw the creature hanging from his hand they said to each other, "This man is obviously a murderer. He has escaped from the sea but justice will not let him live." But Paul shook off the viper into the fire without suffering any ill effect. Naturally they expected him to swell up or suddenly fall down dead, but after waiting a long time and seeing nothing untoward happen to him, they changed their minds and kept saying that he was a god.

Paul's acts of healing: the islanders' gratitude 28.7

In that part of the island were estates belonging to the governor, whose name was Publius. This man welcomed us and entertained us most kindly for three days. Now it happened that Publius' father was lying ill with fever and dysentery. Paul visited him and after prayer laid his hands on him and healed him. After that all the other sick people on the island came forward and were cured. Consequently they loaded us with presents, and when the time came for us to sail they provided us with everything we needed.

Spring returns and we resume our journey 28.11

It was no less than three months later that we set sail in an Alexandrian ship which had wintered in the island, a ship that had the heavenly twins as her figurehead. We put in at Syracuse and stayed there three days, and from there we tacked round to Rhegium. A day later the south wind sprang up and we sailed to Puteoli, reaching it in only two days. There we found some of the brothers and they begged us to stay a week with them, and so we finally came to Rome.

A Christian welcome awaits us in the capital   28.15

The brothers there had heard about us and came out from the city to meet us, as far as the Market of Appius and the Three Taverns. When Paul saw them he thanked God and his spirits rose. When we reached Rome Paul was given permission to live alone with the soldier who was guarding him.

Paul explains himself frankly to the Jews in Rome 28.17

Three days later Paul invited the leading Jews to meet him, and when they arrived he spoke to them,

"Men and brothers, although I have done nothing against our people or the customs of our forefathers, I was handed over to the Romans as a prisoner in Jerusalem. They examined me and were prepared to release me, since they found me guilty of nothing deserving the death penalty. But the attacks of the Jews there forced me to appeal to Caesar—not that I had any charge to make against my own nation. But it is because of this accusation of the Jews that I have asked to see you and talk matters over with you. In actual fact it is on account of the hope of Israel that I am here in chains."

But they replied,

"We have received no letters about you from Judaea, nor have any of the brothers who have arrived here said anything, officially or unofficially, against you. We want to hear you state your views, although as far as this sect is concerned we do know that serious objections have been raised to it everywhere."

Paul's earnest and prolonged effort to win   28.23
his own people for Christ

When they had arranged a day for him they came to his lodging in great numbers. From morning till evening he explained the kingdom of God to them, giving his personal testimony, trying to persuade them about Jesus from the Law of Moses and the Prophets. As a result several of them were won over by his words, but others would not believe. When they could not reach any agreement among themselves and began to go away, Paul added as a parting shot, "How rightly did the Holy Spirit speak to your forefathers through the prophet Isaiah when he said,

Go thou unto this people, and say,
By hearing ye shall hear, and shall in no wise understand;
And seeing ye shall see, and shall in no wise perceive:
For this people's heart is waxed gross,
And their ears are dull of hearing,
And their eyes they have closed;
Lest haply they should perceive with their eyes,
And hear with their ears,
And understand with their heart,
And should turn again,
And I should heal them.

"Let it be plainly understood then that this salvation of our God has been sent to the gentiles, and they at least will listen to it!"

The last glimpse of Paul . . .   28.30

So Paul stayed for two full years in his own rented apartment welcoming all who came to see him. He proclaimed to them all the kingdom of God and gave them the teaching of the Lord Jesus Christ with the utmost freedom and without hindrance from anyone.

THE LETTER TO THE CHRISTIANS AT ROME

This letter comes to you from Paul, a servant of Jesus Christ, called as a messenger and appointed for the service of that gospel of God which was long ago promised by the prophets in the holy scriptures.

The gospel is centered in God's Son, a descendant of David by human genealogy and patently marked out as the Son of God by the power of that Spirit of holiness which raised him to life again from the dead. He is our Lord, Jesus Christ, from whom we received grace and our commission in his name to forward obedience to the faith in all nations. And of this great number you at Rome are also called to belong to him.

To you all then, loved of God and called to be Christ's men and women, grace and peace from God the Father and from the Lord Jesus Christ.

A personal message   1.8

I must begin by telling you how I thank God through Jesus Christ for you all, since the news of your faith has become known everywhere. Before God, whom I serve with my spirit in the gospel of his Son, I assure you that you are always in my prayers. I am constantly asking him that he will somehow make it possible for me now, at long last, to come to Rome. I am longing to see you: I want to bring you some spiritual strength, and that will mean that I shall be strengthened by you, each of us helped by the other's faith.

Then I should like you to know, my brothers, that I have long intended to come to you (but something has always prevented me), for I should like to see some results among you, as I have among other gentiles. I feel myself under a sort of universal obligation, I owe something to all men, from cultured Greek to ignorant savage. That is why I want, as far as my ability will carry me, to preach the gospel to you who live in Rome as well. For I am not ashamed of the gospel. I see it as the very power of God working for the salvation of everyone who believes it, both Jew and Greek. I see in it God's plan for imparting righteousness to men, a process begun and continued by their faith. For, as the scripture says:

The righteous shall live by faith.

The righteousness of God and the sin of man   1.18

Now the holy anger of God is disclosed from Heaven against the godlessness and evil of those men who render

truth dumb and inoperative by their wickedness. It is not that
they do not know the truth about God: indeed he has made it
quite plain to them. For since the beginning of the world the
invisible attributes of God, for example, his eternal power
and divinity, have been plainly discernible through things
which he has made and which are commonly seen and known,
thus leaving these men without a rag of excuse. They knew all
the time that there is a God, yet they refused to acknowledge
him as such, or to thank him for what he is or does. Thus they
became fatuous in their argumentations, and plunged their
silly minds still further into the dark. Behind a façade of
"wisdom" they became just fools, fools who would exchange
the glory of the immortal God for an imitation image of a
mortal man, or of creatures that run or fly or crawl. They gave
up God: and therefore God gave them up—to be the play-
things of their own foul desires in dishonoring their own bodies.

The fearful consequence of deliberate atheism   1.25

These men deliberately forfeited the truth of God and
accepted a lie, paying homage and giving service to the
creature instead of to the Creator, who alone is worthy to be
worshiped for ever and ever, amen. God therefore handed
them over to disgraceful passions. Their women exchanged the
normal practices of sexual intercourse for something which is
abnormal and unnatural. Similarly the men, turning from
natural intercourse with women, were swept into lustful passions
for one another. Men with men performed these shameful
horrors, receiving, of course, in their own personalities the
consequences of sexual perversity.

Moreover, since they considered themselves too high and
mighty to acknowledge God, he allowed them to become the
slaves of their degenerate minds, and to perform unmention-
able deeds. They became filled with wickedness, rottenness,
greed and malice; their minds became steeped in envy, murder,
quarrelsomeness, deceitfulness and spite. They became
whisperers-behind-doors, stabbers-in-the-back, God-haters;

they overflowed with insolent pride and boastfulness, and their minds teemed with diabolical invention. They scoffed at duty to parents; they mocked at learning, recognized no obligations of honor, lost all natural affection, and had no use for mercy. More than this—being well aware of God's pronouncement that all who do these things deserve to die, they not only continued their own practices, but did not hesitate to give their thorough approval to others who did the same.

Yet we cannot judge them, for we also are sinners: God is the only judge   2.1

Now if you feel inclined to set yourself up as a judge of those who sin, let me assure you, whoever you are, that you are in no position to do so. For at whatever point you condemn others you automatically condemn yourself, since you, the judge, commit the same sins. God's judgment, we know, is utterly impartial in its action against such evildoers. What makes you think that you, who so readily judge the sins of others, can consider yourself beyond the judgment of God? Are you, perhaps, misinterpreting God's generosity and patient mercy toward you as weakness on his part? Don't you realize that God's kindness is meant to lead you to repentance? Or are you by your obstinate refusal to repent simply storing up for yourself an experience of the wrath of God in the day when, in his holy anger against evil, he shows his hand in righteous judgment?

There is no doubt at all that he will. "render to every man according to his works," and that means eternal life to those who, in patiently doing good, aim at the unseen (but real) glory and honor of the eternal world. It also means anger and wrath for those who rebel against God's plan of life, and refuse to obey his rules, and who, in so doing, make themselves the very servants of evil. Yes, it means bitter pain and a fearful undoing for every human soul who works on the side of evil, for the Jew first and then the Greek. But, let me repeat, there is glory and honor and peace for every worker on the side of good, for the Jew first and then the Greek. For there is no preferential treatment with God.

God's judgment is absolutely just   2.12

All who have sinned without knowledge of the Law will die without reference to the Law; and all who have sinned knowing the Law shall be judged according to the Law. It is not familiarity with the Law that justifies a man in the sight of God, but obedience to it.

When the gentiles, who have no knowledge of the Law, act in accordance with it by the light of nature, they show that they have a law in themselves, for they demonstrate the effect of a law operating in their own hearts. Their own consciences endorse the existence of such a law, for there is something which condemns or excuses their actions.

We may be sure that all this will be taken into account in the day of true judgment, when God will judge men's secret lives by Christ Jesus, as my gospel plainly states.

You Jews are privileged—do you live up   2.17
to your privileges?

Now you, my reader, who bear the name of Jew, take your stand upon the Law, and are, so to speak, proud of your God. You know his plan, and are able through your knowledge of the Law truly to appreciate moral values. You can, therefore, confidently look upon yourself as a guide to those who do not know the way, and as a light to those who are groping in the dark. You can instruct those who have no spiritual wisdom: you can teach those who, spiritually speaking, are only just out of the cradle. You have a certain grasp of the basis of true knowledge. You have without doubt very great advantages. But, prepared as you are to instruct others, do you ever teach yourself anything? You preach against stealing, for example, but are you sure of your own honesty? You denounce the practice of adultery, but are you sure of your own purity? You loathe idolatry, but *how honest are you toward the property of heathen temples?* Everyone knows how proud you are of the Law, but that means a proportionate dishonor to God when men know that you break it! Don't you know that the very name of God is cursed among the gentiles because of the behavior of Jews? There is, you know, a verse of scripture to that effect.

Being a true "Jew" is an inward not an outward matter   2.25

That most intimate sign of belonging to God that we call circumcision does indeed mean something if you keep the Law. But if you flout the Law you are to all intents and purposes uncircumcising yourself! Conversely, if an uncircumcised man keep the Law's commandments, does he not thereby "circumcise" himself? Moreover, is it not plain to you that those who are physically uncircumcised, and yet keep the Law, are a continual judgment upon you who, for all your circumcision and knowledge of the Law, break it?

I have come to the conclusion that a true Jew is not the man who is merely a Jew outwardly, and real circumcision is not just a matter of the body. The true Jew is one who belongs to God in heart, a man whose circumcision is not just an outward physical affair but is a God-made sign upon the heart and soul, and results in a life lived not for the approval of man, but for the approval of God.

Jews are privileged, but even they have failed   3.1

Is there any advantage then in being one of the chosen people? Does circumcision mean anything? Yes, of course, a great deal in every way. You have only to think of one thing to begin with—it was the Jews to whom God's messages were entrusted. Some of them were undoubtedly faithless, but what then? Can you imagine that their faithlessness could disturb the faithfulness of God? Of course not! Let us think of God as true, even if every living man be proved a liar. Remember the scripture?

That thou mightest be justified in thy words,
And mightest prevail when thou comest into judgment.

But if our wickedness advertises the goodness of God, do we feel that God is being unfair to punish us in return? (I'm using a human tit-for-tat argument.) Not a bit of it! What sort of person would God be then to judge the world? It is like saying that if my lying throws into sharp relief the truth of God and, so to speak, enhances his reputation, then why should he repay me by judging me a sinner? Similarly, why not do evil that good may be, by contrast, all the more conspicuous and valuable? (As a matter of fact, I am reported as urging this very thing, by some slanderously and others quite seriously! But, of course, such an argument is quite properly condemned.)

Are we Jews then a march ahead of other men? By no means. For I have shown above that all men from Jews to Greeks are under the condemnation of sin. The scriptures endorse this fact plainly enough.

There is none righteous, no, not one.
There is none that understandeth,
There is none that seeketh after God;
They have all turned aside; they are together become un-
    profitable;
There is none that doeth good, no, not so much as one:
Their throat is an open sepulcher;
With their tongues they have used deceit;
The poison of asps is under their lips:
Whose mouth is full of cursing and bitterness:
Their feet are swift to shed blood;
Destruction and misery are in their ways:
And the way of peace have they not known;
There is no fear of God before their eyes.

We know what the message of the Law is, to those who live under it—that every excuse may die on the lips of him who makes it and no living man may think himself beyond the judgment of God. 'No man can justify himself before God' by a perfect performance of the Law's demands—indeed it is the straightedge of the Law that shows us how crooked we are.

God's new plan—righteousness by faith,   3.21
not through the Law

But now we are seeing the righteousness of God declared quite apart from the Law (though amply testified to by both Law and Prophets)—it is a righteousness imparted to, and operating in, all who have faith in Jesus Christ. (For there is no distinction to be made anywhere: everyone has sinned; everyone falls short of the beauty of God's plan.) Under this divine "system" a man who has faith is now freely acquitted in the eyes of God by his generous dealing in the redemptive act of Christ Jesus. God has appointed him as the means of propitiation, a propitiation accomplished by the shedding of his blood, to be received and made effective in ourselves by faith. God has done this to demonstrate his righteousness both by the wiping out of the sins of the past (the time when he withheld his hand), and by showing in the present time that he is a just God and that he justifies every man who has faith in Jesus Christ.

Faith, not pride of achievement   3.27

What happens now to human pride of achievement? There
is no more room for it. Why, because failure to keep the Law
has killed it? Not at all, but because the whole matter is now
on a different plane—believing instead of achieving. We see
now that a man is justified before God by the fact of his faith
in God's appointed Savior and not by what he has managed
to achieve under the Law.

And God is God of both Jews and gentiles; let us be quite
clear about that! The one God is ready to justify the circumcised by faith and the uncircumcised by faith also.

Are we then undermining the Law by this insistence on faith?
Not a bit of it! We put the Law in its proper place.

Let us go back and consider our father Abraham   4.1

Now how does all this affect the position of our ancestor Abraham? Well, if justification were by achievement he could quite fairly be proud of what he achieved—but not, I am sure, proud before God. For what does the scripture say about him?

> And Abraham believed God, and it was reckoned unto him for righteousness.

Now if a man *works,* his wages are not counted as a gift but as a fair reward. But if a man, irrespective of his work, has faith in him who justifies the sinful, then that man's *faith* is counted as righteousness, and that is the gift of God. This is the happy state of the man whom God accounts righteous, apart from his achievements, as David expresses it:

> Blessed are they whose iniquities are forgiven
> And whose sins are covered.
> Blessed is the man to whom the Lord will not reckon sin.

It is a matter of faith, not circumcision   4.9

Now the question, an important one, arises: is this happiness for the circumcised only, or for the uncircumcised as well?

Note this carefully. We began by saying that Abraham's faith was counted unto him for righteousness. When this happened, was he a circumcised man? He was not; he was still uncircumcised. It was *afterward* that the sign of circumcision was given to him, as a seal upon that righteousness which God was accounting to him *as yet an uncircumcised man!* God's purpose here is twofold. First, that Abraham might be the spiritual father of all who since that time, despite their uncircumcision, show the faith that is counted as righteousness. Then, secondly, that he might be the circumcised father of all those who are not only circumcised, but are living by the same sort of faith which he himself had before he was circumcised.

The promise, from the beginning, was   4.13
made to faith

The ancient promise made to Abraham and his descendants, that they should eventually possess the world, was given not because of any achievements made through obedience to the Law, but because of the righteousness which had its root in faith. For if, after all, they who pin their faith to keeping the Law were to inherit God's world, it would make nonsense of faith in God himself, and destroy the whole point of the promise.

For we have already noted that the Law can produce no promise, only the threat of wrath to come. And, indeed, if there were no Law the question of sin would not arise.

The whole thing, then, is a matter of faith on man's part and generosity on God's. He gives the security of his own promise to all men who can be called "children of Abraham," that is, both those who have lived in faith by the Law, and those who have exhibited a faith like that of Abraham. To whichever group we belong, Abraham is in a real sense our father, as the scripture says:

A father of many nations have I made thee.

This faith is valid because of the existence of God himself, who can make the dead live, and speak his word to those who are yet unborn.

Abraham was a shining example of faith   4.18

Abraham, when hope was dead within him, went on hoping in faith, believing that he would become "the father of many nations." He relied on the word of God which definitely referred to "thy seed." With undaunted faith he looked at the facts—his own impotence (he was practically a hundred years old at the time) and his wife Sarah's apparent barrenness. Yet he refused to allow any distrust of a definite pronouncement of God to make him waver. He drew strength from his faith, and, while giving the glory to God, remained absolutely convinced that God was able to implement his own promise. This was the "faith" which was 'counted unto him for righteousness.'

Now this counting of faith for righteousness was not recorded simply for Abraham's credit, but as a divine principle which should apply to us as well. Faith is to be reckoned as righteousness to us also, who believe in him who raised from the dead Jesus our Lord, who was delivered to death for our sins and raised again to secure our justification.

Faith means the certainty of God's love,   5.1
now and hereafter

Since then it is by faith that we are justified, let us grasp the fact that we *have* peace with God through our Lord Jesus Christ. Through him we have confidently entered into this new relationship of grace, and here we take our stand, in happy certainty of the glorious things he has for us in the future.

This doesn't mean, of course, that we have only a hope of future joys—we can be full of joy here and now even in our trials and troubles. Taken in the right spirit these very things will give us patient endurance; this in turn will develop a mature character, and a character of this sort produces a steady hope, a hope that will never disappoint us. Already we have some experience of the love of God flooding through our hearts by the Holy Spirit given to us. And we can see that it was while we were powerless to help ourselves that Christ died for sinful men. In human experience it is a rare thing for one man to give his life for another, even if the latter be a good man, though there have been a few who have had the courage to do it. Yet the proof of God's amazing love is this: that it was *while we were sinners* that Christ died for us. Moreover if he did that for us while we were sinners, now that we are men justified by the shedding of his blood, what reason have we to fear the wrath of God? If, while we were his enemies, Christ reconciled us to God by *dying for us,* surely now that we are reconciled we may be perfectly certain of our salvation through his *living in us*. Nor, I am sure, is this a matter of bare salvation—we may hold our heads high in the light of God's love because of the reconciliation which Christ has made.

A brief résumé—the consequence of sin and the gift of God   5.12

This, then, is what has happened. Sin made its entry into the world through one man, and through sin, death. The entail of sin and death passed on to the whole human race, and no one could break it for no one was himself free from sin.

Sin, you see, was in the world long before the Law, though I suppose, technically speaking, it was not "sin" where there was no law to define it. Nevertheless death, the complement of sin, held sway over mankind from Adam to Moses, even over those whose sin was quite unlike Adam's.

Adam, the first man, corresponds in some degree to the man who was to come. But the gift of God through Christ is a very different matter from the "account rendered" through the sin of Adam. For while as a result of one man's sin death by natural consequence became the common lot of men, it was by the generosity of God, the free giving of the grace of the one man Jesus Christ, that the love of God overflowed for the benefit of all men.

Nor is the effect of God's gift the same as the effect of that one man's sin. For in the one case one man's sin brought its inevitable judgment, and the result was condemnation. But, in the other, countless men's sins are met with the free gift of grace, and the result is justification before God.

For if one man's offense meant that men should be slaves to death all their lives, it is a far greater thing that through another man, Jesus Christ, men by their acceptance of his more than sufficient grace and righteousness should live all their lives like kings!

We see, then, that as one act of sin exposed the whole race

of men to God's judgment and condemnation, so one act of
perfect righteousness presents all men freely acquitted in the
sight of God. One man's disobedience placed all men under
the threat of condemnation, but one man's obedience has the
power to present all men righteous before God.

Grace is a bigger thing than the Law   5.20

Now we find that the Law keeps slipping into the picture to
point the vast extent of sin. Yet, though sin is shown to be wide
and deep, thank God his grace is wider and deeper still! The
whole outlook changes—sin used to be the master of men and
in the end handed them over to death: now grace is the ruling
factor, with righteousness as its purpose and its end the bringing of men to the eternal Life of God through Jesus Christ our
Lord.

Righteousness by faith, in practice   6.1

Now what is our response to be? Shall we sin to our
heart's content and see how far we can exploit the
grace of God? What a ghastly thought! We, who have died
to sin—how could we live in sin a moment longer? Have you
forgotten that all of us who were baptized into Jesus Christ
were, by that very action, sharing in his death? We were dead
and buried with him in baptism, so that just as he was raised
from the dead by that splendid revelation of the Father's
power so we too might rise to life on a new plane altogether.
If we have, as it were, shared his death, let us rise and live
our new lives with him! Let us never forget that our old selves
died with him on the cross that the tyranny of sin over us might
be broken—for a dead man can safely be said to be im-
mune to the power of sin. And if we were dead men with him
we can believe that we shall also be men newly alive with
him. We can be sure that the risen Christ never dies again—
death's power to touch him is finished. He died, because of sin,
once: he lives for God for ever. In the same way look upon
yourselves as dead to the appeal and power of sin but alive

and sensitive to the call of God through Jesus Christ our Lord.

Do not, then, allow sin to establish any power over your mortal bodies in making you give way to your lusts. Nor hand over your organs to be, as it were, weapons of evil for the devil's purposes. But, like men rescued from certain death, put yourselves in God's hands as weapons of good for his own purposes. For sin is not meant to be your master—you are no longer living under the Law, but under grace.

The new service completely ousts the old   6.15

Now, what shall we do? Shall we go on sinning because we have no Law to condemn us any more, but are living under grace? Never! Just think what it would mean. You *belong* to the power which you choose to obey, whether you choose sin, whose reward is death, or God, obedience to whom means the reward of righteousness. Thank God that you, who were at one time the servants of sin, honestly responded to the impact of Christ's teaching when you came under its influence. Then, released from the service of sin, you entered the service of righteousness. (I use an everyday illustration because human nature grasps truth more readily that way.) In the past you voluntarily gave your bodies to the service of vice and wickedness—for the purpose of becoming wicked. So, now, give yourselves to the service of righteousness—for the purpose of becoming really good. For when you were employed by sin you owed no duty to righteousness. Yet what sort of harvest did you reap from those things that today you blush to remember? In the long run those things mean one thing only—death.

But now that you are employed by God, you owe no duty to sin, and you reap the fruit of being made righteous, while at the end of the road there is life for evermore.

Sin *pays* its servants: the wage is death. But God *gives* to those who serve him: his free gift is eternal life through Christ Jesus our Lord.

How to be free from the Law   **7.1**

You know very well, my brothers (for I am speaking to those well acquainted with the subject), that the Law can only exercise authority over a man so long as he is alive. A married woman, for example, is bound by law to her husband so long as he is alive. But if he dies, then his legal claim over her disappears. This means that, if she should give herself to another man while her husband is alive, she incurs the stigma of adultery. But if, after her husband's death, she does exactly the same thing, no one could call her an adulteress, for the legal hold over her has been dissolved by her husband's death.

There is, I think, a fair analogy here. The death of Christ on the cross has made you "dead" to the claims of the Law, and you are free to give yourselves in marriage, so to speak, to another, the one who was raised from the dead, that you may be productive for God.

While we were "in the flesh" the Law stimulated our sinful passions and so worked in our nature that we became productive—for death! But now that we stand clear of the Law, the claims which existed are dissolved by our "death," and we are free to serve God not in the old obedience to the letter of the Law, but in a new way, in the Spirit.

Sin and the Law   7.7

It now begins to look as if sin and the Law were very much the same thing. Can this be a fact? Of course it cannot. But it must in fairness be admitted that I should never have had sin brought home to me but for the Law. For example, I should never have felt guilty of the sin of coveting if I had not heard the Law saying "Thou shalt not covet." But the sin in me, finding in the commandment an opportunity to express itself, stimulated all my covetous desires. For sin, in the absence of the Law, has no chance to function technically as "sin." As long, then, as I was without the Law I was, spiritually speaking, alive. But when the commandment arrived, sin sprang to life and I "died." The commandment, which was meant to be a direction to life, I found was a sentence to death. The commandment gave sin an opportunity, and without my realizing what was happening, it "killed" me.

The Law is itself good   7.12

It can scarcely be doubted that in reality the Law itself is holy, and the commandment is holy, fair and good. Can it be that something that is intrinsically good could mean death to me? No, what happened was this. Sin, at the touch of the Law, was forced to expose itself as sin, and *that* meant death for me. The contact of the Law showed the sinful nature of sin.

But it cannot make men good   7.14

After all, the Law itself is really concerned with the spiritual —it is I who am carnal, and have sold my soul to sin. In practice, what happens? My own behavior baffles me. For I find myself not doing what I really want to do but doing what I really loathe. Yet surely if I do things that I really don't want to do, I am admitting that I really agree with the Law. But it cannot be said that "I" am doing them at all—it must be sin that has made its home in my nature. (And indeed, I know from experience that the carnal side of my being can scarcely be called the home of good!) I often find that I have the will to do good, but not the power. That is, I don't accomplish the good I set out to do, and the evil I don't really want to do I find I am always doing. Yet if I do things that I don't really want to do then it is not, I repeat, "I" who do them, but the sin which has made its home within me. When I come up against the Law I want to do good, but in practice I do evil. My conscious mind wholeheartedly endorses the Law, yet I observe an entirely different principle at work in my nature. This is in continual conflict with my conscious attitude, and makes me an unwilling prisoner to the law of sin and death. In my mind I am God's willing servant, but in my own nature I am bound fast, as I say, to the law of sin and death. It is an agonizing situation, and who on earth can set me free from the clutches of my own sinful nature? I thank God there *is* a way out through Jesus Christ our Lord.

The way out—new life in Christ   8.1

No condemnation now hangs over the head of those who are "in" Christ Jesus. For the new spiritual principle of life "in" Christ Jesus lifts me out of the old vicious circle of sin and death.

The Law never succeeded in producing righteousness—the failure was always the weakness of human nature. But God has met this by sending his own Son Jesus Christ to live in that human nature which causes the trouble. And, *while Christ was actually taking upon himself the sins of men, God condemned that sinful nature.* So that we are able to meet the Law's requirements, so long as we are living no longer by the dictates of our sinful nature, but in obedience to the promptings of the Spirit. The carnal attitude sees no further than natural things. But the spiritual attitude reaches out after the things of the spirit. The former attitude means, bluntly, death: the latter means life and inward peace. And this is only to be expected, for the carnal attitude is inevitably opposed to the purpose of God, and neither can nor will follow his laws for living. Men who hold this attitude cannot possibly please God.

What the presence of Christ within means   8.9

But you are not carnal but spiritual if the Spirit of God finds a home within you. You cannot, indeed, be a Christian at all unless you have something of his spirit in you. Now if Christ does live within you his presence means that your sinful nature is dead, but your spirit becomes alive because of the righteousness he brings with him. I said that our nature is "dead" in the presence of Christ, and so it is, because of its sin. Nevertheless once the Spirit of him who raised Christ Jesus from the dead lives within you he will, by the same Spirit, bring to your whole being new strength and vitality.

So then, my brothers, you can see that we have no particular reason to feel grateful to our sensual nature, or to live life on the level of the instincts. Indeed that way of living leads to certain spiritual death. But if on the other hand you cut the nerve of your instinctive actions by obeying the Spirit, you are on the way to real living.

Christ is within—follow the lead of his Spirit   8.14

All who follow the leading of God's Spirit are God's own sons. Nor are you meant to relapse into the old slavish attitude of fear—you have been adopted into the very family circle of God and you can say with a full heart, "Father, my Father." The Spirit himself endorses our inward conviction that we really are the children of God. Think what that means. If we are his children we share his treasures, and all that Christ claims as his will belong to all of us as well! Yes, if we share in his sufferings we shall certainly share in his glory.

Present distress is temporary and negligible   8.18

In my opinion whatever we may have to go through now is less than nothing compared with the magnificent future God has planned for us. The whole creation is on tiptoe to see the wonderful sight of the sons of God coming into their own. The world of creation cannot as yet see reality, not because it chooses to be blind, but because in God's purpose it has been so limited—yet it has been given hope. And the hope is that in the end the whole of created life will be rescued from the tyranny of change and decay, and have its share in that magnificent liberty which can only belong to the children of God!

It is plain to anyone with eyes to see that at the present time all created life groans in a sort of universal travail. And it is plain, too, that we who have a foretaste of the Spirit are in a state of painful tension, while we wait for that redemption of our bodies which will mean that at last we have realized our full sonship in him. We were saved by this hope, but in our moments of impatience let us remember that hope always means waiting for something that we do not yet possess. But if we hope for something we cannot see, then we must settle down to wait for it in patience.

This is not mere theory—the Spirit helps us   8.26
to find it true

The Spirit of God not only maintains this hope within us, but helps us in our present limitations. For example, we do not know how to pray worthily as sons of God, but his Spirit within us is actually praying for us in those agonizing longings which never find words. And God who knows the heart's secrets understands, of course, the Spirit's intention as he prays for those who love God.

Moreover we know that to those who love God, who are called according to his plan, everything that happens fits into a pattern for good. God, in his foreknowledge, chose them to bear the family likeness of his Son, that he might be the eldest of a family of many brothers. He chose them long ago; when the time came he called them, he made them righteous in his sight and then lifted them to the splendor of life as his own sons.

We hold, in Christ, an impregnable position   8.31

In face of all this, what is there left to say? If God is for us, who can be against us? He who did not hesitate to spare his own Son but gave him up for us all—can we not trust such a God to give us, with him, everything else that we can need?

Who would dare to accuse us, whom God has chosen? The judge himself has declared us free from sin. Who is in a position to condemn? Only Christ, and Christ died for us, Christ rose for us, Christ reigns in power for us, Christ prays for us!

Who can separate us from the love of Christ? Can trouble, pain or persecution? Can lack of clothes and food, danger to life and limb, the threat of force of arms? Indeed some of us know the truth of that ancient text:

For thy sake we are killed all the day long;
We were accounted as sheep for the slaughter.

No, in all these things we win an overwhelming victory through him who has proved his love for us.

I have become absolutely convinced that neither death nor life, neither messenger of Heaven nor monarch of earth, neither what happens today nor what may happen tomorrow, neither a power from on high nor a power from below, nor anything else in God's whole world has any power to separate us from the love of God in Christ Jesus our Lord!

The fly in the ointment—the infidelity of my own race   9.1

Before Christ and my own conscience in the Holy Spirit I assure you that I am speaking the plain truth when I say that there is something that makes me feel very depressed, like a pain that never leaves me. It is the condition of my brothers and fellow Israelites, and I have actually reached the pitch of wishing myself cut off from Christ if it meant that they could be won for God.

Just think what the Israelites have had given to them. The privilege of being adopted as sons of God, the experience of seeing something of the glory of God, the receiving of the agreements made with God, the gift of the Law, true ways of worship, God's own promises—all these are theirs. The patriarchs are theirs, and so too, as far as human descent goes, is Christ himself, Christ who is God over all, blessed for ever.

God's purpose is not utterly defeated by this infidelity   9.6

Now this does not mean that God's word to Israel has failed. For you cannot count all "Israelites" as the true Israel of God. Nor can all Abraham's descendants be considered truly children of Abraham. The promise was that "in Isaac shall thy children be called." That means that it is not the natural descendants who automatically inherit the promise, but, on the contrary, that the children of the promise (that is, the sons of God) are to be considered truly Abraham's children. For it was a promise when God said: "About this time I will come and Sarah shall have a son." (Everybody, remember, thought it quite impossible for Sarah to have a child.) And then, again, a word of promise came to Rebecca, at the time when she was pregnant with two children by the one man, Isaac our forefather. It came before the children were born or had done anything good or bad, plainly showing that God's act of choice has nothing to do with achievements, good or bad, but is entirely a matter of his will. The promise was:

The elder shall serve the younger.

And we get a later endorsement of this divine choice in the words:

Jacob I loved, but Esau I hated.

We must not jump to conclusions about God   9.14

Now do we conclude that God is monstrously unfair? Never! God said long ago to Moses:

I will have mercy on whom I have mercy, and I will have compassion on whom I have compassion.

It is obviously not a question of human will or human effort, but of divine mercy. The scripture says to Pharaoh:

For this very purpose did I raise thee up, that I might show in thee my power, and that my name might be published abroad in all the earth.

It seems plain, then, that God chooses on whom he will have mercy, and whom he will harden in their sin.

Of course I can almost hear your retort: "If this is so, and God's will is irresistible, why does God blame men for what they do?" But the question really is this: "Who are you, a man, to make any such reply to God?" When a craftsman makes anything he doesn't expect it to turn round and say, "Why did you make me like this?" The potter, for instance, is always assumed to have complete control over the clay, making with one part of the lump a lovely vase, and with another a pipe for sewage. Can we not assume that God has the same control over human clay? May it not be that God, though he must sooner or later expose his wrath against sin and show his controlling hand, has yet most patiently endured the presence in his world of things that cry out to be destroyed? Can we not see, in this, his purpose in demonstrating the boundless resources of his glory upon those whom he considers fit to receive his mercy, and whom he long ago planned to raise to glorious life? And by these chosen people I mean you and me, whom he has called out from both Jews and gentiles. He says in Hosea:

I will call that my people, which was not my people;
And her beloved, which was not beloved.
And it shall be, that in the place where it was said unto
them, Ye are not my people,
There shall they be called sons of the living God.

And Isaiah, speaking about Israel, proclaims:

If the number of the children of Israel be as the sand of the
sea, it is the remnant that shall be saved:
For the Lord will execute his word upon the earth, finishing
it and cutting it short.

And previously, Isaiah said:

Except the Lord of Sabaoth had left us a seed,
We had become as Sodom, and had been made like unto
Gomorrah.

At present the gentiles have gone further   9.30
than the Jews

Now, how far have we got? That the gentiles who never had the Law's standard of righteousness to guide them, have attained righteousness, righteousness-by-faith. But Israel, following the Law of righteousness, failed to reach the goal of righteousness. And why? Because their minds were fixed on what they achieved instead of on what they believed. They tripped over that very stone the scripture mentions:

Behold, I lay in Zion a stone of stumbling and a rock of offense:
And he that believeth on him shall not be put to shame.

How Israel has missed the way   10.1

My brothers, from the bottom of my heart I long and pray to God that Israel may be saved! I know from experience what a passion for God they have; but, alas, it is not a passion based on knowledge. They do not know God's righteousness, and all the time they are going about trying to prove their own righteousness they have the wrong attitude to receive his. For Christ means the end of the struggle for righteousness-by-the-Law for everyone who believes in him.

Moses writes of righteousness-by-the-Law when he says that the man who perfectly obeys the Law shall find life in it. But righteousness-by-faith says something like this:

"You need not say in your heart, 'Who could go up to Heaven to bring Christ down to us, or who could descend into the depths to bring him up from the dead?' For the secret is very near you, in *your own heart*, in *your own mouth!*" It is the secret of faith, which is the burden of our preaching, and it says, in effect, "If you openly admit by *your own mouth* that Jesus Christ is the Lord, and if you believe in *your own heart* that God raised him from the dead, you will be saved." For it is believing *in the heart* that makes a man righteous before God, and it is stating his belief by *his own mouth* that confirms his salvation. And the scripture says: "Whosoever believes in him shall not be disappointed." And that "whosoever" means anyone, without distinction between Jew or Greek. For all have the same Lord, whose boundless resources are available to all who turn to him in faith. For:

Whosoever shall call upon the name of the Lord shall be saved.

Can we offer the excuse of ignorance on Israel's behalf?   10.14

Now how can they call on one in whom they have never believed? How can they believe in one of whom they have never heard? And how can they hear unless someone proclaims him? And who will go to tell them unless he is sent? As the scripture puts it:

How beautiful are the feet of them that bring glad tidings of good things!

Yet all who have heard have not responded to the gospel. Isaiah asks, you remember,

Lord, who hath believed our report?

(Belief, you see, can only come from hearing the message, and the message is the word of Christ.)

But when I ask myself: "Did they never hear?" I have to answer that they *have* heard, for

Their sound went out into all the earth,
And their words unto the ends of the world.

Then I say to myself: "Did Israel not know?" And my answer must be that they did. For Moses says:

I will provoke you to jealousy with that which is no nation,
With a nation void of understanding will I anger you.

And Isaiah, more daring still, puts these words into the mouth of God:

I was found of them that sought me not.
I became manifest unto them that asked not of me.

And then, speaking of Israel:

All the day long did I spread out my hands unto a disobedient and gainsaying people.

Israel's failure—yet remember the faithful few   11.1

This leads naturally to the question, "Has God then totally
repudiated his people?" Certainly not! I myself, for one,
am an Israelite, a descendant of Abraham and of the tribe of
Benjamin. It is unthinkable that God should have repudiated
his own people, the people whose destiny he himself appointed.
Don't you remember what the scripture says in the story of
Elijah? How he pleaded with God on Israel's behalf:

Lord, they have killed thy prophets
They have digged down thine altars:
And I am left alone, and they seek my life.

And do you remember God's reply?

I have left for myself seven thousand men
Who have not bowed the knee to Baal.

In just the same way, there is at the present time a minority,
chosen by the grace of God. And if it is a matter of the grace
of God, it cannot be a question of their actions especially
deserving God's favor, for that would make grace meaningless.

What conclusion do we reach now? That Israel did not, on
the whole, obtain the object of his striving, but a chosen few
"got there," while the remainder became more and more
insensitive to the righteousness of God. This is borne out by the
scripture:

God gave them a spirit of stupor,
Eyes that they should not see,
And ears that they should not hear,
Unto this very day.

And David says of them:

Let their table be made a snare, and a trap,
And a stumbling block, and a recompense unto them:
Let their eyes be darkened, that they may not see,
And bow Thou down their back alway.

In the providence of God disaster has been 11.11
turned to good account

Now I ask myself, "Was this fall of theirs an utter disaster?" It was not! For through their failure the benefit of salvation has passed to the gentiles, with the result that Israel is made to see and feel what it has missed. For if their failure has so enriched the world, and their defection proved such a benefit to the gentiles, think what tremendous advantages their fulfilling of God's plan could mean!

Now a word to you who are gentiles. I should like you to know that I make as much as I can of my ministry as "God's messenger to the gentiles" so as to make my kinsfolk jealous and thus save some of them. For if their exclusion from the pale of salvation has meant the reconciliation of the rest of man-kind to God, what would their inclusion mean? It would be nothing less than life from the dead! If the flour is consecrated to God so is the whole loaf, and if the roots of a tree are dedicated to God every branch will belong to him also.

A word of warning 11.17

But if some of the branches of the tree have been broken off, while you, like shoots of wild olive, have been grafted in, and share like a natural branch the rich nourishment of the root, don't let yourself feel superior to those former branches. (If you feel inclined that way, remind yourself that you do not support the root; the root supports you.) You may make the natural retort, "But the branches were broken off to make room for my grafting!" It wasn't quite like that. They lost their position because they failed to believe; you only maintain yours because you do believe. The situation does not call for conceit but for a certain wholesome fear. If God removed the natural branches for a good reason, take care that you don't give him the same reason for removing you. You must try to appreciate both the kindness and the strict justice of God. Those who fell experienced his justice, while you are experiencing his kindness, and will continue to do so as long as you do not abuse that kindness. Otherwise you too will be cut off from the tree. And as for the fallen branches, unless they are obstinate in their unbelief, they will be grafted in again. Such a restoration is by no means beyond the power of God. And, in any case, if you who were, so to speak, cuttings from a wild olive, were grafted in, is it not a far simpler matter for the natural branches to be grafted back into the parent stem?

God still has a plan for Israel 11.25

Now I don't want you, my brothers, to start imagining things, and I must therefore share with you my knowledge of God's secret plan. It is this, that the partial insensibility which has come to Israel is only to last until the full number of the gentiles has been called in. Once this has happened, all Israel will be saved, as the scripture says:

There shall come out of Zion the deliverer;
He shall turn away ungodliness from Jacob:
And this is my covenant unto them,
When I shall take away their sins.

As far as the gospel goes, they are at present God's enemies— which is to your advantage. But as far as God's purpose in choosing is concerned, they are still beloved for their fathers' sakes. For once they are made, God does not withdraw his gifts or his calling.

The whole scheme looks topsy-turvy, until 11.30 we see the amazing wisdom of God!

Just as in the past you were disobedient to God but have found that mercy which might have been theirs but for their

disobedience, so they, who at the present moment are disobedient, will eventually share the mercy which has been
extended to you. God has all men penned together in the
prison of disobedience, that he may have mercy upon them all.

Frankly, I stand amazed at the unfathomable complexity of
God's wisdom and God's knowledge. How could man ever
understand his reasons for action, or explain his methods of
working? For:

Who hath known the mind of the Lord?
Or who hath been his counselor?
Or who hath first given to him, and it shall be recompensed
    unto him again?
For of him, and through him, and unto him, are all things.
To him be the glory for ever, amen.

We have seen God's mercy and wisdom: 12.1
how shall we respond?

With eyes wide open to the mercies of God, I beg you,
my brothers, as an act of intelligent worship, to give
him your bodies, as a living sacrifice, consecrated to him and
acceptable by him. Don't let the world around you squeeze
you into its own mold, but let God remold your minds from
within, so that you may prove in practice that the plan of God
for you is good, meets all his demands and moves toward the
goal of true maturity.

As your spiritual teacher I give this piece of advice to each
one of you. Don't cherish exaggerated ideas of yourself or
your importance, but try to have a sane estimate of your
capabilities by the light of the faith that God has given to you
all. For just as you have many members in one physical body
and those members differ in their functions, so we, though
many in number, compose one body in Christ and are all
members of one another. Through the grace of God we have
different gifts. If our gift is preaching, let us preach to the
limit of our vision. If it is serving others let us concentrate on
our service; if it is teaching let us give all we have to our

teaching; and if our gift be the stimulating of the faith of others let us set ourselves to it. Let the man who is called to give, give freely; let the man who wields authority think of his responsibility; and let the man who feels sympathy for his fellows act cheerfully.

Let us have real Christian behavior   12.9

Let us have no imitation Christian love. Let us have a genuine break with evil and a real devotion to good. Let us have real warm affection for one another as between brothers, and a willingness to let the other man have the credit. Let us not allow slackness to spoil our work and let us keep the fires of the spirit burning, as we do our work for the Lord. Base your happiness on your hope in Christ. When trials come endure them patiently; steadfastly maintain the habit of prayer. Give freely to fellow Christians in want, never grudging a meal or a bed to those who need them. And as for those who try to make your life a misery, bless them. Don't curse, bless. Share the happiness of those who are happy, and the sorrow of those who are sad. Live in harmony with one another. Don't become snobbish but take a real interest in ordinary people. Don't become set in your own opinions. Don't pay back a bad turn by a bad turn, to *anyone*. See that your public behavior is above criticism. As far as your responsibility goes, live at peace with everyone. Never take vengeance into your own hands, my dear friends: stand back and let God punish if he will. For it is written:

Vengeance belongeth unto me: I will recompense.

And these are God's words:

If thine enemy hunger, feed him;
If he thirst, give him to drink:
For in so doing thou shalt heap coals of fire upon his head.

Don't allow yourself to be overpowered by evil. Take the offensive—overpower evil with good!

The Christian and the civil law   13.1

Every Christian ought to obey the civil authorities, for all legitimate authority is derived from God's authority, and the existing authority is appointed under God. To oppose authority then is to oppose God, and such opposition is bound to be punished.

The honest citizen has no need to fear the keepers of law and order, but the dishonest man will always be nervous of them. If you want to avoid this anxiety just lead a law-abiding life, and all that can come your way is a word of approval. The officer is God's servant for your protection. But if you are leading a wicked life you have reason to be alarmed. The "power of the law" which is vested in every legitimate officer is no empty phrase. He is, in fact, divinely appointed to inflict God's punishment upon evil-doers.

You should, therefore, obey the authorities, not simply because it is the safest, but because it is the right thing to do. It is right, too, for you to pay taxes, for the civil authorities are appointed by God for the good purposes of public order and well-being. Give everyone his legitimate due, whether it be rates, or taxes, or reverence, or respect!

To love others is the highest conduct   13.8

Keep out of debt altogether, except that perpetual debt of love which we owe one another. The man who loves his neighbor has obeyed the whole Law in regard to his neighbor. For the commandments, "Thou shalt not commit adultery," "Thou shalt not kill," "Thou shalt not steal," "Thou shalt not covet" and all other commandments are summed up in this one saying: "Thou shalt love thy neighbor as thyself." Love hurts nobody: therefore love is the answer to the Law's commands.

Wake up and live!   13.11

Why all this stress on behavior? Because, as I think you have realized, the present time is of the highest importance—it is time to wake up to reality. Every day brings God's salvation nearer.

The night is nearly over; the day has almost dawned. Let us therefore fling away the things that men do in the dark; let us arm ourselves for the fight of the day! Let us live cleanly, as in the daylight, not in the "delights" of getting drunk or playing with sex, nor yet in quarreling or jealousies. Let us be Christ's men from head to foot, and give no chances to the flesh to have its fling.

Don't criticize one another's convictions 14.1

Welcome a man whose faith is weak, but not with the idea of arguing over his scruples. One man believes that he may eat anything; another man, without this strong conviction, is a vegetarian. The meat eater should not despise the vegetarian, nor should the vegetarian condemn the meat eater—they should reflect that God has accepted them both. After all, who are you to criticize the servant of somebody else, especially when that somebody else is God? It is to his own master that he gives, or fails to give, satisfactory service. And don't doubt that satisfaction, for God is well able to transform men into servants who are satisfactory.

People are different—make allowances   14.5

Again, one man thinks some days of more importance than others. Another man considers them all alike. Let every one be definite in his own convictions. If a man specially observes one particular day, he does so "to the Lord." The man who eats, eats "to the Lord," for he thanks God for the food. The man who fasts also does it "to the Lord," for he thanks God for the benefits of fasting. The truth is that we neither live nor die as self-contained units. At every turn life links us to the Lord, and when we die we come face to face with him. In life or death we are in the hands of the Lord. Christ lived and died that he might be the Lord in both life and death.

Why, then, criticize your brother's actions, why try to make him look small? We shall all be judged one day, not by one another's standards or even our own, but by the judgment of God. It is written:

As I live, saith the Lord, to me every knee shall bow,
And every tongue shall confess to God.

It is to God alone that we have to answer for our actions.

This should be our attitude   14.13

Let us therefore stop turning critical eyes on one another. If we must be critical, let us be critical of our own conduct and see that we do nothing to make a brother stumble or fall.

I am convinced, and I say this as in the presence of the Lord Christ, that nothing is intrinsically unholy. But none the less it is unholy to the man who thinks it is. If your habit of unrestricted diet seriously upsets your brother, you are no longer living in love toward him. And surely you wouldn't let food mean ruin to a man for whom Christ died. You mustn't let something that is all right for you look like an evil practice to somebody else. After all, the kingdom of Heaven is not a matter of whether you get what you like to eat and drink, but of righteousness and peace and joy in the Holy Spirit. If you put these things first in serving Christ you will please God and are not likely to offend men. So let us concentrate on the things which make for harmony, and on the growth of one another's character. Surely we shouldn't wish to undo God's work for the sake of a plate of meat!

I freely admit that all food is, in itself, harmless, but it can be harmful to the man who eats it with a guilty conscience. We should be willing to be both vegetarians and teetotalers if by doing otherwise we should impede a brother's progress in the faith. Your personal convinctions are a matter of faith between yourself and God, and you are happy if you have no qualms about what you allow yourself to eat. Yet if a man eats meat with an uneasy conscience about it, you may be sure he is wrong to do so. For his action does not spring from his faith, and when we act apart from our faith we sin.

Christian behavior to one another   15.1

We who have strong faith ought to shoulder the burden of the doubts and qualms of others and not just to go our own sweet way. Our actions should mean the good of others—should help them to build up their characters. For even Christ did not choose his own pleasure, but as it is written:

The reproaches of them that reproached thee fell upon me.

For all those words which were written long ago are meant to teach us today; that when we read in the scriptures of the endurance of men and of all the help that God gave them in those days, we may be encouraged to go on hoping in our own time. May the God who inspires men to endure, and gives them a Father's care, give you a mind united toward one another because of your common loyalty to Jesus Christ. And then, as one man, you will sing from the heart the praises of

God the Father of our Lord Jesus Christ. So open your hearts to one another as Christ has opened his heart to you, and God will be glorified.

A reminder—Christ the universal savior   15.8

Christ was made a servant of the Jews to prove God's trustworthiness, since he personally implemented the promises made long ago to the fathers, and also that the gentiles might bring glory to God for his mercy to them. It is written:

Therefore will I give praise unto thee among the gentiles
And sing unto thy name.

And again:

Rejoice, ye gentiles, with his people.

And yet again:

Praise the Lord, all ye gentiles;
And let all the peoples praise him.

And then Isaiah says:

There shall be the root of Jesse,
And he that ariseth to rule over the gentiles:
On him shall the gentiles hope.

May the God of hope fill *you* with joy and peace in your faith, that by the power of the Holy Spirit, your whole life and outlook may be radiant with hope.

What I have tried to do   15.14

For myself I feel certain that you, my brothers, have real Christian character and experience, and that you are capable of keeping one another on the right road. Nevertheless I have written to you with a certain frankness, to refresh your minds with truths that you already know, by virtue of my commission as minister of Christ Jesus to the gentiles in the service of the gospel of God. For my constant endeavor is to present the gentiles to God as an offering which he can accept, because they are sanctified by the Holy Spirit. And I think I have something to be proud of (through Christ, of course) in my work for God. I am not competent to speak of the work Christ has done through others, but I do know that through me he has secured the obedience of gentiles in word and deed, working by sign and miracle and all the power of the Holy Spirit. I have fully preached the gospel from Jerusalem and the surrounding country as far as Illyricum. My constant ambition has been to preach the gospel where the name of Christ was previously unknown, and to avoid as far as possible building on another man's foundation, so that:

They shall see, to whom no tiding of him came,
And they who have not heard shall understand.

My future plans 15.22

Perhaps this will explain why I have so frequently been prevented from coming to see you. But now, since my work in these places no longer needs my presence, and since for many years I have had a great desire to see you, I hope to visit you on my way to Spain. I hope also that you will speed me on my journey, after I have had the satisfaction of seeing you all. At the moment my next call is to Jerusalem, to look after the welfare of the Christians there. The churches in Macedonia and Achaia, you see, have thought it a good thing to make a contribution toward the poor Christians in Jerusalem. They have thought it a good thing to make this gesture and yet, really, they received "a good thing" from them first! For if the gentiles have had a share in the Jews' spiritual "good things" it is only fair that they should look after the Jews as far as the good things of this world are concerned.

When I have completed this task, then, and turned their gesture into a good deed done, I shall come to you en route for Spain. I feel sure that in this long-looked-for visit I shall bring with me the full blessing of Christ.

Now, my brothers, I am going to ask you, for the sake of

our Lord Jesus Christ and for the love we bear one another in the Spirit, to stand behind me in earnest prayer to God on my behalf—that I may not fall into the hands of the unbelievers in Judaea, and that the Jerusalem Christians may receive the gift I am taking to them in the spirit in which it was made. Then I shall come to you, in the purpose of God, with a happy heart, and may even enjoy with you a little holiday.

The God of peace be with you all, amen.

Personal greetings and messages   16.1

I want this letter to introduce to you Phoebe, our sister, a deaconess of the church at Cenchreae. Please give her a Christian welcome, and any assistance with her work that she may need. She has herself been of great assistance to many, not excluding myself.

Shake hands for me with Prisca and Aquila. They have not only worked with me for Christ Jesus, but they have risked their necks to save my life. Not only I, but all the gentile churches, owe them a great debt. Give my love to the little church that meets in their house.

Shake the hand of dear Epaenetus, Achaia's first man to be won for Christ, and of course greet Mary who has worked so hard for you. A handshake too for Andronicus and Junias my kinsmen and fellow prisoners; they are outstanding men among the messengers and were Christians before I was.

Another warm greeting for Ampliatus, dear Christian that he is, and also for Urbanus, who has worked with me, and dear old Stachys, too.

More greetings from me, please, to:

Apelles, the man who has proved his faith;
The household of Aristobulus;
Herodion, my kinsman;
Narcissus' household, who are Christians.

Remember me to Tryphena and Tryphosa, who work so hard for the Lord, and to my dear Persis who has also done great work for him.

Shake the hand of Rufus for me—that splendid Christian—and greet his mother, who has been mother to me too. Greetings to Asyncritus, Phlegon, Hermes, Patrobas, Hermas and their Christian group: also to Philologus and Julia, Nereus and his sister, and Olympas and the Christians who are with them.

Give one another a hearty handshake all round for my sake. The greetings of all the churches I am in touch with come to you with this letter.

A final warning   16.17

And now I implore you, my brothers, to keep a watchful eye on those who cause trouble and make difficulties among you, in plain opposition to the teaching you have been given, and steer clear of them. Such men do not really serve our Lord Christ at all but are utterly self-centered. Yet with their plausible and attractive arguments they deceive those who are too simplehearted to see through them.

Your loyalty to the principles of the gospel is known everywhere, and that gives me great joy. I want to see you experts in good, and not even beginners in evil. It will not be long before the God of peace will crush Satan under your feet. May the grace of our Lord Jesus Christ be with you.

Timothy, who works with me, sends his greetings, and so do Lucius and Jason and Sosipater my fellow countrymen. (Paul has just told me that I, Tertius, who have been taking down this epistle from his dictation, may send you my Christian greetings too.) Gaius, my host (and the host as a matter of fact of the whole church here), sends you his greetings. Erastus, our town clerk, and Quartus, another Christian brother, send greetings too.

Now to him who is able to set you on your feet as his own sons—according to my gospel, according to the preaching of Jesus Christ himself, and in accordance with the disclosing of that secret purpose which, after long ages of silence, has now been made known (in full agreement with the writings of the

prophets long ago), by the command of the everlasting God to all the gentiles, that they might turn to him in the obedience of faith—to him, I say, the only God who is wise, be glory for ever through Jesus Christ, amen!

PAUL